CW01302637

GREATER TIGRAY AND THE MYSTERIOUS MAGNETISM OF ETHIOPIA

HAGGAI ERLICH

Greater Tigray and the Mysterious Magnetism of Ethiopia

HURST & COMPANY, LONDON

First published in the United Kingdom in 2023 by
C. Hurst & Co. (Publishers) Ltd.,
New Wing, Somerset House, Strand, London, WC2R 1LA
© Haggai Erlich, 2023
All rights reserved.

The right of Haggai Erlich to be identified as the author of this publication is asserted by him in accordance with the Copyright, Designs and Patents Act, 1988.

A Cataloguing-in-Publication data record for this book is available from the British Library.

ISBN: 9781805260233

www.hurstpublishers.com

CONTENTS

Ethiopian Names and Titles		vii
1.	Preface: The Mysterious Magnetism	1
2.	Introduction: Cradle, Gate, Wall, Legacy	5
3.	'Medri Bahri': Defying Emperors, Saving Ethiopia	11
4.	The Era of the Judges: Autonomy and Traditional Structure	19
5.	Their Finest Hour: Yohannes	29
6.	Collapse	57
7.	Back to Center Stage: From War to War	75
8.	Fascists, British: Tigray under Asmara	95
9.	Under Haile Selassie: To Woyane and Back	109
10.	Haile Selassie's Imperial Centralism	123
11.	Three Revolutions: Derg, EPLF, TPLF	137
12.	Restored Hegemony, Inter-Tigrayan War	155
13.	The Grand Dam: The Legacy of Meles Zenawi	165
14.	Non-conclusion: 'The Theory of Disintegration' and the 'Grand Dam'	177
Notes		181
Index of Names		205
Index		211

ETHIOPIAN NAMES AND TITLES

Ethiopians have no family names. They are identified by their first name, often adding to it one's father's name. A certain Makonnen Haile is the son of Haile Mangasha whose father was Mangahsa Walda-Mariam, a son of Walda-Mariam Abebe. The same goes for all other Ethiopians—we shall mention them by their 'first name' and often with their rank or title preceding it, sometimes with their father's name after it.

1

PREFACE

THE MYSTERIOUS MAGNETISM

Whenever I begin the great adventure of delving into the sea of history, I am full of awe. I try to caution myself: remember Benedetto Croce. Namely, the words of the Italian philosopher, that all history is contemporary history, that any serious study of the past is informed by the problems of the writer's own time, and that the more historians are conscious of their contemporary motives, the more balanced their understanding of the past.

These words reverberated in my mind even more forcefully when I was attempting to cope with the subject of this book. Three years after I began working on this study, the Tigray question deteriorated into a bloody conflict. Every chapter in the long history of Tigray surfaced again, colored by the unfolding events. I always tried to refrain from writing on contemporary affairs, and when I did, I later regretted it. Therefore, I brought this discussion of Tigray to a point usefully distant from today. Usefully, but not safely, I am afraid. Historians should aspire to have accurate facts and proper time perspective. When it came to writing on more recent developments, I had less and less of these two traits. The literature on current issues is too vast, and little of it is unbiased. I dared to write the last chapters of this book only because I came to them from the perspective of the longer past. Indeed, this book should also be read as a historical background to today's tragedy in the Horn of Africa rather than as a balanced contemporary record. We have no better key to understanding human affairs other than honest history. The presence is ever chaotic, the future is never predictable.

Fifty-two years ago, I entered the field of Ethiopian studies by working on a Ph.D. in London University. The dissertation (submitted in 1973) was on Ras Alula, the late nineteenth-century hero of Ethiopia and of Tigray. The book came out in 1982, and I was later told that it helped to restore the pride of a young generation in the then-ruined and humiliated Tigray. I was told that it also inspired Tigrayan revolutionary youngsters who, in 1991, toppled Mangistu's dictatorship. They named their advance force that liberated Addis Ababa 'Ras Alula Division.' They led Ethiopia until 2018.

During the five decades after I wrote on Ras Alula, I did not limit my interest to Tigray. I studied and published on general Ethiopian history, on Eritrea, on the Nile, on the Red Sea, and on the historical connection between the Horn of Africa and the Middle East. My last relevant book was on the greatest Ethiopian of Amhara origin, emperor Haile Selassie (Amharic translation published in Addis Ababa, 2021). Indeed, I tried to be as professionally non-biased as a foreign observer can be, never ignoring both the negative and the positive sides of historymakers. Nor did I try to be the advocate of any cause, only a student of the complicated past as I understood it.

As these lines were written (2022), a cruel, fratricidal war was raging in Ethiopia. The ancient entity, which survived in various shapes for two millennia, seemed at risk of falling apart. Would it survive today's tragedy once again? Who can tell? Historians cannot. History never really repeats itself (only some historians do…), but learning it is essential.

One chapter, which will be discussed below in detail, might prove relevant. Eighty-one years ago, the British liberated Ethiopia from Mussolini's occupation. Controlling the land, some of the army officers planned to annex Tigray to their newly administered

PREFACE

Eritrea. A British intelligence officer, Major (later Colonel) R. Cheesman, referred to the then-accepted concept that Ethiopia was a disintegrating anachronism. Acquainted better with Ethiopia's history, he opposed 'the *theory of disintegration.*' He explained that 'the crazy structure of the Ethiopian Empire' was 'held together by a *mysterious magnetism* [emphasis added], which is incomprehensible to one who has no more than a superficial knowledge of Ethiopia.'[1] At that time, Cheesman was proven right—Ethiopia did survive. Would it survive now? Is the ancient 'mysterious magnetism' still working?

Undertaking to present the history of many centuries could prove over-ambitious and result in a titanic volume of little use. I hereby present a succinct discussion, hopefully balanced. I derived a lot from my previous relevant writings,[2] and reread some of the documentary material I gathered in the process. However, I would not pretend I could revisit all the archival and primary sources I used and would therefore often avoid referring to them in the notes. I did consult most of the relevant literature produced by other scholars. The present book is therefore an analytical survey as well as an attempt to rethink the story of people ever conscious of their history's legacies.

I wish I could thank all those who helped me during my long journey as an Ethiopianist. Some of them are no longer with us. I wish that all others continue to enjoy being the children and observers of this unique and fascinating country.

Tel-Aviv, May 2023

2

INTRODUCTION

CRADLE, GATE, WALL, LEGACY

The Cradle

The subject of this book is the history of an ethnic-linguistic group which played and still plays a pivotal role in the Horn of Africa.[1] It aims to present the story of the Tigrinya speakers and their contribution to the shaping of the Ethiopian and Eritrean space.

Today, Tigrinya speakers in both Ethiopia and Eritrea number some ten million at the most. However, they are and were central to the story of a region populated by ten times more, and one that is the home of many other groups.

The space, which is sometimes called 'Greater Tigray,' was the cradle of Ethiopia both as a state and as a concept. In modern geographical terms—history is more volatile—the space in question included, in the mid-nineteenth century, the districts of Hamasen, Seraye, Akkala Guzay (beyond the River Mareb—*Mareb Melash*—in today's Eritrea), Agame, Tigray or Adwa (namely Adwa and Aksum), Shire, Adyabo, Tamben, Enderta, and Wajarat.[2]

In Ancient times, Ethiopia was born around the town of Aksum. In and around Aksum, there developed a state and culture complete with urban life, written language, agriculture, and commerce. The ancient Aksumite entity was also developed by immigrants who had crossed the Red Sea. The tribes of the Habashat and Agazian crossed from Arabia to the Horn of Africa during the first millennium BC. The Agazian brought with them the fundamentals of the Semitic language of Ge'ez, which developed locally and became the written and spoken language of the kingdom.

Most historians of the period agree that the ancient legendary kingdom of Sheba included territories on both sides of the Red Sea, stretching over areas in today's Yemen, Eritrea, northern Ethiopia, northern Somalia, Djibouti, and western Saudi Arabia. By Ethiopian tradition, the queen of ancient Sheba was the mother of their kingdom. That Ethiopia was born when Queen Makeda, the last of the Agazian dynasty, transferred power to her son, Menelik, the first of an Ethiopian dynasty. By this tradition, Menelik was the son of Makeda and King Solomon of Jerusalem. The queen of Sheba, it was said, crossed the Red Sea and came to Jerusalem, met king Solomon, and conceived his son. Ethiopia's kings and emperors, by tradition, were therefore descendants and heirs of King Solomon. Haile Selassie, deposed in 1974, was said to be number 225 in line.[3]

The Gate and Wall

Aksum led ancient Ethiopia for over a millennium, bridging the gap between local and immigrating ethnic groups. Ancient Ethiopia established political and economic institutions and connected with the greater world. It was there that Christianity was adopted in the fourth century, providing the basis for Ethiopia's culture and politics until today. In Ethiopia, relations with the Coptic Church of Egypt as the mother Church of Ethiopia were initiated, and the link to Jerusalem as an indirect bridge to the greater Christian world was formed.

With its port at Adulis (Zula in today's Eritrea), Aksum, became by the sixth century a power in the Red Sea, a junior partner to Byzantium and Persia in the all-'Oriental' sphere. Aksumite Ethiopia even expanded (524–590 AD) to include parts of southern Arabia, and stretched over much of the Horn of Africa.

In Aksum, and under the auspices of an Ethiopian king, there was also the first meeting between Christians and Muslims;

Christianity and Islam. The Arab pioneers of Islam came there from Mecca to seek refuge from their Arab pagan persecutors. The story of the 'najashi,' the king of Aksum, and his relationship with the prophet Muhammad is still influencing Islamic–Christian relations in Ethiopia and the country's foreign relations to this day. However, with the seventh-century rise of Islam in Arabia, the Ethiopians' involvement in the Red Sea began fading. The center of the Ethiopian Christian state moved steadily inland, deeper into the mountains. The Red Sea did remain as Ethiopia's gate to the world, but more so became a wall against it.[4]

With the gradual decline of the Aksumite state, Ge'ez slowly died as a spoken language. It has remained the Ethiopian language of holy scriptures, like Latin in Europe. But gradually, in a process lasting from the seventh to the tenth centuries, two main other languages, stemming from the fading Ge'ez, did develop. One was Tigrinya: purely Semitic, like her mother Ge'ez, yet distinctly different. Tigrinya spread in the core areas of the Aksumite kingdom and survived its decline. The other was Amharic, developed at the same time, but in areas more to the south, to which the center of the Ethiopian entity shifted, especially after its revival under new dynasties. 'Both languages,' summarized Rainer Voigt, 'are roughly speaking descendants of Ge'ez. More strictly speaking they are descendants of closely related daughter languages or dialects of Ge'ez, since there are some modern linguistic features that cannot be traced back to Ge'ez.'[5] Amharic has become, since the late twelfth century, the working language of the new royal courts, the language of the military, trade, and everyday communications. Amharic kept the Semitic roots and the Ge'ez script but was also significantly influenced by other local Cushitic languages. In time, Amharic would become practically the all-Ethiopian language as it is today

The Legacy

As Ethiopia's center moved to the south, Amharic speakers took over leading the country. They reached their medieval climax during the 'era of the Solomonian dynasty,' from the thirteenth to sixteenth centuries. By that time, the regions of Tigrinya speakers had been impoverished. Pushed to the periphery for the first time in our story, although certainly not for the last time.

The Amhara's political culture became different from the Tigrayans'. The latter, striving to maintain their own identity within the Ethiopian world, adopted a pluralistic and diverse vision of the Christian kingdom. It was and still is different from the Amharas' vision. The Amhara strove to create imperial unity around their all-Ethiopian language, and in turn an ideally centralized political system. One may call it 'the Amhara thesis' of Ethiopia.

The Tigrayans, though marginalized and weakened by endless internal rivalries, remained proud of their own identity and went on keeping the gate of the country to and from the Red Sea and the world. Ethiopia's major battles for survival, as I shall describe, were conducted on their soil. In the late nineteenth century, the Tigrayans returned to lead Ethiopia in a formative time, and did so following their 'thesis.' Marginalized and divided again, they made it back to leadership in 1991, and rebuilt Ethiopia on the basis of ethnic federalism. In 2018, they were pushed yet again back to Tigray. In 2021, it became clear that this ancient tension over Ethiopia's system and culture—acquiring many more dimensions over the centuries—still moves the country.

Separately, in 1991, Tigrinya speakers also captured power in Eritrea, having developed a distinct Eritrean identity and nationalism. We shall discuss it below.

The ancient kingdom of Aksum was the cradle of Ethiopia. Can Tigrayans claim it was theirs? That they 'invented' Ethiopia and were later deprived?

The leading Ethiopianist, Edward Ullendorff, wrote: 'Here [in Tigray] is historic Abyssinia *par excellence*, the Semitized people of the plateau with their Semitic language and Old Testament way of life.'[6] In his famous book 'Greater Ethiopia,' cultural anthropologist Donald Levine argued for the same. He discussed the Ethiopian national ethos of the Kebra-Nagast—a Ge'ez language fourteenth-century compilation of traditions on the legend of Queen Makeda of Sheba and King Solomon of Jerusalem—as an ethos which legitimized the Ethiopian royal system. He did so in a chapter titled

INTRODUCTION

'A National Script – The Tigrean Contribution.'[7] Levine wrote that 'the fact remains that those who drafted its terms were Tigreans.' And that 'only in the northern part of Tigrinya-speaking territory does one find a cluster of places celebrated in local lore for having been associated with the legend of Makeda and Solomon ... the Old Church of Saint Mary in Aksum is believed to this day to contain the original Ark of the Covenant brought by Menilek I and Azariah from Jerusalem, locked within seven caskets inside the sanctuary.' Levine added that 'the ancient homeland of the Tigrean people thus possesses a particularly intimate relationship with the two central symbolic complexes that undergird the traditional Ethiopian political order: Solomonic genealogy and Monophysite Christian authority.' Levine also argued 'that it was precisely because Tigray lost political power that it was able to play a distinctive role in the evolution of a national society in Greater Ethiopia.' That 'by the time Aksum's kings were overthrown, a stratum of monks had been securely established who were heirs to the prestige formerly associated with the Aksumite polity. They could more easily diffuse their ideas among peoples farther south who had had little or no contact with the Aksumite imperium, and the Amhara kings could more readily accept their moral authority and ideological formulations because Tigray was no longer a serious political competitor.'

The ancient kingdom of Aksum was and has remained the cradle of Ethiopia, as it was conceived by the Christians. Amharic-speaking emperors—at least some of them—made their way to Aksum to be crowned in the 'Church of Our Lady Mary of Tsiyon [Zion[8]].' This church has been rebuilt at least twice. The last time it was rebuilt was in the 1950s by Haile Selassie, the last of the Amhara emperors.

Even though Tigrinya was probably developed in the later stages of Aksumite history (a variant of the term Tigray first appeared in a tenth-century text; the first text in Tigrinya language known to scholars is dated in the twelfth century), for Tigrinya-speaking people and their leaders, there was never a doubt that their roots stemmed in the glory of the ancient kingdom. The only modern Tigrayan emperor, Yohannes IV, did his best—as we shall see—to identify his legitimacy with ancient Aksum. His coronation was conducted there, in the language of Ge'ez, and he himself ruled the empire in Amharic, but he closely followed the legacy of Tigray's Aksum. Language is one of the main components of any definition of self-identity, but history is flexible. Modern Egyptian identity, to mention just one relevant neighbor, a product of the revival of modern Arabic, has been based on a strong sense of continuity from ancient Egypt, even though Arabic was introduced millennia later. I shall confine myself to reconstructing history in as multifaceted a manner as possible. History does change along periods, and no one theoretical truth can fully define any aspect.

Aksum belongs to all of Ethiopia, which was and is a land of diversity and of dualities. Tigrinya speakers always belonged both to themselves and to Ethiopia. They had no one-dimensional priority, but they did often face dilemmas. Closer to our time, some of the Tigrinya speakers adopted Eritrean nationalism and departed from Ethiopia. In most cases, Tigrinya speakers were motivated by a sense of victimization by Amharas and by the fact that, situated at the gate of Ethiopia, they paid the more costly price of Ethiopia's wars. Still, in the major junctures of history, they did identify with the entire land. Yet their strong sense of uniqueness occasionally led foreigners to believe they may secede. There were indeed cases in which Tigrayans did cooperate with external enemies, but so did members of other Ethiopian groups, a part of the ever-energetic Ethiopian power game.

From their incipience, Tigrayans themselves have developed a rich set of internal rivalries in a ceaseless dynamism of inter-Tigrayan jealousies and conflicts. All throughout, they managed to preserve their traditional world, experiencing their first real sociopolitical revolution only in the 1970s.

3

'MEDRI BAHRI'

DEFYING EMPERORS, SAVING ETHIOPIA

After the demise of the Aksum kingdom, the history of the area in question can hardly be followed systematically. For the centuries up to the fifteenth, we have mostly traditions and fragments of information as well as biased modern interpretations. On one side, the rise of Islam in Arabia turned the Red Sea into a wall rather than a bridge. On the other side, the political center of Ethiopian history moved to the south, away from the sea. We are told that in the second half of the tenth century (960?), a queen named Gudit, hailing from Semien Mountains, destroyed the remnants of Aksum, ruled for over forty years, and passed on the throne to her descendants. The issue of her identity remained controversial (one tradition has it that she was Jewish), but surely she was not a Tigrayan. Her dynasty, if there was one worthy of the term, was finally removed by King Mara Takla-Haymanot, who established the Zagwe dynasty, centered around Lalibela in today's Lasta-Amhara region. The kings of Zagwe (1137–1270) exercised authority over a vast area stretching from Wag, Lasta, and Wallo in the south, to modern day Eritrea and Tigray in the north, and to Lake Tana to the west. Their history is shrouded with mystery, and we have little reliable knowledge about the land between the Mareb River and the Red Sea in their time. Tigrinya speakers among the locals—there were various other groups and entities in the future Eritrea—enjoyed local autonomies. One such autonomous center emerged in the village of Debarwa (not far from today's Asmara, to its south).[1] Meanwhile, in 1270, the Zagwe dynasty was toppled by a new dynasty centered on Shoa, the Solomonians.

Medri Bahri

The great Solomonians led the Christian kingdom of Amhara to its golden age: 1270–1527. They ruled quite effectively, spread Christianity, developed the Church, and implemented authority over much of the Horn of Africa.[2] The Solomonians conquered Muslim principalities to their south and annexed and taxed their peoples. They also opened Ethiopia to the greater world and primarily had complex relations with Egypt, which revolved around a story of mutual dependence. The Ethiopians needed the Coptic Church, which was under Egypt's Muslim sultans, the Mamluks (1250–1517). Without an *Abuna*—the bishop sent from Egypt to head the Ethiopian church—they would have little religious legitimacy. The Egyptians, for their part, became more concretely aware that the Nile's main tributary, the Blue Nile, originates in Ethiopia, and they developed fear that the locals could block their source of life.[3] We mention it here as a background to later chapters in which Tigrayans are more directly involved.

The Solomonians ruled officially over northern Ethiopia and today's Eritrea, but did so indirectly and interruptedly, mostly through local allies. The greatest of the Solomonians, Emperor Zara Yaqob (1434–68), sent a force to Debarwa, backed a local ally, and declared him Bahr Negash, the king of the sea. He also named his kingdom Medri Bahri, the land of the sea.[4] The act can be defined as an official renaissance of a Tigrayan kingdom. In 1520, Debarwa was visited by the Portuguese traveler Francisco Alvares. By his account,[5] the Bahr Negash at the time was named Dori, an uncle and a tributary of the Solomonian Emperor Lebna Dengel. The latter was the last of the mighty Solomonians. And it was a Tigrayan, Bahr Negash Yishak (died 1578),[6] who would save Ethiopia. Twice.

Ahmad Gragn

The sixteenth century was a stormy period for the Red Sea. It became an arena of a global conflict with great consequences. On one side were the rulers of Islam in the Middle East: first the Mamluks of Egypt, then, in 1517, their successors, the Ottomans. The Muslims strove to join forces with Islamic rulers in India and dominate the globally important trade route. On the other side stood the Portuguese, pioneers of European seamanship and masters of oceangoing sailing, who discovered the route to India around Africa (1499, Vasco da Gama) and began dominating the trade of the entire East. There began a naval conflict which lasted for five decades, beginning in 1505. Some of the major battles of this conflict were conducted in the Red Sea. The Horn of Africa and Solomonian Ethiopia became a sideshow, yet the conflict escalated to constitute a double threat to the very existence of the Christian state. The first threat came from the south.

Against the background of the Islamic–Christian conflict in the Red Sea (but not directly connected to it), the early sixteenth century saw also a revival of political Islam in the Horn of Africa. It was inspired by the immigration of Muslim scholars from Yemen and from Mecca, who were motivated by the spirit of a Holy War against Christians, both Portuguese and Ethiopian. The walled town of Harar, the capital of the Islamic sultanate of Adal and of Islamic learning in the Horn of Africa, became the center of a Jihadi momentum. Imam Ahmad Ibn Ibrahim, known by his nickname Ahmad Gragn, led a huge army that united various Islamic groups in modern-day southern Ethiopia and Somalia. Gragn penetrated the heart of Ethiopia by 1529, swept the country, and by 1535 conquered most of it. Emperor Lebna-Dengel survived by fleeing into the mountains, finally dying as a refugee in 1540. Except for churches on the islands of Lake Tana, nearly all other symbols of Ethiopia's Christianity were destroyed by the Muslims. Ethiopian tradition has it that nine out of every ten Christians were forced to convert. Ethiopia, as a Christian culture, never experienced such calamity, before or since.[7]

Ahmad Gragn had the backing of the Ottomans. In 1538, at the prime of his campaign in Ethiopia, Gragn sent to the Ottoman governor in Yemen and asked for 3,000 men. The Ottomans were busy fighting the local Zaydis in Sanaa and preparing a renewed naval campaign against the Portuguese. They sent 900 troops to help Gragn, which seemed suffice to secure the Islamic conquest of the already destroyed Ethiopia. The son of Lebna-Dengel, Emperor Galadewos (1540–59), was still fleeing from Gargn's men. The Christian empire was practically finished, with the exception of Medri Bahri. The armies of Gragn were unable to cross the Mareb River and Debarwa survived under Bahr Negash Yishaq.

The Bahr Negash and Salvation

In January 1541, the Portuguese launched another raid on the Red Sea, aiming to burn the Ottoman fleet in Suez. The mission failed and returned in May to anchor in Massawa. Christopher [Cristóvão] da Gama (son of the great Vasco) established contact with the Bahr Negash. In early July, the Portuguese moved uphill. He led over 400 well-trained fighters, skilled artisans, and slaves who carried munitions and about a thousand arquebuses. They also carried long infantry guns and other war materials. They reached Debarwa on 20 July and were well received by Bahr Negash Yishak. The Tigrayan provided them with whatever they needed and arranged for them to camp in his capital. Yishak strengthened a combined combat unit by adding about 500 local soldiers. He also gave Da Gama vital information about the land and the Muslim invaders. The emperor Galadewos camped somewhere in the south with only some sixty followers. His mother, the widow of Emperor Lebna-Dengel, Queen Seble Wongel, was besieged by Gragn's men at the summit of a nearby mountain (probably in Debra Damo). She had a similarly small number of supporters. This was what was left of the great Solomonian empire. Among those who surrendered to Ahmad Gragn and cooperated with him was also the father of Bahr Negash Yishak.

An account of the Portuguese–Ethiopian campaign was captured in writing by Miguel de Castanhoso, who was an eyewitness to almost everything he recorded.[8] In February 1542, the combined force, with Queen Seble Wongel and her men, clashed with Gragn's army. Two more battles were fought in April. On 28 August, near Lake Ashange, in yet another battle, the Christian force was beaten. Christopher da Gama was taken prisoner, tortured, and executed by Gragn himself. Overly confident that he had finished the Christian empire for good, Ahmad Gragn sent the Ottoman soldiers back to Yemen, leaving only 200 for himself. However, the remnants of the Portuguese soldiers joined the camp of Emperor Galadewos, which meanwhile, as hope had been restored, was swelling. On 21 February 1543, the two armies met near Lake Tana in the battle of Zantara. A bullet fired by one of the Portuguese killed Amad Gragn. With the fall of their great leader, the whole Islamic campaign collapsed. His men dispersed, and some returned to their capital Harar and fortified its walls. Ethiopia, as a Christian country, was saved.

An episode told by Castanhoso is worth mentioning. The father of Bahr Negus Yishak, who had betrayed Ethiopia and his son and collaborated with Ahmad Gragn, sought pardon from Galadewos. The emperor was hardly in the mood. All sides in that conflict were not merciful—prisoners were cruelly executed by the dozen, let alone traitors. Yet despite the emperor's anger at the man's betrayal, he spared his life. It was no doubt out of respect for the son, the Bahr Negash, who had provided such critical help. It was also, we might presume, a calculated step not to overly alienate the people of Medri Bahri, the guardians of the gate. It would not be the last case of mutual grace in the Amhara–Tigrayan story, nor would it be the last episode of collaborating with foreigners.

The Ottomans and the Bahr Negash

After the threat to Ethiopia from the jihadi Islam of Ahmad Gragn, there appeared another threat. This time it came from the north, from the direction of the Red Sea. Once again, the arena of the confrontation was Medri Bahri, and the Bahr Negash played the main role.

The threat came from the Ottoman Empire, one of the strongest powers in the world at that time. The Islamic Ottoman empire, as mentioned, lost the sea war with the Portuguese, but was still at its peak as a land power. Frustrated for not winning the route to India, the Ottomans still wanted to control the Red Sea. They were also looking for alternative sources of gold and silver and to this end had conquered Tunisia in 1551. They now looked to Ethiopia as a land of minerals and gold (and were about to discover the coffee of Yemen as a commercial asset). In 1555, Ottoman General Ozdemir Pasha was tasked with capturing the African coast of the Red Sea.[9]

Ozdemir landed in Suakin and, in 1557, led a force of 3,000 men to Debarwa. Luckily for him, Bahr Negash Yishaq at the time was with Emperor Galadewos in central Ethiopia, where they fought against what was left of Gragn's army. Ozdemir built a mosque in Debarwa and a fortified tower. In July of that year, he declared the establishment of 'Habesh Eyaleti,' the Province of Ethiopia in Turkish.[10] The declaration was tantamount to claiming that Ethiopia was part of the great Islamic empire.

What was planned in Istanbul was foiled on the soil of Medri Bahri, though not immediately. First there was a war of thirty years in which the defenders of Ethiopia also acted as proud Tigrayans, wavering between loyalty to the Amhara-dominated empire and collaboration with the Ottoman foreigners.

In 1559, Bahr Negash Yishaq returned from the south and forced the Ottoman garrison to flee from Debarwa to Massawa. The Ottoman force was also weakened by an influenza epidemic that killed thousands of their troops. Soon after, the son of Ozdemir, Othman Pasha, came to Massawa as his replacement, and hurried to make peace with the Bahr Negash.

For the next three decades, the Ottoman effort was to return to Debarwa and secure Massawa. They could do so only by allying with the Bahr Negash. When Emperor Minas (1559–63), the successor of Galadewos, tried to end Yishaq autonomy, the latter did not hesitate to collaborate with Othman. In the ensuing clash in 1562, their combined army defeated the emperor's, and Minas retreated to Shoa, where he died the following year. His successor, Emperor Serza-Dengel (1563–97), made peace with the Bahr Negash, who broke relations with the Ottomans.

In 1572, Radwan Pasha was sent from Egypt with fresh forces and recaptured Debarwa. Two years later, he was forced out by Bahr Negash Yishaq. In 1577, Ahmet Pasha was appointed over Habesh Eyaleti and marched there equipped with eight cannons. Again, much like sixteen years previously, he proposed an alliance to the Bahr Negash. Again, the old Tigrayan allied with the Ottomans. He and Ahmet fought against the army of Emperor Serza Dengel and were both killed on 17 December 1578. The emperor entered Debarwa and abolished local autonomy. There, Serza Dengel established the first Ethiopian unit, equipped with firearms taken from the Ottomans. The unit was put under a *Turk Basha*, directly under imperial command. Serza Dengel also declared that local governors of the regions beyond the Tekezé River were not allowed the banner, *sandaq,* and the drum, *nagarit*, which hitherto they had used to mobilize armies.

Still the Ottomans did not give up. A force of 7,000 men was dispatched from Yemen, and in 1588 recaptured Debarwa. However, they soon realized that messing with Ethiopia was too costly. Debarwa was abandoned, and the Ottomans appointed over Massawa a member of a local family from nearby Arkiko, who for the next three centuries would hoist their flag over his palace, symbolizing their claim to the Red Sea port.[11]

Debarwa and Massawa would be included in the future Eritrea established by the Italians in 1890. Modern Eritrean nationalists would consider the medieval Medri Bahri as part of Eritrean history. Such a view is not entirely unjustified. Between the coastal Massawa, which would develop and begin prospering as part of the Red Sea space, and Tigray proper, south of the River Mareb, the now marginalized highlands of Hamasen, Saraye, and Akala Guzay developed separately. In the seventeenth to nineteenth centuries, Hamasen enjoyed a period of communal rule under councils of village elders. They enforced traditional laws which had prevailed uniquely in the region alongside feudal authority since ancient times.[12] The region appeared in European maps as 'The Republic of Hamasien.' For the rest of Ethiopia, it was now *Mareb Melash*, namely 'beyond the River Mareb.'[13] Its political centers began rotating between two rival villages of Tigrinya speakers: Tsazega (a little northwest from today's Asmara) and Hazzega. In around 1841 a strongman from Hazzega, Walda-Mikael Solomon,[14] managed for a while to unite the locals. We shall return to his story later. Today he is widely celebrated as a hero of Eritrean history.[15]

4

THE ERA OF THE JUDGES

AUTONOMY AND TRADITIONAL STRUCTURE

Ethiopia was liberated from the conquest of Ahmad Gragn and was saved from an Ottoman attempt to occupy her north. However, the next three centuries were hardly spent recuperating. The failure was not just because of the destruction inflicted by the Islamic warriors. More factors contributed to a gradual weakening of the imperial system of the kingdom. Below, we shall discuss some of them.

Enter the Oromo

While Christian Ethiopia was traumatized, the Oromo people penetrated from their homelands in the south and settled in the highlands. The first Oromo movements occurred in the 1520s. In the 1540s and 1550s, their some fifty clans mixed with other local peoples and occupied vast areas. In the process, they managed to safeguard their identity and retain their language, unique social system, and the political independence of their various entities. In the last quarter of the nineteenth century, they would be conquered by King Menelik of Shoa (1889–1913) and begin playing a very major role in the modern and contemporary developments of Ethiopia. This, for now, is outside of our story of greater Tigray.

However, still in the context of the sixteenth-century migration wave, some of the Oromo groups penetrated the northern central regions of Wallo, between Shoa and Tigray, and joined our scene. Settling there, they absorbed Amhara practices and also began using the Amharic language. They kept their separateness by adopting Islam during the eighteenth century, but in a flexible way that enabled close contact with Christians.[1] The Oromo had already perfected horsemanship and built very useful cavalry, gradually adding firearms to their cold weapons. The Wallo Oromos gained military superiority, especially when they were led in the early eighteenth century by the Mammedoch dynasty, who claimed descendancy from prophet Muhammad.[2] It was enough to dominate the core of the country but not to cross the Takkaze River into the heart of Tigray. Only to the east of the river's source, the Rayya Oromo[3] penetrated into Tigrayans' land, assimilated with locals, and in time also adopted Tigrinya.

Portuguese religious challenge

The decline of the authority of the emperors of the Solomonian dynasty was also due to the Portuguese. After the fall of Ahmad 'Gragn,' some 170 of the Portuguese soldiers stayed in Ethiopia. They married local women, were allotted lands, and contributed to the country in various ways. However, Christian harmony was not created. The Catholic Portuguese, loyal to the Roman Church, had difficulty accepting the Ethiopians' Christianity. They scored a major success on 11 February 1626 when Emperor Susenios, under the influence of the missionary Afonso Mendes, publicly made Catholicism the state religion. Upon Susenios' death in 1632, his son and heir, Fasiladas or Fasil (1632–67), canceled his father's declarations, and in 1634 expelled Mendes and his associates—but not before a costly internal war.

Fasil was quite resourceful. After he expelled the Jesuits and revived the Ethiopian Church, he rebuilt the ancient cathedral of Our Lady Mary of Zion in Aksum[4] (which had been destroyed by Gragn), where he was crowned.

Gondar—the New Center

Fasil also initiated the establishment of a new capital city. It was a renewed concept in Ethiopia. For many centuries, the emperors were used to roving around the country, implementing their authority by appearing in the provinces with their mobile courts and thrones. In 1636, Fasil decided to build Gondar as an urban center. It was a gigantic enterprise in Ethiopian terms. However, the establishment of Gondar also contributed to further decline. In the next two centuries, no emperor capable of implementing authority in the vast realm emerged. The Christian kings mostly closed themselves in the city, relied more and more on Oromo chiefs in the center, and were immersed in power manipulations like in a Byzantine court. By the mid-eighteenth century, these kings had no imperial leadership in the more distant provinces.

Tigray's Rise

While the power of the imperial center in Ethiopia was weakening, Tigray was undergoing two processes that would prepare for future hegemony.

One was the solidification of the social and economic power of the leading families. It had to do with the ancient landownership system of the Ethiopian highlands. The major form of this ownership was a type of communal system known as *Rest*.[5] All descendants (both male and female) of an individual founder were entitled to a share, and individuals had the right to use a plot of family land. *Rest* was inalienable, and inviolable, as the land belonged not to the individual but to the descent group. The other major form of land tenure was *Gult,* an ownership right acquired from the emperor or from provincial rulers. *Gult* was non-inheritable, attached to a governorship in lieu of salary, and granted in return for specific—often military—obligations. In effect, *Gult* reinforced an existing system of political power. Both *Gult* and *Rest* involved military service obligations. Historian Patrick Gilkes studied landownership in Tigray in 1971 and found out that genealogies he reconstructed showed sequences of up to ten or twelve generations of claimed inheritance of both *Rest* and *Gult*. This meant that the late sixteenth to early seventeenth century was a time of significant social and political change in greater Tigray. When the authority of the emperors weakened in the periods leading to the its eighteenth-century collapse, Gilkes wrote, 'the great provincial nobility not only usurped the royal authority to make land grants, but also exerted control over the local soldiers.'[6] By the nineteenth century, 'greater Tigray' (Tigray and present-day Eritrea) was divided into no less than twenty-four independent units, each led by local feudal warlords.[7]

The other was the quicker and better adoption of firearms by the people of Tigray. In 1578, to reiterate, Emperor Serza Dengel declared that local governors of the provinces beyond the Tekezé River were not allowed the banner, *sandaq*, and the war drum, *nagarit*, which traditionally were used to call to arms. However, as imperial power in the center declined and became increasingly dependent on Oromo cavalry, and as new firearms were used by the emperors to defend the far-off Gondar, the Tigrayan leaders became practically independent. They accumulated power to tax their lands, to judge, and to mobilize their people. Settled closer to the Red Sea, especially to the port of Massawa, the Tigrayan chiefs better benefitted from increasing quantities of imported firearms. They also had better access to the salt mines of the Afar desert, a vital source of finance.[8] As it was put by historian Richard Caulk in his 1972 article 'Firearms and Princely Power in Ethiopia,'[9] in the later sixteenth and the seventeenth centuries Tigray and the lands beyond the Mareb River (much of what is now Eritrea) were best placed to master the new technology of war. During the period 1830–50, there were 28,000 matchlock guns in Tigray, while Bagemdir, Shoa, and Wallo had 4,000, 1,000, and 1,000 respectively.[10]

Throughout the nineteenth century, the Ethiopians in general and Tigray in particular could absorb firearms in growing quantities. They could do so based on their traditional social and political structures. The personal gun could replace the personal sword without any need to change or challenge the existing mobilizing systems, the organizing of armed peasants as combat units, discipline, or formations. In many other societies in that period—Egypt is a good, relevant example—the absorption of modern firearms had to be accompanied by revolutionary changes. For example, from aristocracy on horses to mass infantry made up of recruited peasants. Ethiopia's hierarchical old systems could do so without experiencing fundamental restructuring. It was one of the reasons for her victories, along with a long enduring conservatism.

This was even more so the case in Tigray. What was constructed socially and politically in the late medieval to early modern period survived there till recently. In other parts of Ethiopia (and Eritrea), old structures did undergo some changes over the centuries. Tigray, as will be reflected in the following chapters, would only experience her first real revolution in 1974.

Gondar, Shoa, Gojjam, Tigray

The heirs of Emperor Fasiladas hardly ventured out of Gondar, and practically, the empire now consisted of four different political centers: Gondar, with a powerless royal family torn apart by endless intrigues, dependent mainly on the infusion of Oromo families supported by the numerous cavalries of their kinsmen in Yeju and Wallo; Gojjam, defined by the loop of the Blue Nile and led by local hereditary elite families; Shoa in the south led by her kings (who, in time, would restore their country as the center of Ethiopia); and in the north, Tigray, which was growing stronger due to plentiful supply of munitions and many skilled marksmen.

One event in 1769 marked the beginning of the actual demise of the royal institution. Ethiopian tradition, ever inspired by the Hebrew bible, called it 'the Era of the Judges,' zamana masafint, for 'In those days there was no king in Israel but every man did that which was right in his own eyes' (Judges, 17:6). In narrating the story of the period, many scholars used the term 'anarchy.' But in fact, it was definitely not 'every man' for himself.[11] Ethiopia as a Christian state and as a political culture did not disintegrate. Regional princes, the 'nobility,' *masafint*, did control regional hierarchies of loyalties, which maintained legitimacy sanctioned by traditional titles. What happened was that this feudal regional order prevailed at the expense of the Gondarine dynasty, but the sense of affiliation to the same Ethiopian identity and culture survived. Regional warlords went on striving for Ethiopian titles enacted by the court of Gondar, or worked to force the puppet emperors to enact them. They aimed to dominate Ethiopia, not to depart or secede from her. Yet the idea that Ethiopia could disintegrate, and the image and legacy of that period, would persist, and still survives today.

Ras Mikael Sehul

It was a Tigrayan strongman, Mikael Sehul, who, by becoming the kingmaker in Gondar in 1769, opened the 'Era of the Judges.'

Born in Adwa to a leading local family, Mikael was reported in the late 1750s to have an army of some 8,000 men equipped with firearms. Well involved in power struggles in the northern regions, Mikael was recognized by Gondar as Governor of Tigray and was given the title of Dajazmach.[12] He was also involved in Gondar's palace intrigues. Empress Mentwab (1706–73), the strong person in the court, married him to one of her daughters. In 1768, she called him to intervene in a violent crisis in the royal family. Mikael arrived in Gondar with an army of some 26,000 musketeers. What followed was a collision with local forces, a bloodbath in the town, and the execution of Emperor Iyoas I at the order of Mikael, who then appointed the next two emperors: Yohaness II, who was quickly removed, and Tekle Haymanot II.

Terrorizing Gondar, Mikael forced the court not only to promote him to ras,[13] but also to give him the title of *ras biwadad* (literally 'the beloved ras') to distinguish him above all other nobles in the realm. It meant accepting the puppet emperors of Gondar as the source of traditional legitimacy without destroying the by-now merely symbolic Solomonian court.

However, away from Tigray, the army of Ras Mikael was defeated by a coalition of Amhara and Oromo armies. The numerous cavalries of Yeju and Wallo proved still stronger in the open field, especially as only slow-firing weapons were then used to oppose swift and often surprise attacks by cavalry and infantry in large numbers. On 4 June 1771, Ras Mikael surrendered. He had to prostrate himself before the emperor with a stone on his neck—as was the custom—before he was pardoned.[14] After a year, and probably to avoid another invasion from Tigray, Ras Mikael was released and sent back to govern Tigray in Adwa.[15]

Ras Walda-Selassie

Tigray itself was far from stable. Strong families in other corners of it had accumulated feudal power and built strong local armies. Upon the death of Mikael Sehul in Adwa, power went on rotating to other parts of Tigray. Still, the rest of Ethiopia was mostly in a deeper crisis.

The next leader of Tigray, formally as viceroy of the weak emperors in Gondar—like Mikael Sehul had been—was from Endarta.

Walda-Selassie[16] began paving his way fighting against Ras Mikael (who killed Walda-Selassie's father, Kifle Iyasus) and against Mikael's successors. Walda-Selassie was forced to spend years in exile in central Ethiopia, and only in 1788 managed to stabilize his power in Endarta. Two years later, he marched to Gondar to be recognized there as a ruler of Tigray. Like Ras Mikael, he was given the title of *ras bitwadad*, thus declared the strongest non-royal man in Ethiopia. Until his death in 1816, Ras Walda-Selassie had direct authority in Tigray, including the vast spaces between the Rayya and the gates of Massawa. During his lifetime, he was said to have fought in some forty battles. He built palaces, supported the monasteries, and helped spread the Orthodox faith. He also involved himself in Gondar's palace intrigues and in the endless conflicts of the central regions. Moreover, Ras Walda-Selassie was the first ruler of the period to have close contact with Europeans. He hosted British diplomats, among them Henry Salt, with whom he signed a treaty of friendship between Ethiopia and Britain in 1805. Walda-Selassie also succeeded in negotiating with the Egyptians the sending of a new *abuna* from Cairo. He died in his bed in his palace in Hintalo, Endarta, aged eighty.

Dajazmach Sabagadis Woldu

Power in Tigray then shifted to Agame, to Dajazmach Sabagadis Woldu, who ruled 1822–31.[17]

Sabagadis family ruled Agame from the late eighteenth to the early nineteenth centuries. He spent his youth fighting his four brothers and then consolidated his power in Agame by defeating punitive expeditions sent by Ras Walda-Selassie. In 1811, Sabagadis challenged Walda-Selassie and rallied forces from all over Tigray. He then settled with the master of Tigray in turn for his confirmation as governor of Agame. After the death of Walda-Selassie, Sabagadis fought against other regional contenders and acquired the Tigrayan overlordship in 1822, assuming the title of Dajazmach. Making Adigrat his capital, Sabagadis ruled Tigray, Semien, the coastal plains of today's Eritrea, and occasionally parts of the Eritrean highlands. Like his Tigrayan predecessors, he challenged the Orormo Yejju domination in Gondar and aspired to end their control over the weak emperors. To this end, he sought to acquire more firearms, capture the port of Massawa, and build relations with European powers. He also worked to build alliances with other regional chiefs in northern Ethiopia, notably Dajazmach Wube Hailemariam of Semien.[18] However, Ras Marye of Yejju, leading the powerful Oromo cavalry, defeated and captured Wube Hailemariam. In 1830, Sabagadis invaded Semien, appointed his men, and retired to Tigray. In retaliation, Marye, supported by Wube, led his army across the Takazze River and on 14 February 1831 clashed with Sabagadis at the battle of Debra Abbay. *Ras* Marye himself was killed, but Sebagadis had to surrender to Wube. The latter handed the defeated Tigrayan to the Oromo troops. It was said that just before he was beheaded, Sabagadis said to his Oromo prisoners: 'I have only fought in this war to defend my country, which you wished, without cause, to ruin, and of which I was the father. You may kill my body; but my soul is in the hands of God...'[19]

Dajazmach Wube Haile Maryam

THE ERA OF THE JUDGES

The Oromo army then went on to ravage Tigray in revenge for their leader's death. The ceaseless internal conflicts, bloodshed, and constant violent rivalries and betrayals left Tigray weakened. Local leaders would not be able to unite Tigray for the next forty years.

Upon Sabagadis's death, Tigray became the power base of Dajazmach Wube Haile Maryam of Semien who was not, strictly speaking, a proper Tigrayan. Controlling much of northern Ethiopia, Wube was one of the more powerful feuding regional warlords in the empire of that time. He aimed at taking the capital of Gondar, and in 1841, he managed to do so for a while before he was defeated in February 1842 by the Oromo warlord Ras Ali in the battle of Debra Tabor. The two chiefs, however, avoided more serious clashes. Wube tried to take Massawa from the Egyptians but failed and left Tigray in 1846 to focus on the conflicts in the center. In these ceaseless struggles, an ambitious strongman from the peripheral region of Qwara, Kasa Hailu, went from force to force. He defeated Ras Ali II in June 1853, then Wube's army on 9 February 1855, before crowning himself as emperor Tewodros II within a few days. His coming to power is generally considered the end of 'Era of the Judges,' and his reign, a most dramatic chapter in Ethiopian history, is considered the opening of the modern era in the country. Its detailed story is outside our scope.

5

THEIR FINEST HOUR

YOHANNES

The Tigrayan Emperor

The reign of Emperor Yohannes IV (1872–89) marked the climax of the Tigrayans' role in Ethiopian history, at least until 1991.

To understand Yohannes, he is best viewed against the background of his predecessor, Emperor Tewodros. They both obtained power as *shifta*s, namely rebels, bandits. Not an illegitimate way by Ethiopian tradition and practice.[1] In every other way they mostly differed.

Tewodros was an ambitious revolutionary. He chose his imperial name from a medieval legend that an emperor by that name would lead Christian Ethiopia to greatness, defeat Islam and inherit Jerusalem. Tewodros sidelined Gondar and established a new capital on an *amba* (one of Ethiopia's many flat-topped mountains). He defeated the Orormo and founded his new capital at *Amba* Maqdala.

Tewodros strove to centralize Ethiopia and to build a new set of loyalties at the expense of the provincial warlords. His army grew to some 60,000 men, peaking in around 1860. It was strong enough to raid in the countryside, to temporarily back his appointees, and to take hostages back to Maqdala. Provincial leaders frequented Maqdala to be granted lands and titles.

Tewodros is widely credited for reviving the institution of emperorship. However, his real power fell short of centralizing the state. His army, equipped with old muskets and some newer breech-loading rifles, could hardly impose authority on the vast periphery and on the various ambitious leaders with similar equipment. After 1861, Tewodros realized he needed modern arms, especially cannons and mortars, which were essential for conquering fortified mountains. He built an arms factory, forcing European missionaries to work as engineers and his people to pave roads. To finance it all, Tewodros went as far as trying to tax the Church, the biggest landowner in the country. In so doing, he alienated Abuna Salama, the Egyptian-born head of the Church, a man no less tough, who responded by excommunicating the emperor. Tewodros also collided with Britain, a strong global power at that time.

In 1863, Tewodros wrote to Queen Victoria asking for British assistance in modernizing Ethiopia and defeating Islam. When this went ignored, he imprisoned several Europeans in his kingdom, along with protestant missionaries and the two British diplomats sent to appease him. This time, the British did respond. [2] In early January 1868, their army landed in Zula, the ancient Adulis. General R. Napier led a force of 13,000 British and Indian soldiers, 26,000 camp followers, and over 40,000 animals (including 44 elephants). They also carried over four million Maria Theresa silver coins to pay for the services of locals. On 10 April 1868, the British expedition faced the mount of Maqdala, and Tewodros committed suicide rather than surrender. The invaders set Maqdala on fire, released the hostages, and left for India. It all had to do with the rise of Yohannes.

In Tigray, Tewodros was never able to impose effective government. Though he managed to take important figures hostage, such as Ras Araya Selassie Demsu[3] of Endarta, his appointees in Tigray were constantly challenged by their local adversaries. The emperor's men were finally removed in 1865, when it was known that Abuna Salama excommunicated Tewodros, and when the well-armed *Shum* of Wag, Gobaze, temporarily took control of Tigray. Competition for the actual rule of Tigray went on among the descendants of key figures: Ras Mikael Sehul, Ras Walda-Sellasse, and Dajazmach Sabagadis. Their mutual fighting ended in October 1867, with the victory of Dajazmach Kasa Mircha, the *Shum* of Tamben. Kasa was a direct descendent of Mikael Sehul,[4] related to the other two important families, and was for a time an appointee of Tewodros and then of Gobaze.

By 1868, the only serious contenders for national leadership were the *Wag-shum* Gobaze, who, in June 1868, declared himself Emperor Takla Giyorgis II[5]; Menelik of Shoa, who had declared himself king (negus) in 1865; and Dajazmach Kasa Mircha of Tigray.

In February 1868, Dajazmach Kasa met with general Napier when the British were on their way to Maqdala. The Tigrayan provided them with information and other services. Already in their first meeting, Napier arranged for Kasa, whom the British called now 'the prince of Tigray,' a display of artillery practice with cavalry and infantry exercise. The display left an overwhelming impression on Kasa. In May, returning victorious from Maqdala, Napier gave the Tigrayan twelve small guns, several hundred muskets, over 100 rifles, a large supply of powder, caps, and shot, and organized another parade. He also left an English sergeant and artillery expert with Kasa: John Kirkham.[6] It was enough to pave the way to domination.

Though Kasa's army was far smaller than that of Emperor Takla Giyorgis—12,000 men, compared to 60,000—it proved decisively superior. In the final clash in the valley of Asem, near Adwa, on 10 July 1871, Takla Giyorgis's army was ambushed. Terrified by the roars of the new guns, it disintegrated. In late January 1872, Kasa was crowned Emperor Yohannes IV.[7]

Yohannes' seventeen years in power were formative for the country, for Tigrinya speakers, and for the whole region as it faced foreign aggressions, western imperialism, and religious radicalization.[8] At first, Yohannes managed to unite Tigray itself, to impose his authority on greater Tigray, and to dictate his supremacy across the entirety of Ethiopia. He recognized the rulers of Shoa and Gojjam as kings, hoping to stabilize the empire as a federation, and trying to cement this structure by Christian unity. For a while, he was successful. He defeated the invading Egyptians and scored some victories against the Italians as well as against the Sudanese Islamic militants. However, in the mid-1880s, it all began to collapse. Tigray proper was hardly modernized in his time. Yohannes, a sad introvert, rather closed himself off, and in its prime, Tigray did not undergo meaningful urbanization. Shouldering enormous new tasks, Yohannes' Tigray exhausted itself. No real all-Ethiopian unity was achieved in the face of growing external challenges. Menelik of Shoa collaborated with the imperialists, and the Tigrinya speakers proved unable to overcome their own endless feuds. Eritrea was eventually lost to the Italians without a battle. Conducting an overly anti-Islamic policy at home, Yohannes failed to appease the Sudanese jihadists when he wanted to. He was killed by their bullets in March 1889. Altogether, the sad emperor ended as a tragic figure. He led Tigray to its finest hour, then left her destroyed.

Coronation and the heritage of Aksum

Cultural Historian Izabela Orlowska studied Kasa's preparations for the coronation and its significances.[9] She observed that Kasa, conscious of the need to legitimize his claim to the emperorship, was careful with the ideological message that he conveyed. She analyzed the way he identified himself by his seals in 1870. His first seal presented him as 'Dejazmach Kasa, the head of nobles of Ethiopia.' Somewhat later, he added: 'the one who is appointed by God,' and then: 'the Elect of God of the Land of Aksum Tsiyon.' Finally: 'Dejazmach Kasa, the head of the nobles, Elect of God of the land of Aksum Tsiyon, the main place [city] of Ethiopia.' After the January 1872 coronation, he styled himself 'King of Kings Yohannes of Ethiopia and all its territories.'

The evolution of the usage of symbols in his titles, Orlowska added, showed the importance he placed on ideological propaganda that underpinned his claim to Solomonic kingship. By carefully preparing a lavish and highly performative coronation ceremony in the ancient church in Aksum, Yohannes mobilized basic historical and nationalist Christian Ethiopian traditions to legitimize his emperorship. Only five out of fifty-eight Solomonic emperors who reigned between 1270 and 1855—she observed—went to Aksum for their coronation. They did so for the symbolism, but they all had their power base elsewhere. Now it was different. The coronation of Yohannes IV in ancient Aksum, in Tsiyon, Ethiopia's Jerusalem, meant not only a connection to ancient legacies, to Christian, Hebraic biblical Solomonic legitimacy, and to long historical continuity, it also meant that ancient Tigray returned to be the very center of the Ethiopian empire.

The ceremony in Aksum was attended by officials from outside of Tigray. A chronicle housed in the Dabra Berhan Sellase, a modest church in Adwa, affirms that 'there was no one from among the clergy and secular officials living between Shoa and Massawa who was not present.'[10] Even the recently deposed emperor Takla Giyorgis was present, albeit in chains. (He was then blinded and put on an *amba*, where he soon died, or was murdered.)

Wearing a golden crown decorated with diamonds, Yohannes went on singing for Tsiyon, imitating King David dancing before the Lord when the people of Israel brought the Ark to Jerusalem.[11] As he approached the ancient church, the clergy challenged him three times on his identity. 'Who are you?' to which he responded, 'I am the king of *Tsiyon* of Ethiopia.' Abuna Atnatewos[12], together with the bishops, priests, deacons, and monks, were inside the church. Yohannes sat on the stone seat, accompanied by the *abuna* to his right and the *echage* (head of the monks) to his left. He recited the Psalm of David while a battery of cannons fired to mark the occasion.

By reinforcing the centrality of the Zionist ideology for the Ethiopian monarchy, the entire process placed emphasis on the continuity of the Solomonic monarchy and on Yohannes' association with it. Yohannes also worked to restore his Ethiopian Christian position in Jerusalem, in the ancient monastery of Dayr as-Sultan, and by initiating, in 1884, the building of a new church in West Jerusalem.[13]

Under Yohannes, the coronation in Aksum was a loud and clear declaration that Tigray was restored as the cradle of the Ethiopian empire.

Yohannes reigned till his violent death in 1889. Throughout those 17 years, he changed Ethiopia in many ways. Primarily, he shifted the center of power back to the north, to the area of the medieval Medri Bahri and the Mareb Melash. However, this time the northern area was not just the peripheral borderland, the gate, and the wall. Global changes which occurred at that time revived the Red Sea as a strategic arena in which powerful forces competed for domination. Greater Tigray became the arena in which Ethiopia's struggle for survival was again to be conducted.

Defeating the Egyptian challenge

In 1869, as 'the Prince of Tigray' was making his way to emperorship, the Suez Canal was opened in Egypt. The Red Sea, which had been on the sidelines of global history since the sixteenth century, became a main strategic waterway. It connected the northern hemisphere to the southern one, the major road for imperialists. Unlike Napier, who invaded Ethiopia aiming at disconnection, from the opening of Suez Canal imperialists came to stay. Tewodros wanted Europe to come and help. Yohannes had to face powerful foreigners who threatened to invade and conquer. Ethiopia was involved in wars throughout the last quarter of the nineteenth century. She would emerge victorious, but Yohannes would pay with his throne and his life, and Tigray would be impoverished, divided, and pushed to the sidelines for another century.[14]

Egypt was the first challenge facing Yohannes.

In the years just prior to the opening of the Suez Canal, *khedive* Ismail (1863–79), 'the impatient Europeanizer' of his country, renewed Egyptian government in Sudan. Ismail dreamt of an Egyptian African empire which would further connect his westernizing enterprise to Europe. To build such an Egyptian empire, he conquered vast territories in the Nile basin. His main problem was communication. The trek along the Nile was not suitable for running an empire. The only valid option to build modern transportation between Egypt and Sudan was via the Red Sea. Already, in 1865, Ismail leased Suakin and Massawa from the Ottomans. In the first half of the 1870s, Egyptian expedition forces crossed Bab al-Mandab, occupied Zeyla and Berbera, and proceeded down the Somali coast. In 1875, the Egyptians penetrated inland and occupied the walled town of Harar, the capital of Islam in the Horn of Africa (and of Ahmad 'Gragn.'[15])

The hub of the enterprise was Massawa. From Massawa, westward to Sudan, through Kassala and then Khartoum, there was a relatively easy road along which a railway could be laid. Controlling this space was essential for Ismail. This strip—the future Eritrea, in 1890—and its mountainous heart, the regions of Hamasen, Saraye, and Akelle Guzay, was the core of the medieval Bahri Meder. It was inhabited by Tigrinya-speaking Christian people; an integral part of greater Tigray. In 1871, the task to open this road from the Red Sea to Sudan was given by Ismail to the Swiss Werner Munzinger, who worked on developing the telegraph and laying rails. This was just when Yohannes was about to be crowned in nearby Aksum. The collision became inevitable.

The first move was by the Egyptians. At the end of the rainy season of 1875, Munzinger was sent to Menelik, in Shoa, to offer a deal against Yohannes but was killed in the Afar desert. At the same time, a 2,500-strong Egyptian army, commanded by the new governor of Massawa, Arakil Bey, and the Danish mercenary Colonel A. Ahrendrup, penetrated deep into Ethiopian territory. An Ethiopian ambush destroyed the force at Gundet on 13 November 1875. Some 1,800 Egyptians were reported killed, and 2,200 rifles were captured by the Ethiopians. [16]

A new Egyptian military expedition was prepared in Suez. It was 15,000-men-strong and led by the commander of the Khedive's army, Muhammad Ratib Pasha. His second-in-command was the American mercenary General William Loring (the headquarters of the force included 19 American officers). In December 1875, the expedition army landed in Massawa and began marching inland. At Gura[17], 100 kilometers south of Massawa, the Egyptians entrenched themselves. The ensuing battle from 7–9 March ended again in an Egyptian defeat. Yohannes mustered some 50,000 warriors, the majority carrying firearms. His 'Turk Basha,' Ras Alula, the commander of the advance guard, provoked the Egyptians and staged a hasty retreat. Ratib Pasha was enticed to order his men to venture out and chase the Ethiopians, and they were ambushed by Yohannes' army. An Egyptian scholar later estimated the number of casualties at Gundet and Gura to be 8,500.[18]

The Egyptians did not recuperate from their Gura defeat. The dream of controlling the corridor to Sudan (today's Eritrea) was not to materialize. Still the Egyptians stayed in Massawa and in posts along the strip connecting it to Sudan for another nine years. They went on clashing with the Ethiopians over the future Eritrea. Ismail Pasha twice sent his hired governor of Sudan, the famous British General Charles Gordon, to negotiate some arrangement, to no avail. Yohannes entrusted the Mareb Melash to Ras Alula, and in any case was not ready to compromise on parts of greater Tigray. Alula, for his part, did his best to humiliate and mock the Egyptians, also demonstrating his sense of superiority to them as Muslims.[19]

The African empire Ismail hoped to build was supposed to cover the debts Egypt was accumulating in her impatient modernization. The ensuing bankruptcy deepened Europeans' interference in Cairo, which ignited popular unrest. It was led by Colonel Ahmad Urabi, who returned embittered from the Gura defeat. In 1879, the European powers removed and exiled Ismail, and the officers' protest movement gradually turned into a popular revolt. In September 1882, the British, fearing for their interests in the entire region, invaded Egypt, and would not leave again until 1956.[20]

The humiliating defeat in Gura in 1876 was never forgotten by the Egyptians, especially their army officers,[21] nor did Tigrayans forget the legacy of that victory. We shall mention it later in the more recent story of the Renaissance Dam.

A long war of attrition between the Egyptians in Eritrea and Ras Alula in Asmara led nowhere. Then, in June 1884, the Egyptians, their own country already conquered, and the Ethiopians signed a treaty in Adwa overseen by the British. Under the Heweet Treaty, the Egyptians evacuated Massawa in February 1885.

The Heweet Treaty was the only international treaty Yohannes ever signed. It was disastrous. As put by Sven Rubenson, Yohannes traded one weak enemy, Egypt, with two strong ones—imperialist Italy and Islamic militant Mahdist Sudan.[22] His decision to do so would prove fatal.

Ethiopia as a federation

Until his fall in 1889, Yohannes enjoyed military superiority over all internal rivals. His army in Tigray and in central Ethiopia was strengthened by the Oromos' cavalry. A good part of his forces was entrusted with Ras Alula beyond the Mareb River. This land would continue to be threatened by the Egyptians up to 1884, then by the Sudanese Mahdists and the Italian imperialists. The local Tigrayans in Hamasen strove to retain their old autonomy and hardly accepted Alula's regime. We shall also come to that below as an initial chapter in the history of modern Eritrean identity.

Yohannes, by most descriptions, was quite an introverted person, occasionally moody. He was ever suspicious of potential conspirators, even in Tigray proper and in his close circle. His main problem in the Ethiopian empire was Menelik, King of Shoa, who had a claim to the imperial throne. While Yohannes had his hands full in the north, Menelik accumulated power with no interruption. Initially, the Shoans under him were free to expand to the south, then, as of 1875, in all directions. Much of what is today's southern Ethiopia was occupied by Menelik as he enriched his treasury and expanded his armed forces. In time, Menelik would inherit Yohannes' lands, but till then, strictly in military terms, the Tigrayans were more powerful.

Yohannes could rebuild Ethiopia his way. He did not follow the failure of Tewodros and refrained from trying to impose a central government. Rather, Yohannes conceived Ethiopia as a sort of a federation under his imperial leadership and recognized the rulers of Shoa and of Gojjam as kings. He strove to cement this structure by unifying the Church around the same Christian tradition. He also sought to impose Christianity on the Muslims of the country, especially on the Oromos of the center. He conducted internal

Ethiopian affairs (outside Tigray) and foreign affairs in the all-Ethiopian Amharic language and did not try to impose Tigrinya on others.

Yohannes did not even centralize his regime in Tigray proper, nor did he build a capital city or administrative branches. Like medieval emperors, he preferred to have a roving court. His mobile throne, the traditional *alga*,[23] contained the state archive and was the center of power. He was especially fond of his stations in Maqale, Adwa, and more to the center in Debra Tabor, between which he traveled with his entourage, nobles, and priests. Foreigners were occasionally forced to spend long weeks searching before they could find where Emperor Yohannes camped.

In March 1877, Menelik challenged Yohannes openly. He marched northward aiming to join hands with Ras Adal of Gojjam.[24] Yohannes sent Alula with 10,000 riflemen in the direction of Gojjam, where Menelik lay siege on Ras Adal. The threat of Yohannes' army forced Menelik back to Shoa. The emperor proceeded to Wallo, where tens of thousands of Oromo horsemen under the Imam Muhammad Ali[25] joined his camp. He ordered Alula to threaten Shoa and sent priests to Menelik to offer peace. In February 1878, under renewed threat, Menelik surrendered.[26] He was then summoned to an all-Ethiopian conference in Boru Meda, Wallo.[27] It was also attended by Ras Adal of Gojjam, Ras Alula, and Imam Muhammad Ali of the Mammedoch dynasty of Wallo. Menelik had to experience a humiliating traditional ceremony of submission. Carrying a stone on the back of his neck, he prostrated before Yohannes, who then nodded to Alula to remove the stone in a sign of forgiveness.[28]

In time, the wheel of fortune would turn, but meanwhile history was made in Boru Meda. Among the clergy and monks of Ethiopia there had been a split regarding the interpretation of Monophysism. Was Jesus, as both God and a man, born twice or three times? In the meeting, Yohannes declared that the version prevalent in the north—two births—was the national one and dictated it to all.

In working to enhance Ethiopian Christianity and Church, Yohannes also initiated a renewed dialogue with the Egyptian patriarchate in Cairo. Despite tensions in the Mareb Melash, Yohannes managed to convince the Egyptian patriarch Cyril V to send a replacement for Abuna Antanewos, whom Yohannes had suspected as siding with the Egyptians and so had eliminated after the battle of Gura. This marked the first time since the days of Zara-Yaqob that four bishops were sent from Egypt since the Ethiopians undertook to be a branch of the Coptic Church. In 1881, the four bishops arrived at Massawa. Abuna Petros (died 1917)[29] remained with Yohannes, Abuna Matewos (died 1926) was sent to Menelik's court in Shoa, Abuna Luqas (died 1900) was sent to Gojjam, and Abuna Markos was sent to Gondar but died soon upon arrival. Petros was officially the metropolitan, but the bishops in Shoa and Gojjam had the same religious authority and were not answerable to him. Thus, the arrangement further underlined the federal structure Yohannes envisioned for his empire.[30]

Yohannes and Islam

No less important than trying to unify Christianity in Ethiopia was the policy Yohannes adopted at Boru Meda towards Islam. When Kasa was younger, he was reputed to be a religiously tolerant person. He found shelter among the Muslim Afars, befriended their chiefs, and married one of their daughters, Halima, who was then baptized as Tebaba Sillase.[31] In 1869, she gave birth to a son, Araya Selassie,[32] later Ras. The Afars indeed proved loyal to Yohannes, also when the Egyptians invaded from Massawa.

However, the 1875–6 Egyptian invasion aroused Yohannes' suspicion of Muslims. He viewed Ismail of Egypt as a religious enemy and the fighting against him as a crusade. According to one account, before the battle of Gura there were some 4,000 priests and monks in Yohannes' camp, 'all praying together with their emperor.' After Gura, Yohannes' policy was marked with a strong anti-Islamic element as he aimed to convert all Muslims of Ethiopia to Christianity. His policy included harsh measures, such as the destruction of mosques. Many Amharic or Tigrinya-speaking Muslims, now called *Jabarti*,[33] in towns such as Gondar and Aksum were forced to convert. Others fled by the thousands to nearby Sudanese territory. The more powerful Oromo Muslims of the central highlands presented a major problem. Some of them participated as a cavalry in Yohannes' army. Nevertheless, Yohannes was determined to convert them all. In May 1878, at Boru Meda, he summoned two of the major Oromo chiefs. According to an Ethiopian chronicler, Yohannes told them: 'We are all apostles. All this used to be a Christian land until Gragn ruined and misled it all. Now... believe in the name of Jesus Christ! Be baptized! If you wish to live in peace preserving your belongings, become Christians!' Imam Muhammad Ali was renamed Ras Mikael. It is estimated that by 1880, some 50,000 Jabartis and 500,000 Oromos had been forced to renounce Islam and convert to Christianity.[34] 'There was no room for Islam in his ideological world,' concluded historian Bahru Zewde.[35] His alienation of Muslims in the territories under his direct government had far-reaching consequences for the urbanization and modernization of northern Ethiopia, or rather lack of. This policy would also backfire in Yohannes' foreign relations in the coming years.

Arrangement with Menelik

Yohannes gave the rulers of Shoa and Gojjam political-religious legitimacy but also worked to drive a wedge between them. In January 1881, he declared Ras Adal as King Takla-Haymanot of Gojjam.[36] He also declared him King of Kaffa, a region long claimed by Menelik. Yohannes' manipulation was successful for a while. On 6 June 1882, the two kings of Shoa and of Gojjam, met in battle. Menelik won the day and took the Gojjami and his army as prisoners. He thus controlled the entire south. The following July, Yohannes, alarmed, marched from Debra Tabor in the direction of Shoa. Again, as in 1878, the priests intervened and a clash was avoided. In early August, both kings—Menelik and Takla-Haymanot—arrived at Yohannes' camp in Wara-Ilu, in Wallo. The Gojjami was not allowed to leave until he surrendered his firearms to Ras Alula. As for Menelik, his control of Wallo was transferred to Yohannes' son, Ras Araya Selassie, with the local Oromo Ras Mikael (formerly Imam Muhammad Ali) as his deputy.

A bond was then sealed between the emperor and the king of Shoa. On 24 October 1882, the son of Yohannes, Ras Araya Selassie (aged 13), married the daughter of Menelik, Zawditu (aged 6). A full Christian ceremony sanctioned the new alliance between the house of Tigray and the house of Shoa. It would not last long.[37]

Dominating the future Eritrea

While in the south, Yohannes tolerated kings under his imperial crown, it was different in the Mareb Melash. The future Eritrea was the gate from which foreigners threatened to invade. We mentioned the Egyptians. The Italians and Sudanese would follow.

The highlands of the Mareb Melash, inhabited by fellow Christian Tigrinya speakers, remained practically autonomous since the days of Bahr Negash Yishaq. The Leadership of Hamasen rotated between local rival families of the villages of Hazzega and Tsazega. In 1868, Walda-Mikael Salomon[38] of Hazzega won the backing of Kasa Mircha and restored his position as the strongman of the area. He was recognized as Dajazmach and Governor of Hamasen and Saraye and attended Kasa's coronation as Emperor Yohannes. Yet he was not fully trusted by Yohannes. In the battle of Gundat (November 1875), Walda-Mikael led the guard which captured some 700 Remington rifles from the fleeing Egyptians. Still he did not win Yohannes' trust and was ordered to hand the rifles to *shalaqa* Alula.[39] This action would prove a turning point in the history of Tigrinya speakers to this day.

When the Egyptians returned in full force to fight Yohannes, Walda-Mikael arrived in their camp, heading 2,500 troops from Hamasen. The Egyptian commander, Ratib Pasha, declared him Ras. In return, Walda-Mikael accompanied the invaders to their defeat at Gura (March 1876). Partially recuperating, the Egyptians built a chain of forts along the line from Massawa to Keren and encouraged Walda-Mikael to declare Hazzega the capital of the region. In September 1876, Yohannes marched again across the Mareb and appointed Alula over Hamasen and Saraye on 9 October, promoting him to Ras. Walda-Mikael fled to Egyptian-held territory.

In March 1877, Alula was summoned by Yohannes to Debra Tabor to help him in facing Menelik and Ras Adal. In Alula's absence, Ras Walda-Mikael reoccupied Hamasen. In late September 1878, Alula, back in Aksum, invited Walda-Mikael to travel to Yohannes in Debra Tabor. Yohannes, always looking for a compromise, pardoned Walda-Mikael. He recognized him as ras and appointed him in January 1879 as deputy of Alula over the Mareb Melash.[40] Ras Alula was less happy with the arrangement. In August 1879 he tricked Walda-Mikael to send his troops to face the Egyptians, put him in chains, and accused him of treason. The two of them were summoned to Yohannes in Debra Tabor. In January 1880, Yohannes imprisoned Walda-Mikael on top of an *amba*, where he would stay until 1894. Ras Walda-Mikael Solomon was the last native governor of Eritrea until 1991. Eritrean modern nationalists remember him today as their hero, betrayed and humiliated by the people of Tigray.

Asmara—the beginning of Eritreanism

In the second half of 1884, Alula moved his capital of the Mareb Melash from Addi Taklai to Asmara, a small village at the time.[41] Asmara is located on the road from Tigray to Massawa, better suited for both defense and economic development. The village of Asmara was described as having 150 inhabitants in 1830. In an English map of Ethiopia, probably drawn for or after the 1868 campaign, Asmara appears as a little village, smaller than Sa'zega or Aylet. In 1873, the town was described as 'almost deserted.'[42]

The initiative to build a new urban center was in tune with developments in the empire as a whole. In the south, as mentioned, Menelik annexed new territories and accumulated resources. In 1886, he established Addis Ababa, and a year later he occupied Harar. Both towns turned into centers of modernization. Yohannes was slower. He hardly developed urban life in Tigray proper. Asmara, however, was a new enterprise. For Yohannes and Alula, Asmara was the best center of defense against foreign invaders, the hub of a new regime in the Mareb Melash.

In the eyes of many Eritreans in later years, the new Asmara was part of Tigrayan colonization of their country—a center for a new military elite that came to settle and inherit their land. Indeed, Yohannes authorized Alula to confiscate one-tenth of the Mareb Mellash lands for himself and his officers. Alula's effort to create large *Gults* was fiercely and often successfully opposed by the local inhabitants. The fiefs that were established were too small to cover the expenses of maintaining an army as large as Alula's. Consequently, Alula tried to attack the hereditary land tenure system in the Mareb Mellash, which was based largely on *Rest*. During his government in the Mareb Mellash, Alula managed to make a few inroads into the *Rest* system to enable newcomers to join the feudal upper-class. For example, one loophole was to give the right of inheritance to local women, many of whom married the Tigrayan newcomers. Still Alula could not really destroy the well-established agrarian elite of the Mareb Mellash.

Alula was therefore forced to rely upon the proceeds of urban commerce. After returning to Hamasen, he began trading with Massawa in 1879. Ten years after the opening of the Suez Canal (1869), Massawa was now a major Red Sea port.[43] Alula established contacts with Massawa traders and tried to secure the road for their caravans. His main concern was importation of firearms, which Greek and Indian traders of Massawa were actively involved in. Massawa, we may assume, was the model of urban life Alula wanted for Asmara. The beginning was slow. In 1881, a visitor reckoned that the population of Asmara as numbering a 'few hundred.'[44] In early 1884 another guest estimated 'three hundred houses ... built haphazard on two low hills or mounds above the ordinary plateau level ... the only clearing in it being near the church, towards which most of the lanes that represent streets run out.'[45]

To enhance trade, Alula refrained from the anti-Muslim policy of Yohannes, and cultivated Muslim communities in the Mareb Melash. But mostly he cared for his armed followers from Tigray. They were salaried and enjoyed privileges at the expense of locals. By 1884 Asmara turned into a big barrack city. Three stone buildings were built on top of the central hill surrounded by a wall. They were inhabited by some 2,000 soldiers and ready to host five times more. All of Alula's main aides were from Tigray, from his native region of Tamben, (For example, *blata* Gabru his lieutenant, and Dajazmach Hailaselassie, his son-in-law). They were all of humble origin, like Alula himself, happy to become a new elite, grateful and loyal to their master. The old local elite of Hamasen was now reduced to a middle class—village heads, tax collectors. Alula and his men monopolized trade and centralized it in the Asmara market.

Alula's government in the Marab Mellash lasted only four years after the establishment of Asmara. During 1885–9, when Alula had to struggle for the future of Ethiopian government over Eritrea, the majority of Christians hardly opposed him. During his time, the Muslim tribal zones, later included in the future Eritrea, Assawurta, Habbab, Mansa, Banu 'Amir[46], were actually part of his raiding zone. They were not directly governed by Asmara and naturally resisted any central government, especially Alula's, which only taxed and raided them. It was mainly the peripheral Muslim tribes which later supported the Italians during the struggle to take the Mareb Mellash from Alula.

Enter the Italians

The last five years of Yohannes were the most eventful. After the June 1884 Heweet Treaty, two of the most powerful powers in modern history replaced the weakened Egypt as the greatest enemies of his kingdom.[47]

We shall soon address the Islamic militant Mahdist Sudan in Ethiopia's west. European imperialism, represented by Italy, presented itself from the direction of the Red Sea. Though not as powerful as Britain, Italy was now a united modern state, hungry and ready to participate in the 'Scramble for Africa.' Namely, in the momentous European competition for dominance in the continent. From 1882, when the British occupied Egypt, Africa was divided between western colonizers. The continent's map was quickly colored with British red and French blue. Germany and Belgium managed to snatch some pieces, and Italy strove for a substantial share. Rome had its reasons to aspire for colonies in Africa, such as national dignity in Europe and controlling emigration (which mostly went to America). The British, who had enough to handle, backed the Italians, especially in the Red Sea.

After the opening of the Suez Canal, to reiterate, the Red Sea became globally important. Controlling it was vital for imperialists. After occupying Egypt, the British controlled its two gates: Suez in the north and Aden, which they had occupied in 1839, in the south. Their main concern was to deprive France from settling along the coasts, so they helped the Italians to do so. In masterminding the Heweet Treaty, the British committed Yohannes to fight the Sudanese. They also let him assume that they themselves would operate Massawa and as friends and allies. But on 5 February 1885, as the Egyptian flag was about to be lowered in the city, the Italians landed and hoisted theirs. Yohannes was surprised. In June, he wrote to Queen Victoria asking for Massawa, but in practice he could do little. He would never sign anything with the Europeans, and trusted Ras Alula in Asmara to deal with the Italians.

Yohannes clearly preferred workable relations with the newcomers, who, for their part, had little respect for the Ethiopians and began a slow encroachment inland. The heat and humidity of Massawa was unbearable for them, and they needed water available in the hinterland. They also began cultivating relations with local Muslim tribes as well with Ethiopian rivals of Alula and *shiftas*—deprived members of Tigray's nobility jealous of Alula, the arrogant and prospering son of a peasant. Prominent among the latter was *fitawrari*[48] Dabbab Araya,[49] the son of Ras Araya Selassie Demsu, and Alula's brother-in-law. Ras Alula, for his part, grew stronger in Asmara. He had little respect for the Italians and was angry at their interference in local affairs. All this was to prove fateful for all involved.

Enters the Mahdia

At the same time, the Mahdia in Sudan presented no less a threat to Yohannes and to Christian Ethiopia.[50]

The Mahdia was one of the movements for Islamic revival that emerged during the late nineteenth century. Prominent similar movements included the Wahhabia in Arabia, the Sannusia in north Africa, and the Salihia of the Somalis. These movements revived fundamental Islam to unite tribal societies against western imperialism and against westernization of Islamic societies. They all began in the name of universal Islamic values but were later identified with local nationalisms. The Mahdia would become the formative experience of the modern Sudanese. However, initially, under Muhammad Ahmad, the *'mahdi'* ('the one guided by God to continue the mission of prophet Muhammad') movement was essentially radically militant. It aimed at ending the Egyptian occupation of Sudan (which had begun in 1820), then at liberating Egypt of her westernization, and later at restoring the whole Islamic world to the model of the prophet's state. Colliding with next-door Christian Ethiopia was not an immediate priority. The Mahdi, identifying with the mission of Muhammad, believed in the legacy of 'the righteous najashi,' namely, the prophet's contemporary Aksumite king, who gave shelter to the pioneers of Islam and, by Islamic tradition, converted to that religion. The Mahdi wanted to convince Yohannes to follow his medieval predecessor.

In January 1885, a few weeks before the Italians landed in Massawa, the Mahdists captured Khartoum, replaced it with Umm Durman, and established their Islamic state (it would survive till 1898). On 16 June 1885, the Mahdi wrote to Yohannes. He praised the Ethiopian emperor as a 'modest listener,' wished him all the best, and called him to be a Muslim. The Mahdi ended his letter with a threat,[51] which did not go well with Yohannes. But compared to letters the Mahdi sent at the same time to Muslim leaders, it was almost polite. In any case, circumstances soon led to a fatal Ethiopian–Sudanese conflict, which developed simultaneously alongside the conflict with the Italians.

The Sad King

'Emperor Yohannes IV,' wrote historian Bairu Tafla, 'was a nobleman by birth, a cleric by education, a zealot by faith, a moralist by tendency, a monk by practice, a nationalist by policy, and a soldier and emperor by profession.'[52] His last four years, facing growing challenges, were particularly unhappy. Yohannes grew lonelier, evidently more melancholic, and suspicious. He was an intimidating and angry man. Already in his youth, as *shifta*, he won the name 'Bazbez,' translating as 'taker of booty day after day.'[53] His chroniclers tried to attribute his bursts of rage to patriotism: '... he was called the angel of wrath, for this leading warrior, Yohannes, became infuriated if other men wanted his wife, and he would roar like a lion to fight, as Ethiopia, his legal espouse, was to him alone...'[54] However, he was also well-feared at home. His authority, it seems, stemmed from a mixture of intimidation and his strong sense of conviction. It proved enough to unite greater Tigray (for a while), but not the entire Ethiopian empire. The kings of Shoa and of Gojjam were seldom cooperative, and in major historical juncture avoided help. Even his loyal Alula in the Mareb Melash was too independent.

Yohannes, apparently an introvert, had no close family to rely upon. His only wife, hardly his close friend, died in 1871, a year before his coronation, and he never married again. His chroniclers wrote:

'When he was ready to be crowned ... he gathered the chosen fathers from all corners of the land to bless him... Gathering together, these holy people said to him: Yohannes, you should marry a wife according to the royal law. He told them: Have you not heard what Paul the Apostle, said: He who has a wife does not serve God, but he lives serving his wife. Having said this he was crowned alone, according to the tradition of the monks, for he had weakened the power of his lust and did not see the face of a woman. His steward was a monk... Thus was the life of Yohannes up to his end.'[55] He never smoked, forbade smoking, and prohibited raising tobacco.

Yohannes' only son, Ras Araya Selassie,[56] died in 1888. His three brothers and his nephews were apparently not his soulmates. The emperor preferred a kind of self-isolation. Foreigners who wanted to meet with him were mostly unsuccessful; they were never sure where he was at any certain time. Those who managed to find out had to travel many days before arriving to one of his capitals. These capitals were more roving camps than urban centers. The devout Yohannes invested more in building churches and monasteries, mainly trusting Italian architect G. Naretti with the works,[57] who left for Massawa after the Italian landing. Prior to that, Naretti was also behind Yohannes' more famous castle in Maqale. It was a beautiful structure, symbolically more like a medieval fortress than a royal palace. 'It was said of him—wrote his chroniclers—that Yohannes did not have a treasury of silver and gold like all other kings for he dispersed his wealth among the needy and the poor.'[58] Nothing around Yohannes resembled the Byzantine court in Gondar, with Empress Mentwab and her manipulations, or *Amba* Maqdala, the capital of Tewodros, with all its accumulated treasures. Nor did they resemble Menelik's Addis Ababa, established in 1886, with his wife Taitu as closest confidant. Or later, the palaces of Haile Selassie, with his faithful wife Mennen, seven children, dogs, and pompous ceremonies. Yohannes was surrounded by priests. They were good for mental comfort and for occasionally mediating with insubordinate vassals. They were less good for understanding the greater world, the encroaching Italians, and the Islamic militants of the Mahdia. Yohannes, it seems, wanted peace. He wanted to head an empire kept by religious unity rather than by a state apparatus.

Yohannes tried to avoid the powers now involved in his affairs. After the 1884 Hewett Treaty, and the landing of the Italians in Massawa, he signed no other treaties. He had little respect for the Italians, about whom he was most probably informed of by the French. In November 1885, he wrote to Menelik: 'They are not people of good faith, they are intriguers... The Italians have not come here because they lack pastures and fat in their own country, but they come from ambition to better themselves, because there are many of them and they are not rich. With the help of God, they will depart again, humiliated and disgraced in the eyes of the world'[59]

Yohannes never forgot that the British (namely, Napier back in 1868) helped him to power. However, following their backing of the Italian landing in Massawa, he gradually lost trust. In April 1886, he wrote to Queen Victoria: 'We had no quarrel before [with the Italians] because you told me to be in friendship with the Italians. Now I do not know how to be in friendship with them. Write to me explaining how to do it.'[60] But the British did little to restrain their Italian allies. Rather, they went on diverting Yohannes' attention to fighting the Mahdia in his west.

The Massacre of the Baria, Eritrea

While Menelik was going from force to force in the south, Takla-Haymanot of Gojjam was facing the Mahdist General Hamdan Abu 'Anja in the central west. Ras Alula was the man in Eritrea (still the Mareb Melash), facing both the Italians and the Mahdists there. Alula was the one Yohannes trusted, but they differed. Yohannes wanted stability even based on some compromise. Alula was younger, more militant, and better informed in local Eritrean matters and on the concrete steps taken by the Italians. However, he had his local and personal considerations. Alula had accumulated enmities with local rivals, Muslim or Tigrayan Christians—notably Dabbab Araya, the frustrated son of Ras Araya Selasse Demsu—who often collaborated with the Italians. Moreover, he attached importance to small places occupied by the Italians in the hinterland of Massawa. These places, such as Saati and Wi'a, were part of Alula's taxing sphere but of marginal importance to Ethiopia as a whole. The escalating dynamism that Alula developed with the Italians around such issues had a significant impact on the history of Ethiopia and Eritrea.

While Alula in Asmara had his eyes on the Italians' encroachment, the British and Yohannes pushed him westward to stem the Mahdists. On 23 September 1885, Alula, heading an imperial army (Yohannes sent him more forces) in a place called Kufit, decisively defeated the army of *amir* Uthman Diqna, the commander of the Mahdia in her northern section. It was a great relief for Yohannes, and Alula returned, confident, to Asmara to face the Italians. In their meeting in Maqale in late April 1886, the emperor expressed his trust with the ras, but ordered him not to overly provoke the Italians. Rather, still believing that Britain would restrain the Italians, Yohannes again diverted Alula to the Mahdist front. This time, he ordered Alula to capture the Sudanese town of Kassala (promised to Ethiopia by the Hewett Treaty). Militarily, it was a mission impossible, and so it failed.

Alula's huge army reached western Eritrea exhausted, exposed to malaria, and underequipped to storm the walled Mahdist town. No provisions were prepared for the Ethiopians by the local tribesmen. Frustrated, Alula ordered his forces to massacre the local Baria and Kunama tribes. Between 22 November and 1 December 1886, two-thirds of the people and cattle of these two tribes were destroyed.[61] Modern Eritrean nationalists keep the memory of this brutal massacre alive to this day.

Dogali and the Italians—a disastrous stalemate

Yohannes was angry at Alula for the massacre of the Baria and for failing to reach Kassala. Prominent figures in Tigray, ever jealous of Alula, the son of a peasant, were speaking to the emperor to remove him. But it was not to be—not now. [62]

On 23 November, as Alula was busy in the west, the Italians advanced and occupied Saati. Yohannes put Alula at the head of all available troops in northern Ethiopia. A massive Ethiopian attack on Saati on 25 January 1887 met Italian artillery and ended with hundreds dead but only four Italians wounded. The next day, an Italian battalion of 500 men marching from Massawa to Saati was ambushed by thousands of Ethiopians and destroyed. Only eighty wounded men managed to flee back. Yohannes was apparently unaware of this. According to an Italian prisoner of the Ethiopian ras, Yohannes wrote to Alula: 'Who gave you permission to go there and ignite a war? The soldiers are mine, not yours. I shall cut your right arm!'[63] Indeed the massacre of the Baria, and more so the humiliation of the Italians in Dogali, began a quick countdown towards the Ethiopian loss of Eritrea and the fall of Yohannes.

Italy could not contain the humiliation. All throughout 1887 a new Africa Corpus was built. In December, a British envoy, G. Portal, met with Yohannes in Lake Ashange in a bid to prevent war. The message from London sided with the Italians and was rejected by Yohannes. He refused to sacrifice Alula and sent harsh words to Queen Victoria: 'The Italians want war, but the strength is with Jesus Christ. Let them do as they will, so long as I live I will not hide myself from them in a hole.'[64]

Threatened by an Italian army and feeling deserted by the British, Yohannes called for a national war. 'The whole country is under arms,' Portal reported on his way back. By his account, Ras Alula had 16,000 men at Asmara; Ras Hagos Mircha, 20,000; Ras Mikael, 25,000 (largely Oromo cavalry); Yohannes, some 5,000 imperial guardsmen; his nephew (the son of his brother Gugsa), Dajazmach Mangasha, about the same size of force; Ras Haila-Mariam Gugsa (Yohannes' nephew, brother of Mangasha), over 16,000; Ras Araya Selassie, Yohannes' son, an army of 40,000.[65] This was not an all-Ethiopian army. The two kings, Menelik and Takla-Haymanot, stayed away. It was the army Yohannes could mobilize; the maximum power under his direct authority. The sad king apparently trusted Ras Alula, Ras Mikael, and his closest relatives, brother, and nephews. Still, it was a huge army, well over 100,000 troops, the majority of them possessing firearms.

However, the Ethiopians soon discovered they could not successfully storm a fortified modern force. The Italians had constructed a rail line from Massawa to their fortifications in Saati. They had artillery and machine guns behind barbed wires, mines, observation balloons, and searchlights. By March 1888, it was painfully clear to Yohannes he could not dislodge the Italians. His forces sustained heavy losses as they fed on the impoverished peasants of northern Ethiopia and destroyed the land.

The Mahdia and the burning of Gondar

While helplessly facing the power of western imperialism, Yohannes had his share in escalating relations with Ethiopia's Muslims, and with the Mahdist Islamic state.[66] His anti-Muslim policy at home had triggered Islamic revolts in Wallo, beginning in the late 1870s. The most important leader of the Ethiopian Islamic anti-Yohannes jihad in the 1880s was *Shaykh* Talha bin Ja'far, a scholar and military leader who built his connections with the Mahdia soon after its appearance. *Shaykh* Talha began his revolts in July 1884 and intensified his activity in November 1885, raising jihadi slogans, burning churches, and harassing priests. Talha's forces were finally uprooted from the center of Wallo in January 1886 by the son of

Yohannes, Ras Araya Selassie, and Talha moved his headquarters to Walqayt, nearer the Sudanese border. From there, he continued what was already a close alliance with the Khalifa, the successor of the Mahdi (1885–98).[67]

Soon the border shared by Ethiopia and Sudan was on fire. In January 1887, *Negus* Takla-Haymanot invaded the Sudanese Qallabat and by the order of Yohannes killed prisoners before sending a provocative letter to the Khalifa.[68] The latter, in response, declared in Umm Durman: 'When Yuhanna established himself on the Ethiopian throne he became arrogant ... and he invaded Islamic territory ... and conquered from the land of Islam and he is the most hateful of the Ethiopians towards Islam ... so do not leave them alone, oh you the people of Islam, but fight them.'[69]

On 6 January 1888, the Mahdia commander of the Ethiopian front, the *amir* Hamdan Abu 'Anja, defeated Takla-Haymanot's army and invaded Gondar on 23 January. His men massacred all those who failed to flee, burnt all the churches, and returned to Sudanese soil.[70]

The news of the burning of the historic Ethiopian capital reached a traumatized Yohannes. Finding himself threatened by a strong Italian army on the coast of the Red Sea and by the Mahdist aggression led by Abu 'Anja to the west, he now also had to deal with growing subordination of both Menelik and Takla-Haymanot to the south.

Menelik's defiance

A few days after receiving the news about the destruction of Gondar, and as he realized he could not defeat the entrenched Italians, Yohannes decided to lead his forces against the Mahdists. He was also angry at Ras Alula, whom he blamed for Dogali and its consequences. Alula was ordered to go to Asmara and prepare to return to the emperor's camp. Yohannes also ordered *negus* Menelik to march from Shoa northward. Menelik had been in close contact the Italians for a long time, who for their part assumed that he wanted Yohannes to be defeated. The Shoan king with his army did march north, and on 18 April 1888 they camped near the ruined Gondar. In May, Yohannes ordered Menelik to return to Shoa, but Menelik crossed to Gojjam. He made an alliance with Takla-Haimnot, the two swearing to one another never to obey Yohannes.[71]

Another disaster followed. On 10 June 1888, Ras Araya Selassie, Yohannes' only son, was taken ill and died. His sudden death was the last blow to whatever was left of Tigrayan–Shoan relations. The prince was officially married to Zawditu, Menelik's daughter. But more so, it was a terrible blow to Yohannes. The isolated emperor, never really at peace with himself, was traumatized. Alula joined him in Maqale a few days later, but even the faithful ras was now hardly trusted. He was again ordered to return to Asmara and come back with all he could mobilize. More news came on 17 June that Abu 'Anja was marching again in the direction of Gondar.

On 8 August 1888, Yohannes crossed the Abbay into Gojjam and lay siege on Takla-Haymanot, who found shelter on top of an *amba*. Menelik, back in Shoa and fearing a Tigrayan invasion, wrote to the emperor. He put the blame on the Gojjami, who finally, on 17 January 1889, climbed down from the *amba* and was pardoned by Yohannes.[72]

No peace with the Mahdia

In order to secure his wing facing Menelik, on 25 December 1888, Yohannes sent a very appeasing letter to Abu 'Anja. The Ethiopian decided to avoid battle and preferred now to selectively remember the Khalifa's words to him earlier that year: 'Now let bygones be bygones; we still have a liking for you ... become one of us [be a Muslim], and let us cease warfare, and instead let us become friends...'

Yohannes' letter to the Khalifa was a call to unite against the European imperialists: 'The truth is that the *faranji*s [the Europeans] are our enemies as well as yours. If they destroy us, they will turn to destroy you, and if they defeat you, they will then defeat us. The sensible thing is to agree between us to face them together....'[73]

However, sent in the second or third week of January 1889, Abu 'Anja's reply was aggressive: 'If you are as brave as you claim, come out, do not fear ... and if not, stay where you are and be inevitably destroyed by the victorious party of Allah ... your throne will burn and all your decisions will come to nothing.'[74]

It was apparently too late for mutual understanding. The option of non-violent dialogue was given one last chance by Yohannes, but the old legacies of religious militancy proved stronger.[75]

Yohannes faced a dilemma: invade Shoa to defeat Menelik, or respond to the Mahdist provocation. The priests in both the Shoan and the imperial camps continued to play a major role. They fulfilled their traditional role as mediators between Christians and managed to prevent civil war.[76] They did so by appealing to Yohannes' emotions as an anti-Muslim crusader: the monks, wrote Heruy Walda-Selasse, were said to have told him, 'you may go to Shoa, for you will be victorious there, but your soul will never benefit. Go to Matamma, you will die but that will be to the benefit of your soul.'[77] Arriving on the scene of Takla-Haymanot's defeat, Yohannes vowed to fight the Mahdists. He was quoted as declaring: 'If I am defeated, I will receive the martyr's crown; if I am victorious, I will have avenged Christian blood.'[78]

The fall of Asmara

At the time Yohannes was facing the Mahdia, the Mareb Melash was falling to the Italians.

Throughout the previous two years, Yohannes was wavering as to Ras Alula. He was angry at him for the disastrous consequences of Dogali but still trusted his loyalty and his military abilities. Yohannes wanted Alula in his imperial camp and thus away from Asmara. Ironically, Yohannes began trusting Dabbab Araya, the son of his old uncle, Ras Araya Dimtsu. Dabbab was a lifetime enemy of Alula, collaborating first with the Egyptians and then with the Italians. In February 1888, Dabbab, admonished by his old father, crossed lines in an effort to win the heart of Yohannes. The emperor, much to Alula's frustration, appointed Dabbab over Akele Guzai in the Mareb Melash and promoted him to Dajazmach.

Dabbab, however, aspired to have much more. Pretending to be loyal to Yohannes, he went on collaborating with the Italians in Massawa. On 9 February 1889, Dabbab marched to Asmara and destroyed the small garrison Alula had left there. The next day, he wrote to General O. Baldissera in Massawa: 'The king gave me a title, but I was not convinced he was my friend... I have half of Ethiopia in my hands. You and I should help each other to our victory...'[79] Courtesy of Dabbab Araya, the Italians could now march safely into Asmara. They would soon take the whole of the Mareb Melash (Eritrea) without firing a shot. There was no way they could have managed this if Alula and his men had stayed there.

The end of Yohannes

On 9 March 1889, Yohannes' army met with the Mahdists in Matamma (Al-Qallabat). The left wing, under Ras Haila-Mariam, failed to penetrate their lines, and the ras was killed. On the right, under Alula, it went better. Mangasha,[80] the emperor's nephew recently promoted to ras, advised Yohannes to move there and help exploit the success. The *echage* Tewoflos described six days later that Yohannes had hurried, firing his rifle, when a bullet hit his right hand. He had ignored it and moved on when another bullet hit his left arm and penetrated his chest. Yohannes was carried to his tent, and the demoralized Ethiopians panicked and retreated, suffering heavy loses. 'That night' wrote the chronicler of Ras Alula, 'the king passed the time in great pain. When it was morning Ras Alula came to him to know his condition. He, Yohannes told him secret mysteries concerning the house of the kingdom and concerning the house of his son Mangasha.' Namely, that Mangasha was his own son, not his brother's, and that he, Ras Mangasha, should be his successor. 'Having spoken like this Yohannes made a promise, and rested from the toil of this transitory world.'[81] The Mahdists seized Yohannes' corpse and sent his head to decorate their celebrations in Umm Durman. 'The Khalifa's delight knew no bounds.'[82]

The fall of Yohannes resulted in the disintegration of Tigray as the political-military center of Ethiopia. It was now in total chaos. The fall of Yohannes also led to the Italian conquest of all of Eritrea without Ethiopian resistance, and the transfer of imperial power to Shoa, where Menelik crowned himself emperor the following November.

6

COLLAPSE

When marching to Matamma in the first week of March 1889, Yohannes was still the more powerful leader in Ethiopia. Tigray was still seemingly hegemonic, but her power was already hollow. Yohannes' army avoided colliding with Menelik and had to retreat when facing the Italians. The country which remained under Yohannes' direct authority was economically devastated. Peasants were starving, and soldiers—after so many wars in the area of greater Tigray—were nearly out of ammunition. When deciding to fight the Mahdia, the desperate emperor was gambling on the wrong side. He took his chance and was killed. For the next several decades, the new rulers of Ethiopia would do their best to marginalize Yohannes' role in history. Moreover, the imperial system that had been built around Tigray collapsed with him. It was now beyond repair.[1]

King Takla Haymanot of Gojjam and Ras Mikael of Wallo survived the battle of Matamma and hurried to join king Menelik of Shoa. They further strengthened what was already the bigger and richer army in Ethiopia, and under a more astute politician.

After Matamma, Menelik could confidently wait before officially crowning himself emperor. The Shoans, who had long been in fruitful contact with the Italians, now solidified their alliance. On 2 May 1889, in the small Ethiopian town of Wichale,

Menelik signed a treaty with Italy by which he recognized the Italians' gains in Eritrea in return for Italy's recognition of his imperial power and supplying of twenty-eight guns and 38,000 rifles. The treaty also sealed off the north and the Tigrayans from import of arms by binding the Italians at Massawa to sell them only to Menelik.

Meanwhile, all of Eritrea was falling into Italian hands. Dabbab Araya, who had occupied Asmara, was aspiring to inherit Tigray. He worked to obtain Italian help and eventually opened the gates of Asmara to them. On 2 August 1889, the Italians under General O. Baldissera entered the city and established their headquarters in the old compound of Ras Alula. By the end of that year, the Italians advanced down to the River Mareb and declared their Colony of Eritrea on 1 January 1890.[2]

Kefu Qan

With Menelik in the south and the Italians in Eritrea, the divided and impoverished Tigrayans had to face another catastrophe. Between 1888 and 1892 the country—mainly the north—experienced one of the worse famines in Ethiopian history. It became known as the *Kefu qan*: the bad day.[3] The disaster was probably caused by cattle disease that began with herds that the Italian army of 1888 brought from India. These cows carried bovine cholera, an epidemic that started in South-central Asia. In addition to the destruction of cattle, Ethiopia now experienced a plethora of droughts and plagues, and altogether some one-third of the population died over those four years.

The south was less exposed; Menelik managed to minimize the damage there. However, in Tigray, the *Kefu qan* proved a major catastrophe. No united leadership emerged in Tigray to handle the situation there, and the region was exposed to endless fratricidal wars. Soon it became nearly impossible to keep an army; even one of just a few hundred men.

Back to the Era of the Judges

Only a few Tigrayan chiefs survived the battle of Matamma. Ras Alula and Ras Mangasha managed to flee to Tamben and proceeded to Aksum. They reached the ancient capital on 20 April 1889. Alula planned to crown Mangasha as the heir of Yohannes, but it was just an illusion. Mangasha, hitherto known as the nephew of Yohannes, was accepted in Tigray as his son, but he himself was realistic, understanding that he stood no chance of reviving the devastated and divided region. In fact, Tigray returned now to the 'Era of the Judges,' except in a far worse condition. The unity under Yohannes disappeared, the glory never forgotten.

Indeed, we must return to chapter 4, 'The Era of the Judges,' and take it from there. Below is a succinctly summarized, complex story.

The internal struggle in Tigray was resumed between three rival old regional dynasties.

One was headed now by Ras Mangasha Yohannes, hailing from Tamben and related to the house of Ras Mikael Sehul, who had dominated Tigray till 1780.

The second was related to the house of Ras Walda Selassie of Endarta, who dominated Tigray till 1816 and was the grandfather of Ras Araya Dimtsu (killed in Matamma). It was now led by his son: Dabbab Araya.

The third was the family of Dajazmach Sabagdis from Agame, who dominated Tigray from 1818–31. It was now led by Dajazmach Sebhat Aregawi.[4]

Ras Alula continued to play a key role. But he was not a member of Tigray's nobility and had lost his base in Asmara. Still, Alula remained identified with the legacy of Yohannes and with the military victories of his time. More concretely, Alula became a protector and mentor of Mangasha, who, he hoped, would be able to restore Tigray's autonomy.

In Adwa, in May 1889, Mangasha and Alula managed to gather a force of some 8,000 men. Lacking food, however, many started deserting. On 10 May, Alula opened the last emergency store of Aksum—a few hundred rifles and forty boxes of ammunition.

He then ordered his men to cross the Mareb and feed themselves there. As more and more men deserted, Alula was left with just 200 armed followers. In July, Mangasha and Alula camped in Tamben with some 1,500 men. Dabbab Araya crossed the Mareb from Asmara to fight them. They avoided battle and traveled to Maqale, to Yohannes' castle. Mangasha then invited Dabbab to the castle, promising to declare him the heir of Yohannes. But once there, Alula arrested Dabbab and sent him in chains to *Amba* Salama. The act did not improve relations between the leading families of Tigray.

After the Italians captured Asmara, Alula changed his strategy. Left with only 700 hungry followers, and dreading having to accept Shoan hegemony, he started courting the Italians. But the response he got from Asmara was that he should first recognize Menelik as emperor. Mangasha was ready to do that, but Alula would not. In November 1889, together they managed to defeat a small expedition near Aksum sent by Menelik. Defending the pride of Tigray, their army grew for a while. They marched to Agame, where Dajazmach Sebhat Aregawi was helped by both the Italians and Menelik. A three-day battle, from 2–5 December, waged eastward to *Amba* Zion in Agame, resulted in the defeat of Mangasha and Alula. They fled back to Tamben. Sebhat, with Italian backing, now took Adigrat. Dajazmach Seyum Gabra-Kidan, Yohannnes' nephew and now Menelik's man, took Maqale.

Menelik's Tigrayan policy

Soon things went from bad to worse. Menelik himself led a strong Shoan army to Maqale and entered Yohannes' castle on 23 February 1890. Earlier, on 26 January, the new Italian governor of Eritrea entered Adwa and ceremoniously commemorated there three years since Dogali. With the two historical capitals fallen, Mangasha and Alula, isolated and hungry in Tamben, had their differences. Mangasha wanted to surrender to the emperor, while Alula insisted on fighting for Tigrayan autonomy and with Italian help if possible.

The tension which grew between Menelik and the Italians determined what happened next. Menelik was furious that the

Italians had penetrated Adwa, and Rome instructed General B. Orero to pull back to Eritrea. It helped a little. Rome interpreted the Treaty of Wichale as an Ethiopian acceptance of Italian protectorate. Menelik would have none of it. The issue, which had begun already in October 1889, would develop over the next years into an all-out conflict that would only be settled following the Ethiopian victory in Adwa in March 1896.

Against this background, advisers in Menelik's court began arguing for appeasing Tigray rather than destroying it. In late February 1890, as Alula stayed behind in Tamben, Mangasha submitted to Menelik in Maqale. The astute emperor declared Mangasha governor of Tigray, but to ensure his loyalty, Menelik appointed two of his devotees under Mangasha: Dajazmach Seyum Gabra-Kidan in Maqale on eastern Tigray, and the Shoan Dajazmach Mashasha Warqe[5] in Adwa over western Tigray. On 19 March 1890, Menelik headed back to Addis Ababa.

Italian Politica Tigrigna

Policymakers in Rome also began reassessing their Ethiopian policy. They had named their old strategy *Politica Scioana*. This was the mid-1880s strategy of supporting Shoa and of helping negus Menelik against Emperor Yohannes, encouraging and arming him to conquer the south, away from Eritrea. Italian diplomat Count P. Antonelli resided in Addis Ababa to oversee this policy, the climax of which was the Treaty of Wichale.

However, against what we described above, there developed in Rome a counterstrategy: *Politica Tigrigna*. Namely, that supporting the autonomy of the now weakened Tigray would better serve the interest of securing Eritrea, and that the impoverished and proud Tigrayans would be dependent on Eritrean economy and serve as a buffer entity between Asmara and Addis Ababa. *Politica Tigrigna* was mostly adopted in 1890s by the governors of Eritrea and the Ministry of Colonies in Rome. *Politica Scioana* was mostly preferred by the Italian foreign ministry. This duality would be behind much of the story of Tigray, down to the 1935 crisis and Mussolini's war.

More internal fighting

Menelik, for his part, played it carefully. He initiated his own 'Tigrayan Policy,' which would be continued by him and his successors till 1974. This policy operated by giving a vague promise to the successors of Yohannes that they would be crowned as kings of Tigray in Addis Ababa. This was now the hope of Mangasha: to become *negus*. However, Alula was strongly against submitting to the Shoan emperor. He would rather cooperate with the Italians and their *Politica Tigrigna*. To prevent Mangasha from leaving for Addis Ababa, Alula worked to create instability in Tigray and waited for a rupture between Menelik and Italy. In March 1891, Alula confronted Mangasha in Maqale, and as the latter insisted on going to Shoa, Alula left for his base in Tamben, from which he offered the Italians an agreement with an autonomous Tigray.

Tigray knew no moment of peace. Dabbab Araya, practically free on *Amba* Salama, secretly made an alliance with Dajazmach Sebhat Aregawi[6] in Agame. The two offered to Mangasha that, as the three seniors of Tigray hereditary families, they would submit to Menelik and fight the Italians. In May 1891, Dabbab managed to escape from *Amba* Salama, and demanded from the other two that Alula, his nemesis, surrender to him. Alula prepared for battle in the name of independent Tigray. The priests intervened, and an all-Tigrayan clash was avoided.

At the end of July 1891, Mangasha, Alula, and Dabbab entered Adwa amid a big popular demonstration of Tigrayan unity. Mangasha wrote to Asmara swearing eternal friendship, but Dabbab differed. He wanted to invade Akkele Guzay, his old territory, now part of Italian Eritrea. Soon the differences turned into a battle. On 29 September 1891, near Abba Garima monastery, Dabbab Araya was killed by Alula's men. He was buried in the Trinity cathedral in Adwa.

An Alliance with Asmara?

A new series of clashes in Tigray only delayed negotiations between Mangasha and the Italians. Yet a moment of opportunity came:

the new governor of Eritrea, A. Gandolfi, was a man of *Politica Tigrigna*. On 6 December 1891, on the Mareb River, a meeting took place between Gandolfi and the Tigrayans: Mangasha, Alula, Ras Hagos Mircha, and Ras Walda-Mikael, now freed from prison. The presence of the latter, the old hereditary prince of Hamasen, and Alula signified Tigrayan acceptance of the loss of Eritrea, the Mareb Melash.

Gandolfi hugged Alula and praised his courage, and Alula apologized for Dogali. The Italians refused to sign any document so as to not provoke Menelik. However, they might as well have done so albeit inadvertently. In the meeting, Mangasha appointed Gandolfi as a ras. The Italian press regarded it with humour, but for the Ethiopians, it was tantamount to recognizing Mangasha as a king. Only a *negus* could promote someone to a ras. On 8 March 1892, Mangasha, dressed like a king, accepted the submission of Dajazmach Sebhat Aregawi, and also promoted him to ras in a full royal ceremony.

In between them, the rases of Tigray now had some 10,000 riflemen. Gandolfi, as a gesture, had sent to Mangasha 35,000 rounds of ammunition. But it was hardly enough to challenge Menelik. Tigray was starving, and Rome would not permit Gandolfi to send the 20,000 sacks of grain Mangasha had asked for. Moreover, on 28 February 1892, Gandolfi was replaced with O. Baratieri, an overt opponent of *Politica Tigrigna*. Upon arriving at Asmara, Baratieri sent an appeasing letter to Ras Makonnen, Menelik's right hand.

Mangasha orienting on Menelik

Baratieri went on pretending he was committed to Gandolfi's policy, but he sent no grain and no ammunition. It was only in July that Mangasha realized the change and decided to go to Addis Ababa and submit to Menelik. Alula and Sebhat threatened to depose Mangasha if he went. Baratieri envoys promised to send grain if he did. On 9 November 1892, an envoy of Mangasha to Addis Ababa was promised by Menelik that no harm would be done to the Tigrayans and was handed an invitation to Mangasha and Alula to come to the capital. The envoy returned to Maqale on 12 December, but Alula opposed the idea forcefully. However, his starved soldiers began deserting. *Echage* Tewoflos,[7] the head of Tigray's priesthood, hitherto the most loyal supporter of Alula and a living soul of Tigrayan identity, marched demonstratively to Mangasha's palace in Maqale. Alula retreated with his fifty followers to his birthplace in Mannawe but was chased by Mangasha and Hagos leading 2,000 riflemen. Alula fled and asked for mercy. After the intervention of the *echage,* Alula submitted in January 1893 to Mangasha in the main church of Adwa. He carried a stone on his naked shoulders and put a rope around his neck. Alula was pardoned, allotted a sum of money, and swore to stay away from politics. A few weeks later, he rebelled again and had to flee back to an *amba*. In May, he had to undergo the same humiliating ceremony of submission. From Asmara, Baratieri urged Mangasha to get rid of the troublemaker, the man who remained a stubborn fighter for Tigray's autonomy. Alula was saved, however, due to a major historical change.

Submission and acceptance of Shoan hegemony

Throughout all this the relations between Menelik and the Italians deteriorated. The latter, to reiterate, not only expanded their colony of Eritrea down to the River Mareb—contrary to the Wichale Treaty—but also kept insisting that its article 17 meant that Menelik must consult them on his foreign affairs. Menelik, relying on the Amharic text, negated it categorically. In February 1893, he declared the abolishment of the treaty. Against growing diplomatic tensions and the possibility of a war, Menelik sent to Mangasha to spare Alula's life. He wanted the reputed warrior on his side.

Stuck between the two strong rivals, Tigray went on starving. In early April 1894, after being pressed again and again by Menelik, and frustrated by Italian passivity, Ras Mangasha decided to submit to the emperor. Alula was no more in a position to resist. On 2 June 1894, Mangasha and his rases entered Addis Ababa. 12,000 well-armed troops, equipped with twenty-five cannons, were concentrating to impress the visitors. Conti-Rossini, deriving from the Ethiopian chronicler of Menelik, described the scene: 'Ras Mangasha, preceded by the clergy of the holy church of Aksum, who carried the shrine of Mary, and followed by his rases, Alula, Hagos, and Walda-Mikael, modestly advanced towards the Royal residence, where, seated on the throne, with the Royal crown on his head, surrounded by his major chiefs and Europeans, the king of kings awaited him. At the door, the four rases of Tigray, like rebels who came to submit, loaded a big stone on their naked shoulders: they arrived in front of the king and bowed down to the ground asking pardon. With one word, Menelik declared that he granted it. Mangasha was seated; the others were firstly taken away, but after a few moments were called back and were seated. For a quarter of an hour a dead silence prevailed. Everyone gazing in absolute immobility, as if immersed in his thoughts… For the Tigrayans the sacrifice was completed. Only Alula, his shoulders turned to the king, with one hand on his mouth, still seemed to represent the old Tigrayan pride.'[8]

The humiliated Tigrayans gave Menelik a modest gift: 100 rifles and 6,000 Maria Theresa thalers, which must have been a poor gesture in his eyes. The emperor let them sleep and then presented his demands: Tigray would pay an annual tax directly to his treasury; the region of Tselemti would be transferred to his wife Taytu; the *Gult* rights in Endarta would be given to his daughter Zawditu, the widow of Yohannes' son Ras Araya; and, more symbolically, the *nebura-id*[9] of Aksum, the priestly governor of the ancient capital, the heart and soul of Tigray, would be appointed by him, the emperor.[10]

When Ras Mangasha left Addis Ababa to head back to Tigray, 600 of the Tigrayan soldiers, headed by Ras Alula, preferred to stay under the powerful Menelik in his capital.

In Tigray, Mangasha declared that Alula was a traitor. He himself began challenging the Italians and moved Dajazmach Bahta Hagos to revolt in Akkele Guzay against the authorities of Asmara. Moreover, in January 1895, Mangasha led a force of some 10,000 troops across the Mareb into Eritrea. He sustained heavy losses and pulled back. Ras Hagos Mircha then defected to the Italians.

Menelik and the victory of Adwa

Relations between the Italians and Menelik continued to deteriorate. Rome insisted on her interpretation of the Wichale Treaty, and for a while even blocked Ethiopia's communications with the outside world. In March 1895, Menelik appointed Alula, with Ras Mikael as deputy, over a force of 12,000 troops and allotted 50,000 Maria Theresa thalers for recruiting more. Some 12,000 thalers were sent for this purpose to Mangasha in Tigray. The Italians responded. On 25 March, Baratieri invaded Tigray, captured Adigrat, Maqale and Adwa, and declared their annexation to Eritrea. On 2 May, Alula was sent to the north, but the approaching rainy season stopped the campaign. In September 1895, at the end of the rains, Menelik concluded that a war with the Italians was inevitable.[11]

Eight years after Yohannes could not face the Italian army in Saati, it was now very different. The Italians were far deeper inland, in Tigray's major towns. Their supply routes were much longer and in difficult terrain. In contrast, it was no longer the impoverished Tigray behind the Ethiopian army but the vast empire of Menelik. Ras Alula was a tactical adviser of the emperor and contributed in terms of intelligence and morals. But no less important was the logistical dimension. As supervised by Ras Makonnen, Menelik's chief aide, the conqueror of Harar (1887) and the father of the future Haile Selassie, the Ethiopian forces were better organized. After defeating the Italians in *Amba* Alaje (7 December 1895) and in Maqale (January 1896), some 100,000 or more Ethiopian armed soldiers were concentrated east to Adwa. They did not have to feed at the expense of the poor peasants. Huge herds, prepared by Makonnen's men, were brought from all over the empire. The soldiers were salaried by Menelik's treasury.

This time, the Ethiopians could take their time, but the Italians could not.[12] The Italian supply caravans were ambushed. Ras Sebhat of Agame deserted the Italians and joined the Ethiopian effort, as did Ras Hagos Mircha. Baratieri, heading a force of 18,000 men, was confident that once they were entrenched the Ethiopians could do them no harm. But the government in Rome wanted a quick victory. On 26 February, Prime Minister F. Crispi sent an angry message to Baratieri. He was ordered to act decisively in the name of the army and the king. Three days later, Baratieri ordered his generals to move and outflank the Ethiopians. It was a double mistake. First, the Italians misread the maps, moved in the wrong direction, and tried to correct it too late. Second, they were caught in the open. Ras Alula and his scouts, familiar with the terrain, were quick to grasp the situation, and alerted Menelik.

1 March 1896 turned into a one-sided battle. 7,000 of the Italian soldiers were killed and many were wounded, and 3,000 prisoners were forced to march to Addis Ababa. Some died on the road; others were finally released after long negotiations involving the Pope's pleading. Less fortunate were the Eritreans recruited by the Italians. Some 800 of them were among the prisoners. They were treated like traitors—sent home but not before their right hands and left feet were mutilated (not all survived the cruel punishment). The Ethiopians suffered some 5,000 dead and 8,000 wounded.

The victory of Adwa was first and foremost the victory of Emperor Menelik. He was sophisticated and perceptive, and he played his cards wisely when facing all the other players in the game of the Horn of Africa—Europeans, Ethiopians, foreigners, and locals. He did so successfully before Adwa as well as after. It was primarily due to him that Ethiopia could mobilize forces the extent of which no other African society could dream of.

The day in Adwa sealed a period of two decades during which Ethiopia fought for her survival. From Gundet and Gura against Khedival Egypt, to Kufit and Metemma against the Sudanese Mahdia, to Dogali and Adwa against the Italian imperialists. The country managed to defend herself in the north, while expanding in the south, doubling her power, assuring her independence. In Adwa, Menelik introduced Ethiopia to the twentieth century as a proud African empire, and it was recognized as such by the European powers. Within two years after Adwa, treaties in this spirit were signed in Addis Ababa with the British, French, Italians, and others. The conquerors of other Africans and Asians came to the Ethiopian capital to open legations and embassies. The legacy of the period for most Ethiopians was of victory, and there, it still is.

Ruined Tigray, prosperous Shoa

The sense of victory evaded the Tigrinya speakers. For them, the last two decades of the nineteenth century were a period in which they paid the dearest price for Ethiopia, and ended deprived, marginalized, and divided.[13]

After Adwa, the situation in Tigray worsened. The following day, Alula advised Menelik to cross the Mareb and liberate Eritrea. The emperor thought first to proceed in the direction of Akele Guzay but changed his mind and marched back to Addis Ababa. He must have realized that no success was waiting for him, only entrenched Italians that he would not defeat with his exhausted troops that lacked ammunition and supplies. Moreover, even if he could liberate a part of Eritrea, it would only mean strengthening the Tigrayans. On 26 October, he signed with the Italians a peace agreement recognizing the Mareb as the border between Ethiopia and Eritrea.

Before leaving Tigray, Menelik made a vague promise to Ras Mangasha that he would declare him *negus*. Menelik also married him to a niece of Taitu and gave him 32,000 Maria Theresa thalers. However, without bothering to ask Mangasha, Menelik appointed new governors in the divided Tigray. A brother of Dabbab Araya over Endarta, to reside in Maqale and report on Mangasha; Ras Hagos Mircha over Tamben; Ras Sebhat over Agame; and Ras Alula over Adwa (and Aksum).

In June 1896, the British newspaper correspondent A. Wylde, who had been in Adwa back in 1884, in the heyday of Yohannes, saw the town again: 'It was [back in 1884] a flourishing town of about 15,000 inhabitants, the commercial center of the district. Now it is a ruin and a charnel-house. War and pestilence have done their work, leaving their mark in ruined houses and blackened walls. I do not think there were a thousand people left in Adowa.'[14] Ras Alula told Wylde he could hardly maintain 300 soldiers. He himself fought a short, senseless battle with Ras Hagos in January

1897. Hagos was killed, and Alula died of his wounds on 15 February.

Tigray was in total anarchy. Ras Mangasha remained powerless and frustrated. He had Menelik's empty promise to be recognized as *negus* of Tigray and thought he could play between Rome and Addis Ababa. On 22 April 1896, he wrote to Queen Victoria, signing himself 'the Son of Yohannes,' and asking for British mediation with the Italians. Menelik learned about it. In January 1897, just before Alula and Hagos destroyed each other, the emperor sent for Mangasha inviting him to Addis Ababa to be crowned. Mangasha went to the capital, returned empty-handed, and revolted. In September 1898, Ras Makonnen was sent by the emperor to Tigray heading a large army. In February 1899, Mangasha surrendered and was sent to Addis Ababa to spend the rest of his days in prison, where he died in 1906.

Ras Makonnen himself was assigned to govern Tigray and located his headquarters in Yohannes' castle in Maqale. He stayed in Tigray till early 1900, the first and last Shoan governor of Tigray. Makonnen left behind a new order which assured that the Tigrayans would remain captive to their endless local rivalries, divided, and indirectly ruled from Addis Ababa. Menelik avoided treating Tigray like an occupied area. He and his Shoan successors preferred not to overly humiliate the Tigrayans. Unlike most of the other parts of the empire, Tigray remained under her local hereditary leaderships.[15] The local contenders were left to control different areas, as governors or as aspirants to governorship, in Agame, Adwa, Tamben, and Endarta. They enjoyed the same medieval feudal system we mentioned above when we discussed the 'era of the Judges.' This system would last in Tigray until 1974. The Church continued to play its role in upholding this structure of the society, in encouraging the paying the obligations of service and the need for deference and obedience to the heads of old, leading families. The Church remained the largest *Gult* landowner; it was owed dues and services, tribute, and deference. Its teaching went on supporting the existing structure.

A new generation of Tigrayan princes persisted with their internal rivalries. Dajazmach Seyum Mangasha, the son of Ras

Mangasha; Dajazmach Gugsa Araya Selassie, the son of Ras Araya Selassie Yohannes; Dajazmach Abraha Hagos, the son of the Ras Hagos; Dajazmach Abreah Araya, the son of Ras Araya Dimtsu and the brother of Dabbab Araya; Dajazmach Gabra-Selassie Baria-Gaber,[16] who entered Alula's service just before the Alula died and inherited his followers.

In 1909, Abraha Araya, brother of Dabbab, and governor of Endarta and Tamben in 1902 (he built the famous palace at Maqale, 'Abraha Castle') was imprisoned in Shoa (and served later in Menelik's government). In 1914, Ras Sebhat of Agame fought Dajazmach Gabra-Selassie of Adwa and was killed. Gabra-Selassie, for his part, was defeated a little after by Seyum Mangasha of Adwa and took refuge in Eritrea (he would return to Ethiopia). Seyum was made ras in the same year by the new ruler of Ethiopia: Lidj Iyasu. He would be rivaled (as detailed below) by Ras Gugsa Araya Selassie of Endarta, the other grandson of Yohannes. Tigray was now quite a remote province in the vast Ethiopian Empire.

Ethiopia under Menelik and after Adwa prospered. Ten years after the victory, Addis Ababa was a town of some 50,000 inhabitants, with new buildings and foreign embassies in huge compounds. It held a sizable community of diplomats and traders: Western Europeans, Indians, Greeks, and Armenians. The town had been developing as a political and commercial center for the past two decades, prospering from Ethiopia's newly annexed regions. Members of the Shoan elite ruled the provinces—with the exception of Tigray. They grew confident in their superiority over other groups in Ethiopia. In contrast, a new generation in impoverished Tigray began rather experiencing misery and humiliation. A native of Adwa who became a leading scholar during Menelik's reign, Gebrehiwet Baykedagne, wrote in 1912: '... there are hardly any Tigrayan youth left in their birthplace, Tigray. Like a swarm of bees without their queen, they are aimlessly scattered in four corners of the earth. Some people ridiculed their widespread poverty. Unfortunately, whilst other people live in tranquility, Tigray has never been free from wars, leave alone outlaws and bandits.'[17]

In Eritrea under colonialism

As of 1889, the Tigrinya speakers were not only fighting each other in their impoverished Tigray. They were also separated from fellow Tigrayans beyond the Mareb. The latter were included now in Italian Eritrea, where they became just a section of a diversified Eritrean colony.

In Tigray, the old elite went on governing the province, maintaining their leaderships (though under the imperial domination of Addis Ababa). In contrast, the leading Tigrayan elite of Eritrea was now removed. The process had begun earlier, in the days of Yohannes and Ras Alula's government in Asmara. We have already mentioned the most important case in point: Alula's imprisoning and exiling to Tigray of the hereditary leader of Hamasen, Ras Walda-Mikael. Alula also removed other local chiefs in Saraye and Akelle Guzay, installing his men, who were mostly from his native Tamben of Tigray.

Many members of the deposed Tigrayan Eritrean elite opposed Alula, whose regime is still considered in today's Eritrea a colonial enterprise. Some fled to the coastal or western periphery, lived among Muslim tribes, collaborating with the Egyptians and then with the Italians. The most important of these was Dajazmach Bahta Hagos[18] of Akkele Guzay. He collaborated with the Egyptians in 1875, then with the Italians, whom he helped marching to Asmara in 1889.

The Italians, for their part, tolerated the Muslims in the new colony,[19] but were not slow to destroy whatever positions the old local Tigrayan Christian elite of Eritrea still held. As presented by historian Tekeste Negash, the Italians proceeded immediately to eliminate those chiefs whom they suspected of potential resistance. Between August 1889 and December 1890, the Italians killed about a dozen chiefs together with some 800 of their followers. Only three notable chiefs, Dajazmach Tesfa-Mariam of Serae, Dajazmach Bahta Hagos of Akele-Guzay, and Blatta Beraki of Asmara, survived the initial Italian pacification. In those years of drought and famine, the Italians succeeded in their pacification policy without arousing much alarm amongst the starved peasantry. Between

1889 and 1893, Italy initiated an extensive recruitment of an indigenous army, which offered many peasants means of livelihood (as mentioned, many of these recruits would suffer in the battle of Adwa and after). The law-and-order measures of the Italian administration transformed collaborationist elites into salaried employees of the colonial state.

Of the three who survived the pacification, it was Bahta Hagos who won a name in Eritrean history for revolting against the colonialists. In December 1894, he established contact with Ras Mangasha who, as mentioned above, was sent by Menelik back to Tigray to prepare an advance guard against the Italians. More importantly, Bahta Hagos won the trust of the peasants in Akkele Guzay, who were embittered by the Italians' extensive land confiscations. He asked the collaborating chiefs, as well as the peasantry, to join him in resisting the Italians through what later became a historical idiom: 'there is no medicine for the bite of a white serpent.'

In December 1894, Bahta led his force of 1,600 men in an open revolt against the Italians. He captured Italian administrators and declared an independent Akkele Guzay. On 15 December, the telegraph wires to Asmara were cut. The Italians dispatched an army of 3,500 from Asmara and Massawa and killed Bahta Hagos in a battle on 19 December. Partly in order to suppress Eritrean resistance completely, the Italians decided to invade Tigray, where the followers of Bahta were regrouping. This invasion escalated relations between Rome and Menelik, which led to the battle of Adwa in March 1896.[20]

Modern nationalism in today's Eritrea revives and glorifies the memory of Bahta Hagos, Walda-Mikael, and others. (In 2007, the remains of Bahta Hagos were moved to a newly constructed memorial.) These figures became pillars of an Eritrean identity, the roots of which go back to the days of Medri Bahri and beyond. However, it must be also emphasized that modern Eritrea, like many others, came into being not so much as the political fulfillment of old local identities. As a modern political entity, Eritrea was born as an imposition by a foreign government and its administration over a collection of diverse ethnic, linguistic, regional, and religious sectors.[21] Tigrinya speakers would be part of Eritrean history, and in time would regain leadership there, much as they enjoy today.

The Italian colony of Eritrea existed until the middle of World War II.[22] However, the Italian dream of colonization by channeling Italian emigration to Eritrea instead of to the United States hardly materialized. At the same time, Eritrea proved to be too poor in resources to be of much economic worth. As from the outset, its importance continued to be its being a source of pride to Italian imperialist sentiment.[23]

Italy's impact on Eritrean society was not that significant. The Italians' only real concern was to make Eritrea a strong military base that could serve as a strategic springboard for expansion. They therefore constructed an impressive road and railway network and developed urban centers. Asmara was made the capital city of Italian Eritrea in 1897, and a growing Italian community developed in the city. With its Italian new look, it was also known as 'little Rome.' (By the end of the 1930s, Asmara had a population of 98,000, of which 53,000 were Italians; only 75,000 Italians lived in all of Eritrea, making the capital city by far their largest center.)

Other than that, the Italians were not interested in development per se. Although they contributed to the maintenance of law and order, subsidized the economy, and promoted health care, the tribal system of the Muslim nomads, with its feudal undertones and political overtones, remained largely intact.[24] The members of the great Tigrinya families and regional warlords who had led the Christian community, however, were deprived of their political leadership, and leading personalities were reduced, at best, to the status of low-ranking bureaucrats.[25] Later, as we shall discuss below, Eritrean identity and nationalism would first rise among the local Muslims.

The period of Italian rule up to 1941 contributed by its very length to the strengthening of Eritrean awareness, especially among those who underwent urbanization or served in the bureaucracy and army, although the Italians did very little to promote internal social cohesion.[26] Because of the Italians' undisputed dominance, their rule was relatively free of internal political, social, and economic tensions.

7

BACK TO CENTER STAGE

FROM WAR TO WAR

During World War I, the Tigrayan people went on with their lives on the sidelines. Tigray's affairs were hardly noticeable outside the province. The entire Horn of Africa, to be sure, did experience a political drama, but it developed mostly in the center and south of Ethiopia, away from Tigray. It was only in the 1930s that the province returned to center stage. As the world began escalating toward its second global conflict, Tigray and its internal rivalries gained global importance. The fascist Mussolini, by returning to active *Politica Tigrigna*, made an initial, meaningful step in the direction of World War II.

World War I—Out of the game

During World War I (1914–18), no face-to-face collision between the battling powers occurred in the Horn of Africa. Yet Ethiopia was directly affected. The war in the nearby Middle East, and in other parts of Africa, had a religious dimension. The Ottomans worked to render it an Islamic Holy War against the British and their allies. In the Ethiopian context, the central figure was Lij Iyasu, the heir of Menelik.[1]

Iyasu (born 1895) was the grandson of Menelik and the son of Ras Mikael, formerly *Imam* Muhammad Ali, the leader of the Wallo Muslims, who had been Christianized by Yohannes in 1878. In 1909, when Emperor Menelik's health began deteriorating, he decreed that Iyasu (his only male descendent) would inherit his throne. Upon Menelik's death in December 1913, Iyasu formally became the head of the state. He was supposed to be guided by the leaders of the old Shoan establishment but refused to be their puppet.

Iyasu's reign can be divided into two phases: prior to the outbreak of the war in late 1914, and then after this point.

In the first phase, he worked to build coalitions in defiance of the 'Shoan nobility.' Seeking new local allies, mostly in Ethiopia's periphery, Iyasu also flirted with Islam, as if returning to the faith of his father and ancestors in Wallo. Wallo's Islam, flexible and moderate,[2] had co-existed for centuries with Ethiopian Christian political culture and rulers. Iyasu's new connections and behavior irritated the leading elite but did not yet cause an open crisis. For his part, he avoided being officially crowned as a Christian emperor, and rather symbolized his being a king of kings by having his father crowned, on 31 May 1914, as king, *negus* Mikael.

The outbreak of WWI seemed to have changed Iyasu's perspective on Islam. As conveyed by the Ottoman's declaration of a Holy War (14 November 1914), Islam was now a political ideology fighting for victory. The story of Iyasu flirting with this kind of Islam is still controversial. According to my findings, Iyasu did gamble on an Ottoman victory and on his building of a new Ethiopian empire at the expense of the Shoan establishment. It was in this context that the old guard of Menelik's men deposed Iyasu on 27 September 1916. Menelik's daughter, Zawditu, was proclaimed empress, and Ras Tafari Makonnen was declared heir to the throne. The whole story is beyond our scope here.[3] In October 1916, the army of Iyasu's father, *Negus* Mikael, was defeated by a coalition also headed by Ras Tafari. Iyasu fled to the Afar desert, and Tafari would continue to develop as the strong man of Ethiopia before crowning Emperor Hayla-Selasse I in 1930.

All this drama unfolded in the center of the country, mostly between Addis Ababa and Harar. It also involved the Somalis under their Islamic warrior Muhammad bin Abdalla Hassan (the so-dubbed 'mad Mullah'). Eritrea under the Italians was relatively peaceful, and the impoverished Tigray had a far secondary role.

The successors of Yohannes could have been happy with one aspect of Iyasu's policy. Namely, the prospect of destroying Shoan domination, and that Tigray would be revived in the framework of a decentralized Ethiopia, an empire somewhat reminiscent of Yohannes'. However, the Islamic dimension of Iyasu's vision was something they must have dreaded.

On 31 May 1914, prior to the outbreak of the war, Iyasu, as mentioned, crowned his father as king: 'Negus Mikael of Wallo and Tigray.' Mikael symbolized his new authority by promoting *Dajazmach* Seyum, son of Mangasha and grandson of Yohannes, to ras. Earlier, in 1909, Iyasu had married a sister of Seyum, but like Iyasu would do many times, the union was just for political purposes and was not consummated. Seyum, for his part, married a sister of Iyasu.

The coronation of Mikael as their king went against the very grain of the Tigrayans' Christian identity. Though *negus* Mikael went on behaving like a Christian, he did not hide his intention to revive Islam politically. He had been, to reiterate, the *Imam* Muhammad Ali, whom Yohannes had forced to convert to Christianity back in 1878. As Ras Mikael, he led the powerful Oromo cavalry of Wallo, played a major role under Yohannes, and then, switching loyalties, under Menelik. He married Menelik's daughter (Shoaraga) and fathered Iyasu.

Here again, we can only speculate what would have been the future of Ethiopia had the Ottomans won the war and Lij Iyasu reshaped the country. Negus Mikael did not hide the options. His new seal, after his coronation, included an inscription in both Ge'ez and Arabic. The Ge'ez words were the biblical quotation: 'The government shall be upon his shoulders.' But the Arabic read: 'Mikael, the king of Wallo and Tigray, the son of Imam Ali, the king of Wallo.' Arguably, he entertained the idea of reviving Islam politically, and, through his son, the king of kings, making it dominant in Ethiopia.[4] The very notion that the king of Tigray was 'the son of Imam Ali, the king of Wallo,' must have been painful to the grandchildren of Yohannes.

When the war ended and the Shoan establishment remained safely in power, the two grandchildren of Yohannes, Seyum Mangasha[5] and Gugsa Araya,[6] remained the two meaningful leaders in Tigray. Seyum—made ras by *negus* Mikael—was apparently slow to discern the growing power of Ras Tafari. In 1921, Seyum failed to surrender Iyasu to Tafari when Iyasu was trying to find shelter in his territory. Consequently, Seyum had to spend most of the 1920s as an exile in the capital, (and, more importantly—would be suspected by Tafari/Haile Selassie in the future as not fully loyal). Gugsa Araya, in contrast, was made ras by the Shoan group in February 1918, a group with which he continued to ally himself during the 1920s. Having married a niece of Tafari, in January 1921, Ras Gugsa captured Iyasu and handed him over to the future emperor.[7] In 1928, when Tafari was crowned as *negus*—still under empress Zawditu—he organized a new order in Tigray. Ras Gugsa, residing at Maqale, was appointed over the eastern regions of the province, and Ras Seyum, in Adwa, over the west.

Haile Selassie's centralization

On 2 November 1930, Tafari was crowned Emperor Haile Selassie and began intensifying his policy of centralization at the expense of the regional warlords. In Tigray, the leading families, entrenched for centuries as provincial chiefs, were to adjust to the challenge of the emerging absolutist.[8]

On 14 April, 1930, Tafari ordered the two rival chiefs of Tigray to report to Addis Ababa for his coronation. Belatedly understanding the situation, Seyum ordered a huge ceremony to be held in Adwa on coronation day, at which speeches flattering the new emperor were to be made. The two Tigrayans, and many of the other provincial chiefs, were forced to stay in the capital until the proclamation, on 16 July 1931, of the country's first modern constitution (which was in itself a step towards centralization at the expense of their power). To further reinforce his position, Haile

Selassie appointed Ras Seyum, whom, as mentioned, he trusted less than Ras Gugsa, to the new twenty-seven-member senate, and prevented him returning to the north.

Meanwhile, in Tigray, the emperor started exploiting the absence of Seyum and Gugsa to strengthen his indirect control. In October 1930, the emperor's consul in Asmara, Wadaju Ali, was given imperial right to reorganize the Tigray customs and to control the monopoly on alcohol there. More significantly, he was also given jurisdiction over the holy city of Aksum. While the two chiefs were in the capital, the emperor sent various envoys to take charge of the town. Another important event was the appointment of an Amhara—*Abuna* Yishaq[9]—as bishop to the province.

Only in November 1931 was Ras Gugsa permitted to return to Tigray, but not before paying the equivalent of one million Italian lire and accepting that his deputies be appointed by the emperor. His humiliation proved disastrous. On his way back to Maqale, Gugsa, passing through Asmara, started building friendly relations with the Italians. The Tigrayan ras, renowned in the 1920s for his anti-Italian attitude, was changing his orientation in the face of Haile Selassie's growing centralism. His health had long been deteriorating and he was pinning his hopes on Italian doctors. Nevertheless, the emperor still considered him loyal.

Meanwhile, Seyum was confined to the capital, unable to return to Adwa. He went on trying to prove his loyalty and instructed his men in Tigray to demonstrate a tough anti-Italian policy. He made sure that information from Adwa on this, as well as on ceremonies and speeches praising the emperor, would be published in the capital's newspaper *Berhanena Salam*. In Addis Ababa, Seyum organized parties and ceremonies in the emperor's honor. Haile Selassie remained suspicious but rewarded him with the empty title *leul ras* (i.e., His Highness the ras).

Appeasing Tigray—intermarriages

In 1932, Haile Selassie began to feel a growing aggressive tendency on the part of the Italians. He therefore tried to build better relations with Tigray's leadership. An event of a symbolic nature seemed to underline this effort. Earlier the same year, the emperor's agent in Matamma, the town on the Sudanese border where the 1889 battle with the Mahdia took place, had announced the discovery on Sudanese soil of a grave containing three headless bodies. These were presumed to be the remains of Emperor Yohannes and two other Tigrayan princes killed in the famous battle. (As mentioned, the Mahdists seized Yohannes' corpse and sent his head to decorate their celebrations in Umm Durman). An expedition organized now by Seyum under the auspices of the emperor was sent from Addis Ababa and returned in the middle of the year with Yohannes' cross, verifying the grave's authenticity.[10] Even more important than this paying of respects to Tigray's greatest hero was the return to the old Ethiopian political tradition—marriages between the houses of Shoa and Tigray.

On 5 May 1932, in a European-style royal ceremony, the emperor's elder son *Maridazmach* Asfa-Wossen married Seyum's daughter Walata-Israel. Speeches made on the occasion emphasized the significance of the event. Asfa-Wossen was the officially proclaimed heir,[11] and thus the house of Yohannes was again to have a share in the emperorship. Haile Selassie was said to be paying an old Shoan debt—in 1882, Yohannes had married his son Araya Selassie, Gugsa's father, to Menilek's daughter Zawditu. The fact that the groom, Asfa-Wassen, was a sixteen-year-old boy, and the bride (the widow of Dajazmach Gabra-Selassie[12]) already had two children, did not bode well for the future of the marriage. Nevertheless, it was supposed to lay a foundation for constructive coexistence between Tigray's fictitious autonomy and the emperor's policy of centralization.

To further stabilize the situation in Tigray, a similar step was taken regarding Ras Gugsa. When the marriage of Seyum's daughter was proclaimed in early May, the emperor promised his daughter Princess Zanaba-Warq to Gugsa's son, Haileselassie Gugsa.[13] On 16 June 1932, in a similarly pompous ceremony, the thirty-two-year-old groom, who was to play a pivotal role in forthcoming events, married the emperor's beloved fourteen-year-old daughter.

At the same time, Seyum and Gugsa, both once again in Addis Ababa, had another opportunity to express loyalty to the new master of Ethiopia. Ras Hailu Takla-Haymanot, the hereditary prince of Gojjam, was accused of engineering the escape of Lij Iyasu from prison. Both Seyum and Gugsa did their best to praise the emperor and condemn Hailu as a traitor deserving capital punishment. The death sentence was indeed imposed, although afterwards it was commuted to life imprisonment. Meanwhile, the emperor exploited the situation in two ways: he appointed a Shoan over Gojjam (his most trusted friend and relative, Ras Imru Haile Selassie); and he further strengthened his position by taking care to publicize Seyum's association with Lij Iyasu in the early 1920s. As the province of Bagemdir had also come under Shoan control in 1930, the emperor's campaign against provincial autonomy seemed to be approaching success in the north.

On 25 September 1932, the emperor ordered the two Tigrayan chiefs to return to their territories. They were the only hereditary chiefs in the empire left in practical control of their province. Although they represented traditional provincialism, the emperor felt that their mutual opposition effectively neutralized their threat to him. Tigray was not to be affected directly by centralization, and her hereditary chiefs had now seemingly strong interest in the constructed compromise. This was to have served in the long run as the basis for the gradual integration of the province into the regime which the emperor hoped to build. However, this preservation of traditional patterns also invited foreign involvement, which the system was too weak to withstand.

Back to Politica Tigrigna

From the beginning of their involvement in our story, Italian policymakers—to reiterate—faced a major dilemma between two contradictory options which they called *Politica Scoiana* and *Politica Tigrigna*. In general, it was natural that the Italian Foreign Ministry and the legation in Addis Ababa pursued *Politica Scioana*, while the governors of Eritrea and the Colonial Office pressed for *Politica Tigrigna*. In practice, the emphasis occasionally shifted, but never to the extent to which it became a consistently pursued line. The period 1927–32 saw the culmination of this confusion.

During these years, from 1926, Italian minister to Addis Ababa, G. Cora, became the most influential foreigner in the country. He saw Tafari as a progressive leader deserving Italian support. This policy supported centralization in Ethiopia by giving aid in fields such as communications and banking. It culminated in the Friendship Agreement signed between Italy and Ethiopia on 2 August 1928. (In 1930, Cora was replaced by Paterno Di Manchi, who followed the same line until his dismissal in 1932).

At the same time, the energetic Governor Cornado Zoli of Eritrea, a sworn fascist, was doing his best to build subversive options. He was backed by the new Minister of Colonies, Emilio De Bono, himself a dedicated pursuer of this option. Zoli tried to promote relations with Seyum and Gugsa. In April 1930, when they passed through Asmara on their way to the coronation ceremony, Zoli tried to smooth the relations between them in order to pave the way for a new chapter in *Politica Tigrigna*.

In early 1932, Rome decided to abandon the policy of supporting the emperor and instead adopt a policy of subversion. The emergence of a modern Ethiopia went against the imperialist interests of the increasingly aggressive Fascist regime. The emperor worked to destroy Ethiopia's traditional political fluidity, aiming at stopping the constant competition between the center and the various provincial chiefs, which facilitated foreign penetration. If the country was to be invaded, it was high time for the Fascists to prepare the ground in Tigray.

Both the Ministry of Foreign Affairs and the Ministry of Colonies were asked to prepare reports assessing the options in the Horn. In March 1932, De Bono left for the region. His report made a strong case for intensive subversion. He concluded that Ethiopia, and Tigray in particular, was ripe for such action and that the emperor could thus be goaded into initiating a war that he would lose. In submitting their report in August, the Foreign Ministry experts also recommended the conquest of the country, although they emphasized the importance of taking into full consideration the reaction of the European powers and warned not to underestimate Haile Selassie's emerging position in Ethiopia.

Mussolini, though still personally uninvolved, chose a line combining the two approaches. While the main effort was to be conducted in Europe, intensive subversion in Ethiopia was to be coordinated by a political office centered in the Addis Ababa Legation and an intelligence office coordinating the activities of the various Italian consulates (Adwa, Dessie, Dabra-Markos, Dire-Dawa, and Gondar). Each consulate had technicians able to monitor and translate Ethiopian telephone conversations and telegraph cables. The consulates also had doctors and medical staff who rendered an important political service by treating Ethiopian provincial chiefs.

Tigray was to be the main target of this policy. In the eyes of Italian policymakers, observers, and propagandists, so much had been invested politically in Tigray that it was now Italy's right to interfere actively in her affairs. Furthermore, it was also apparent that due to the so-called 'Adwa Complex,' stemming from Italy's 1896 defeat by Ethiopia on Tigrayan soil, any future war with Ethiopia must begin with an invasion of Tigray. From then on, the domestic policies of this province, the only one in Ethiopia to remain practically untouched by Haile Selassie's centralization, would play a crucial role in the escalation toward what became internationally known as 'the Abyssinian Crisis.'

The death of Ras Gugsa

In spite of his efforts and early successes at centralization, Haile Selassie was far from being all-powerful in the period before World War II. In 1934, he was still facing difficulties in making appointments even in provinces such as Gojjam, Bagemdir, and Sidamo. To some extent, this was due to growing Italian interference. In Tigray, he avoided even a token effort at centralization. The arrangement he had made there seemed to be working: governed by two chiefs, equally influential and mutually hostile, each marrying into the emperor's family and each aiming at obtaining his support to overcome his rival and become Tigray's *negus*. In a span of a few months, however, this carefully balanced arrangement was destroyed: first Princess Zanaba-Warq died, then the death of Ras Gugsa followed.

Ras Gugsa had started improving relations between himself and Asmara after Haile Selassie's coronation. Back in Maqale, he demonstrated his friendliness to Italy, taking little care to hide his growing resentment towards the emperor's policy throughout 1932.

In early 1933, Gugsa's health, always problematic, deteriorated. This enabled him to develop his relations with the Italians openly through their medical services. Early in February 1933, Gugsa met with an Italian doctor in Maqale and confided his decision to throw in his lot with the Italians. The emperor, he said, was afraid that he would conspire against him and refused to let him go to Europe for medical purposes. But he could go to Cairo and Jerusalem, he said, and sought to exploit the opportunity to remain in Asmara.[14] This was not to be, however. Apparently, his health deteriorated, and he was unable to take to the road. Instead, an Italian physician, Dr. P. Lecco, came to take care of him. Dr. Lecco arrived at Maqale on 17 February 1933 and stayed with Ras Gugsa for the next months.

Lecco's report[15] leaves little doubt as to Gugsa's plan to ally himself with Eritrea against Haile Selassie. Being both strong minded and cautious (the doctor was most enthusiastic about his personal merits), he avoided stating it plainly or committing himself. Yet Gugsa was reported by Lecco to have described Haile Selassie as Emperor Tewodros in the last years of his reign. In this context, Gugsa went as far as saying that nobody in Ethiopia would help the hated emperor face an Italian invasion—an obvious analogy to his grandfather Yohannes' alliance with the British enemies of Tewodros.

On 25 March, while Dr. Lecco was attending to Gugsa's pneumonia, Gugsa's daughter-in-law, Princess Zanaba-Warq, died, also in Maqale, of the same illness. Lecco's report casts a serious shadow over Haileselassie Gugsa's role in the two weeks of her sudden illness and death. Ras Gugsa openly disliked his son Haileselassie Gugsa. It was widely rumored, and in fact partially established, that the prince was not Gugsa's son. In any case, the dying ras did not let him approach his death bed. Haileselassie Gugsa reacted to this by keeping Zanaba-Warq's pneumonia a secret. Strangely enough, he even misled her father, the emperor, in this matter. When the emperor finally learned of it, he did all he could to save the life of his daughter, but to no avail. Her body was flown to Addis Ababa together with Haileselassie Gugsa.

Following the death of his daughter, Emperor Haile Selassie finally gave the ailing Gugsa permission to go to Asmara. The ras took the road on a rainy day on a mule (the priests objected to his being carried on a stretcher) and died on the road on 26 April 1933.

According to Dr. Lecco's report, the fates of Gugsa and Zanaba-Warq amounted to a series of tragic errors stemming from political intrigues and superstitions. In any case, it did upset the balance on which the emperor's Tigray arrangement rested. Gugsa's son, Haileselassie Gugsa, was no match for Seyum. Being a son of an important person or the son-in-law of the emperor did not in of itself carry very much weight in Ethiopian politics. He would have to work hard to fill his father's shoes. The political game in Tigray was now open again, and this time with Italy's purposeful and intensive interference.

A new arrangement

After Ras Gugsa's death in April 1933, a full year of intrigue was to pass before the emperor made a decision concerning the territories of the late ras. Meanwhile, the two Tigrayan chiefs tried to undermine each other's position and gain favor. Seyum wanted the whole of the province, while Haileselassie Gugsa worked to obtain at least his father's domain. Shoan advisers of the emperor tried to persuade him to install elements of modern administration over the province, but the emperor was of the belief that only the traditional leadership could work in Tigray.

Of the two rivals, the emperor seemed to favor Haileselassie Gugsa. When he arrived in Addis Ababa with the body of his wife, he was most warmly received as a son by the mourning imperial couple. For his part, he saved no effort in expressing gratitude and humility. The emperor appointed him temporarily over his father's domains, but as Haileselassie Gugsa was ordered to stay in the capital, the region quickly fell into anarchy.

Meanwhile, Seyum and Haileselassie Gugsa started a campaign of defamation. The rumor that Haileselassie Gugsa was not really Gugsa's son was now embellished by the revelation that Gugsa himself was not the son of Araya Selassie, the son of Yohannes. On the other hand, there were others who claimed that Seyum was not the son of Ras Mangasha, and that Mangasha was not the son of Yohannes. The Shoans were not entirely displeased by all this.[16]

What really mattered was actual politics. Haileselassie Gugsa thought he could advance his cause by flattering Emperor Haile Selassie while plotting with the Italians. In June 1933, still in Addis Ababa, he wrote confidentially to the governor of Eritrea, R. Astuto, and asked to purchase a house in Asmara. He was permitted to do so by the Italians. The emperor, unaware of this, continued to take him for granted.

With Seyum, it was the other way round. Although he was doing his best to prove his loyalty by making speeches flattering the emperor as the most enlightened modernizer and by demonstrating strong anti-Italian feelings, Seyum remained suspect by Haile Selassie. Throughout 1933 and the first half of 1934, the emperor sent all sorts of agents to spy on Seyum. Seyum's maltreatment of the Italians of the Adwa consulate was to no avail, and in Addis Ababa he was widely and unfoundedly regarded as an ally of the Italians. Ironically, this was to enhance his nuisance value. His position as such grew stronger when he refused throughout 1933 and early 1934 to obey the emperor's command and report to the capital. He had already experienced some ten years of exile in Addis Ababa. His suspicion grew stronger when the emperor did not allow him to take his wife W. Atsada to the capital. Atsada was reported to be a very clever person, virtually 'the brain' behind the ras. When, in March 1934, he finally felt that he was pushing his refusal to the verge of revolt, Seyum took the road to the capital, convinced—like many others—that he was not to see Tigray again.

But Haile Selassie, in the face of a growing Italian threat, thought nothing of trying conclusions with Tigray's traditional leadership. Though the Italian consul at Adwa presumed that the local population was ripe for a radical step against their old leaders and that the emperor could successfully install a new administration, the emperor himself apparently had a different understanding of Tigrayan affairs. Thus, on 12 May 1934, he appointed Seyum as military commander of the whole province and enlarged his territories to include Aksum, which had belonged to Ras Gugsa in the 1920s, and also Bora and Seloa, which he took from Haileselassie Gugsa. With this arrangement, in time of war, Haileselassie Gugsa was to be under Seyum's command. At the same time, the emperor also allowed Haileselassie Gugsa to return to Tigray, appointing him over Endarta, Agame, Enda Makonni, and Wadjerat and Azebo. Haileselassie Gugsa returned in the same month via Asmara, where his resentment was to lead him to take a very crucial step.

The traitor and Italian strategy

After the arrangement of 12 May 1934, Ras Seyum stayed in Addis Ababa to help the emperor with preparations for the coming war. Haile Selassie still treated him coldly, and Seyum worked to cultivate a friendship with the emperor's heir (and now son-in-law). He entertained the idea of sharing a grandson with the emperor. If ever there was going to be a Tigray *negus,* Seyum probably thought, he was the man. In the war council, he was advocating a preemptive strike and conquest of Eritrea. In August, he returned to Adwa.

Earlier, on 27 May 1934, Haileselassie Gugsa arrived secretly at Asmara. The next day, he met with governor R. Astuto and declared that he came to ally himself with Italy. The emperor, he said, left no hope for the Tigrayans. He was purposely fomenting hatred between him and Seyum, aiming at creating total anarchy in Tigray. To prevent this calamity, he, Haileselassie Gugsa, would collaborate with the Italians and take orders from them. He suggested an immediate Italian invasion of Tigray and guaranteed an open road to Quarram in southern Tigray. When Astuto responded that Italy had friendly relations with the emperor, the Tigrayan chief said that everyone in Addis Ababa saw war as inevitable, and that the Shoans were just using Italy's friendship to cover up their intentions. Astuto concluded the conversation by saying that the Italians were

87

always happy to know that a descendant of Yohannes was ruling in Eastern Tigray, and that unlike Seyum, he, Haileselassie Gugsa, was cleverly choosing the right policy.

The two men met again secretly three days later. This time, Haileselassie Gugsa read out a fully elaborated military plan. Claiming to have command of over 30,000 soldiers, he said he was ready to lead the Italian army to Quarram right away. He pointed out the importance of making such a move before Seyum returned from the capital. Tigray would fall without bloodshed, he promised, and this would spark a revolt all over Ethiopia. The emperor was hated for his tyranny. He would have no alternative but to escape to Europe, where he would spend the money that he was stealing from the people. If Seyum returned before the invasion commenced, Haileselassie Gugsa promised to attack what he called 'Seyum's small force of only 5,000 men,' and kill his rival.

The meeting ended with Astuto advising the Tigrayan to keep his hatred for the emperor to himself. The emperor, Astuto said (he was still calling him Tafari), was leading Ethiopia into chaos, and it was indeed high time to prepare the salvation of Tigray. In Astuto's reports to De Bono on these meetings, he concluded that Haileselassie Gugsa was sincere and shared in the spirit of his father, as had been reported by Dr. Lecco, and that he would be a reliable partner. Astuto recommended preparing diplomatic ground with Britain and France and then using the excellent military start provided by Haileselassie Gugsa. He accepted the latter's opinion that the emperor would be isolated just as Tewodros had been. Furthermore, Astuto analyzed, Haileselassie Gugsa gave Italy a workable option in the event of diplomatic difficulties with other European powers. In such a situation, the Tigrayan prince would be easily convinced to proclaim himself a *negus* and ask for Italian protection. Britain and the League of Nations ('if still existing...') would have to stomach Italian control of Tigray. The emperor, he felt, might give up Tigray in such a case. If he reacted militarily, the road to Addis Ababa would be open for the counter-attacking Italians.[17]

The timing of Haileselassie Gugsa's betrayal was arguably historic. In that same May of 1934, the *duce* had been taking a closer look at the Ethiopian issue. In retrospect, it is quite probable that he took seriously Haileselassie Gugsa's suggestion. It was perhaps not a mere coincidence that on May 31, Mussolini summoned his closest devotees, ordered them to escalate the situation with Haile Selassie and keep it secret from France and Great Britain.[18] In July, Mussolini began personally supervising the policy of subversion in Ethiopia.[19]

Ethiopian failure in preparing for war

Haileselassie Gugsa's secret meeting with Governor Astuto in May 1934 remained unknown to the emperor. The traitor was able to continue strengthening his relations with the Italians. From late September to mid-November 1934, Haileselassie Gugsa hosted Italian agent and spy Virgilio Scotti, an engineer whose cover story was the construction of a monument for the late Ras Gugsa. In reality, Scotti was mapping the roads to Quarram. He reported that the Tigrayan prince was ready to improve the existing roads from Eritrea down to the heart of Wallo. Upon Scotti's departure, Haileselassie Gugsa gave him a written declaration of loyalty to the Italians.

Ironically, the emperor went on suspecting Seyum. In July, with Seyum still in the capital, the emperor sent his consul at Asmara, *Lij* Tedla Haile, as a special envoy to Tigray. A sworn enemy of Seyum, Tedla was authorized by Haile Selassie to appoint new administrators in Tigray. The man toured the province, intimidated the locals, and made intensive changes in the name of the emperor. He was also ordered to find incriminating material on Seyum, mainly to substantiate the rumor that Seyum had intended to proclaim himself a *negus* of Tigray. Though he found no evidence to this effect, Lij Tedla was most successful in preparing the ground for Seyum's return, creating an atmosphere that made Seyum less confident than ever. It was a very nervous ras who returned to Tigray in August to assume command of the Eritrean front.

Back on home ground, Seyum started accusing Haileselassie Gugsa of collaborating with the Italians. His accusations were ignored, and he rather had to prove his own innocence. He did so by demonstrating an anti-Italian line, making speeches full of praises to the emperor as the savior of the country.

The situation soon deteriorated. On 5 December 1934, Mussolini staged an incident in a remote place on the border of Italian Somalia and Ethiopia. A skirmish between a Somali garrison in the service of Italy and Ethiopian troops resulted in over 150 deaths. Rome issued a humiliating ultimatum to Haile Selassie. All Ethiopian efforts at reasonable appeasement were rejected. The case was put to the League of Nations and developed into crisis in January 1935. Ethiopia was a sovereign member, and thus the League's ability to prevent war and impose mediation and reason was at stake. Britain and France worked to save the League, but as Mussolini grew bolder, they became more afraid he would join with Hitler. Ethiopia and Italy's drama was studied and researched thoroughly.

Back in Tigray, Seyum went out of his way to prove his loyalty. In early January 1935, he even aimed a cannon at the Italian consulate in Adwa from a nearby hill. Meanwhile, Haileselassie Gugsa was secretly preparing to help the invaders.

Realizing that direct confrontation with the Italians would be disastrous, the emperor prepared for a guerilla campaign: to let the Italians in and then conduct hit-and-run operations. Tigray was ideal terrain for guerrillas, and it had to be sacrificed. Ras Seyum refused to accept it. In January 1935, he wrote to Haile Selassie saying he would rather attack and invade Eritrea. At the end of February, Italian intelligence intercepted the emperor's answer: 'It is not necessarily going to be like in Adwa in 1896. We have to position our troops in the mountains and the forests, in valleys and caves, without concentrating them in masses... We have to act like rebels and block their lines of communication... Do not allow your men to face the tanks. They have instead to move from one trench to another...' [20]

The emperor's distrust of Seyum continued to grow. On 14 March 1935, another special envoy arrived in Aksum from Addis

Ababa. This was *nagadras* Wadaju Ali, a former consul to Asmara. Wadaju, a sworn enemy of Seyum, was to settle in Adwa and assume responsibility over political affairs related to relations with Italy. In fact, he was to act freely in the name of the emperor. Seyum's prestige and authority in Tigray was seriously undermined.

To make sure that Ras Seyum would do as he was ordered, Haile Selassie sent his military adviser, Colonel T. Konovaloff, an ex-officer in the Czar's army. He came to Adwa in early July and stayed with Seyum until a month after hostilities began. His memoirs shed light on the events that ensued. Seyum did try to follow the emperor's instructions, but with difficulty. He and his men did not follow Konovaloff's advice for preparing for guerrilla warfare. According to Konovaloff, Seyum could not read a map and knew nothing about modern warfare.[21] When the Fascist divisions crossed the River Mareb on 3 October 1935, Seyum was hardly the commander to face them.

The Italians were equipped with not only a modern army, but also bribe money: one million Maria Theresa (MT) silver coins. They failed to bribe Seyum but succeeded with some of his men. They prepared 150,000 MT for Haileselassie Gugsa and his followers. The emperor started to suspect Haileselassie Gugsa only in late August, but the spy he sent had been bribed by the Italians as well. More spies sent more lists of suspected persons to Haile Selassie, who in August and September was busy finding traitors in Tigray. He cabled to Seyum and Haileselassie Gugsa demanding reports. The latter knew how to respond and flatter the emperor. In his memoirs, Haile Selassie even quoted one of his cables: 'If by any chance the Italians should invade us by military force, I shall resist them to the utmost in my province, until I die.' He also reported he was in contact with Eritrean soldiers in the Italian army, and that they would cross lines and join him when the invasion began.

The fall of Ethiopia

The British were convinced that Ethiopia's disintegration was inevitable, that Tigray was shortly to fall into Italian hands, and that it was pointless to develop a conflict with Mussolini over the country's integrity. In June and July of 1935, a British committee concluded that Italian conquest of Ethiopia would not be that bad: 'In the north, Italy would eventually acquire a protectorate over Tigre[...] British interests lie [...] in acquisition of control over Lake Tana[...] It is believed that provision could be made somewhat on this line for a partition of interests between Great Britain and Italy in anticipation for the collapse of the Abyssinian administration, which many authorities consider to be probable.'[22]

The Italian invasion began on 3 October 1935 on two fronts: from Eritrea and Somalia. The major effort was from Eritrea into Tigray. One reason for this was that if the British intervened, at least Tigray would fall into Italian hands. But the 'Tigray first' strategy gave Ethiopia its only chance. If the Ethiopians could conduct efficient guerrilla attacks in this difficult area and could hold the Italians till the rainy season of 1936 (beginning in June), it was possible that Britain and France would finally interfere in some way. For the Ethiopians, it meant letting the invaders capture Tigray's main towns and avoiding direct confrontation. Under pressure from the emperor, Ras Seyum pulled back, and the Italians were happy to march to Adwa. They entered the town—the symbol of their 1896 defeat—on 6 October 1935.

In the eastern Tigrayan front, Marshal Emilio De Bono, now commander in chief, had instructed Haileselassie Gugsa to wait for the Italian attack and then cross the lines—he and his men. However, on 9 October, the Ethiopian traitor panicked and crossed the lines that night. For the Italians, the road to Maqale was now open, but it was a mixed blessing. The premature betrayal of Haileselassie Gugsa prevented the confrontation they desired. On 15 October, the Italians entered Aksum, and on 8 November, they took Maqale. Nearly the whole of Tigray was now theirs. Ras Seyum was ordered to move to the mountainous Tamben. Together with forces under the command of Ras Kasa Haylu, he managed to frustrate the invaders. An angry Mussolini replaced De Bono with the tougher Pietro Badoglio, yet the Ethiopians managed to avoid a decisive confrontation. Thus, 1935 ended, at least according to some British and American experts, in an Italian failure.[23]

Ras Seyum in Tamben was not pleased. According to a British military observer, he was 'still imbued with the medieval idea that the only methods of attack were shock movements, either a frontal attack in mass or wide encircling movement to take the enemy in the flank or the rear.'[24] 'Ras Seyum,' wrote Konovaloff, 'had to conduct a guerrilla war, a word which the Ethiopians translate 'shiftannet,' meaning brigandage. Poor Seyum ... possessing all to live in comfort ... and now, over fifty he became by force of circumstances a 'shifta.' I recall that in a telegram from the emperor advising him not to engage in open battles, Seyum had replied: 'I am too old and too tired to become a shifta.'"[25]

Guerrilla warfare against the Italians—during that war, and later under occupation—was led mainly by minor chiefs, seldom by sons of elite families.

After the early success of late 1935, the generals of Haile Selassie, headed by Adwa 1896 veteran Ras Mulugeta Yigezu, began pushing for a frontal battle. The Fascists used poisonous gas in a way they would not dare to in Europe. Their military superiority now proved overwhelming. From 11–15 February 1936, the Ethiopian armies assembled in *Amba* Aradam were defeated. On 27 February, the armies of Ras Seyum and Kasa Haylu were routed in Tamben. On March 31, the rest of the Ethiopian forces, led by the emperor himself, were destroyed at Maichaw.[26] On 5 May, the Italians entered Addis Ababa. Mussolini completed his conquest prior to the rainy season.

8

FASCISTS, BRITISH

TIGRAY UNDER ASMARA

For the first time since the sixteenth-century Ahmad Gragn, Ethiopia was occupied. Foreign occupation officially lasted the five-year period under the Italian Fascists, 1936–41, but in practice it persisted a little longer. Though Haile Selassie returned to the throne in May 1941, it was still during World War II, and his liberators, the British army, remained in control of the whole of the Horn of Africa. They supported the emperor and helped him rebuild his government in Ethiopia, but not yet in Tigray. It remained pivotal throughout the period as a stage on which much of Ethiopian history was determined.

The Italians, during their occupation, annexed Tigray to Eritrea. The British officers, those who replaced the Italians in Asmara, wanted to continue this arrangement. They envisioned a 'Tigrai State' under their auspices, not under Haile Selassie. The descendants of Yohannes, the traditional leaders of Tigrayan society, proved more than just pawns in this power struggle, which eventually resulted with the return of Tigray from Eritrea to Haile Selassie's empire.

Italian East Africa—Tigray in Eritrea

In facing her Fascist aggressors, Ethiopia was to pay the price of conservatism. The province of Tigray, we discovered, epitomized this failure. Haile Selassie's attempts at some partial modernization did not extend to Tigray's traditional system. On the contrary, the old political game in Tigray not only enabled foreign penetration, but was a factor contributing to the making of Italian aggressive policy. Haileselassie Gugsa's secret ties to the Fascists did influence the process that led to the war.

Militarily, Ethiopia of the mid-1930s was still equipped with nineteenth-century concepts and little-improved arms. Her only chance of coping with a mechanized enemy lay in conducting prolonged guerrilla warfare in the hope of political salvation. This was the case especially in the Tigrayan front. The Italians themselves knew they could penetrate and swiftly take the major urban centers of Tigray, but in the mountainous inlands their tanks were hardly of use. Indeed, the Italian strategists prepared camels (bought from Saudi Arabia) for transportation and supplies in such terrain.[1] When the Ethiopians resorted to guerrilla tactics, they were not unsuccessful. Unintentionally, Haileselassie Gugsa's treason helped shape such strategy in the initial stages. But the traditional system was inimical to such strategy. The Tigrayan chiefs were apparently at pains to retreat from their towns to the mountains in order to conduct guerrilla attacks, as ordered by an emperor they regarded as a Shoan centralist.

The Fascists Italian occupiers erased the name of Ethiopia and established the colonial 'Italian East Africa.' King Vittorio Emanuel III was declared 'king of Italy and emperor of Ethiopia,' and the name of Ethiopia also survived in the name of the local Church. In their new colony of 'Africa Orientale Italiana,'[2] the Italians favored the Muslims, and compensated the Christians by disconnecting the Ethiopian Church from the Egyptian Coptic Church.[3] They paved roads and coped with local resistance by resorting to racist cruelty.[4]

'Africa Orientale Italiana' was divided according to Ethnic criteria into six governorates: Shoa; Galla[Ornomo]-Sidama; Amhara; Harar; Somalia; and Eritrea. In this new order, Tigray, extended to the west and to the southeast, was annexed to Eritrea, with its capital in Asmara.

For a short while, Tigrinya speakers along the two banks of the Mareb River were seemingly unified. But it was no more than an empty arrangement enforced by the Fascists and tailored for their own purposes. Locally, the two societies had now little in common. The Eritreans, whose traditional elite was politically and economically eliminated in the 1890s, had long been pacified. The Eritrean public would be politically revived in the 1940s and then rejoin our Tigrayan-Ethiopian story. Tigray proper, to reiterate, remained under its traditional elite, and they would return to lead the region up until 1974.

The Italians and the descendants of Yohannes

During the five years of Fascist imperialism, the Tigrayan elite was temporarily tore from Tigrayan society. With the descendants of Yohannes exiled, the people of Tigray, under the Fascists, were pacified. Resistance to the Italian imperialists by Ethiopian patriots was conducted mostly in the center, mainly in Shoa and Gojjam, and very seldom in Tigray. A popular uprising in Tigray—the Woyane revolt—would not occur until 1943.

In his article, 'Italy and the Treatment of the Ethiopian Aristocracy, 1937–1940,' Alberto Sbacchi[5] explained that prior to the conquest of Ethiopia, Italian authorities anticipated placing the country under a form of government that would allow the Ethiopian aristocracy to maintain its status and keep intact the old sociopolitical structure. In Tigray, as soon as 16 October 1936, the Italians proclaimed Haileselassie Gugsa as ruler, and General P. Badoglio promised him that he would be promoted from dajazmach to ras. However, once in power, the Fascists became reluctant to use the Ethiopian aristocracy in their government. They began considering its members not as potential collaborators but potential enemies whose power was to be eliminated.

The Italians failed to formulate a consistent policy and responded to the chaotic situation in their new colony. They were motivated by their racism and at times were confused by differences between policy dictated in Rome and the reality in the field. More to the point, they also differed in their attitudes towards the two main personalities of Tigray. Haileselassie Gugsa, ever bold and proud, was liked by Mussolini (the way he had been liked by Haile Selassie before his betrayal was exposed). But the Tigrayan was never trusted by the local Italian administration and was effectively prevented from exercising power as governor of Tigray. 'He lives in obscurity in Addis Ababa' the British reported, 'and is fast dissipating the stipend in cars and wines.'[6] The promised rank of ras was finally given to him by the Italians only in 1938.

Ras Seyum, softer and more cautious, remained suspected by Mussolini to the end (in the same way that he never learned to trust Haile Selassie). After the occupation of Addis Ababa and the emperor's departure into exile, Seyum, whose wife and children had been captured by the invaders, saw no point in conducting guerrilla warfare and surrendered to the Italians in July 1936. He was suspected by the new governor, now Viceroy R. Graziani, of stirring up anti-Italian feeling and was exiled again, this time for nearly two and a half years. Seyum, for his part, remained resentful of Emperor Haile Selassie for what he regarded as a cynical war strategy of sacrificing Tigray. At the same time, he himself remained suspected by Haile Selassie—the emperor was in exile in England—as a collaborator with the occupiers.

After the assassination attempt on Graziani on 19 February 1937, and following his most brutal retaliation acts against the Ethiopians, Graziani was removed by Mussolini. He was replaced in December by Prince Amedeo, Duke of Aosta, who followed a conciliatory policy. The duke recommended that the nobles be pardoned gradually to be used in his administration, which was to be based on Italian institutions, especially the judicial system. He thought that the nobles, assured of some respect, their traditional titles, and good life, would support such a change. The first two to assume some of their old positions were Dajazmach Haileselassie Gugsa of Tigray and Ras Hailu of Gojjam.

The atmosphere in Italy was not compatible with the duke's ideas. From July–October 1938, the more radical fascists in Italy managed to pass new racist laws. These laws were mostly anti-

Semitic but also had much to do with the African population. Intermarriages with locals, quite common between Italians and Eritrean–Ethiopian women, were forbidden. In his visit to Rome in June 1938, the duke was reminded by Mussolini that Ethiopian traditional leaders were to be confined to Addis Ababa, away from positions of political importance, and that they were to be paid generous salaries but only be consulted individually on questions concerning the Ethiopian people.

However, despite Mussolini's strict instructions, under the Duke of Aosta, the condition of the Ethiopian nobility improved. In 1938, he even kept the promise made by Badoglio in 1936 and promoted Haileselassie Gugsa to ras. The duke was anxious to impress the local aristocracy with the greatness of Italy's culture and sent delegates from all over Italian East Africa to Rome. In May 1939, Ras Seyum and Ras Haileselassie Gugsa were among the guests of Mussolini.

Back in Ethiopia, in July 1939, Seyum started cooperating with the Italians. He made speeches praising their activities and was reported even to be helping them to pursue resistance leaders. Not entirely unjustifiably, he was now more strongly regarded by Emperor Haile Selassie as collaborating with the Italians.

With the entrance of Italy into World War II on 10 June 1940, the rulers of Africa Orientale thought they had won the goodwill of the Ethiopian nobles. Ras Seyum was declared the 'prince of northern Ethiopia.' Ras Haileselassie Gugsa was given responsibility for the defense of Endarta. However, the appointments had the opposite effect. The return of Ras Seyum to Tigray provoked an internal crisis in the district. The old followers of Haileselassie Gugsa refused to accept his authority. Seyum responded by removing local chiefs and replacing them with his men. There began fighting among the Tigrayans. In an attempt to correct the balance of power in northern Ethiopia, Ras Haileselassie Gugsa was declared by the Italians the 'prince of eastern Tigray.'

The appointment came too late to ensure Ras Haileselassie Gugsa's loyalty to the Italians. By this time, he was totally disillusioned with the colonial government. He had been assured the status of an Italian citizen and a generous salary in place of the tribute he was no longer able to collect on his lands. These promises were hardly kept. Haileselassie Gugsa also resented the racist attitudes he had suffered when in Italy.

Ras Seyum in particular had no reason to thank the Italians. He had not been treated generously, and he had received no special titles. The Italian viceroy knew that in the face of the British, Seyum would run to save himself. His suspicions were well founded. Back in Tigray, Ras Seyum regained control of his capital, Adwa, and made sure of the loyalty of his fighting force, which had grown to 20,000. In April 1941, with this force behind him, he presented himself to the British commanders. His defection to the British had a significant demoralizing effect on the Italian forces. In any case, the Italian East African empire fell to the British by November 1941.

The British liberators: Politica Scioana *and* Politica Tigrigna

Following Italy's entry into WWII in June 1940, the British began an effort to destroy Africa Orientale Italiana.[7] On 5 May 1941, exactly five years after he had fled from Addis Ababa to exile in England, Emperor Haile Selassie reentered his capital. The British army restored the sovereign to his imperial throne. But just as hostilities were about to end, a political struggle began on the strategic future of the region. The main arena of this struggle was Ethiopia's northern province of Tigray, and three factors participated in it. The first was Haile Selassie, a representative of the old concept of divine emperorship along with modern, imperial, absolute power. Second were the British, who, while restoring the Ethiopian throne, were also pursuing the promotion of British strategic interests in the region. Those interests were not always compatible with an integral and centralized Ethiopia. Third, were the people of the Tigray and their traditional leaders. They, too, were motivated by a set of long-entrenched local values and interests, which led some of the British to believe in the existence of Tigrayan nationalism. The rivalries within both the British and the Tigrayan camps were to play a major role in moving the ensuing tripartite struggle toward the victory of Haile Selassie. Emerging victorious, Haile Selassie secured both the inclusion of Tigray in Ethiopia and the future establishment of a new order in the whole country. Furthermore, his victory in the struggle over Tigray enabled the emerging absolutist to prepare for the restoration of Eritrea to Ethiopia at the beginning of the following decade.

Reentering his capital in May 1941, Haile Selassie's real power was almost negligible. Accompanied by the British-trained small 'Gideon Force,' and supported by local anti-Italian resistance groups, he hardly had independent military or financial power. It was still the period of the global war, and the British army was the dominant factor in the Horn. Many of the leading British officers—especially those who administered Eritrea—had other ideas than the building of Haile Selassie's absolutism. Also, some of the provincial chiefs in Ethiopia had long-entrenched differences with the emperor. Because of British policy from Asmara, for a while the Tigrayans seemed to have the chance to shape their future in their own way.

While the British army was destroying the Italians in the Horn, the British government in London made public its intentions for the future of Ethiopia. On 4 February 1941, Anthony Eden, secretary of state for foreign affairs, stated that the British 'would welcome the reappearance of an independent Ethiopian State and recognize the claim of the Emperor Haile Selassie to the throne. [And that the British] reaffirm that they have themselves no territorial ambitions in Abyssinia. [And that in the meantime] the conduct of military operations in parts of Abyssinia will require temporary measures of military guidance and control. These will be carried out in consultation with the Emperor, and will be brought to an end as soon as the situation permits.'[8]

But this clearly phrased statement was not followed by a clearly coordinated British policy. London was too busy and too far off to follow local developments, and Ethiopian affairs were seldom on its agenda. In the Horn itself, in our story, the British were divided politically into two well-defined camps. One camp consisted of Haile Selassie's British advisers, Foreign Office staff, and members of the newly reopened British legation in Addis Ababa. Prominent among these throughout this period were Brigadier D. A.

Sandford,[9] Major (later Colonel) R. E. Cheesman,[10] and British Minister R. G. Howe. These personalities had been long acquainted with Ethiopian affairs, some having served in the country for decades. They were all in favor of fulfilling Eden's statement to the letter. Familiar with the Ethiopian reality of the 1920s and 1930s, they regarded Haile Selassie as the only progressive Ethiopian and judged him capable of imposing his will on the whole country. Fostering his path to absolutism, they thought, would be the best way of serving British interests. A modern and centralized Ethiopia ruled by a grateful emperor would create stability and encourage cooperation in a region of British presence and vital interests.

This camp, however, at that time had little influence on actual policymaking. It was a war, and political officers in uniforms, answerable to the War Office, were in charge of the practical conduct of Ethiopian affairs. They had a different opinion to that of the emperor on the desired future of the country.

The situation of competing British camps resembled the rivalry that had existed ever since the late nineteenth century among Italian policymakers in the region. Namely, the previously discussed tensions between *Politica Scioana* and *Politica Tigrigna*. The policy of the British military in Ethiopia throughout the 1941–3 period was—from our point of view—a continuation of Italian *Politica Tigrigna*. The strategic goal of the military was to ignore the Eden statement and annex Tigray to the British-administered Eritrea. Eritrea, as an ex-Italian colony, was not considered a part of Ethiopia. It was now put under British Military Administration and would remain so until 1952. The Eritrean population, to reiterate, consisted of two major sectors: Tigrinya-speaking Ethiopian Christians, who inhabited the highlands neighboring Tigray, and Muslims inhabiting Eritrea's western parts and the coast. According to one British idea, the former Italian colony was to be dismembered. Most of the Muslim territories were to be annexed to Sudan, which was considered at the time to be a safe British base for the post-war period. The Eritrean Christian Tigrayan territories were to be united with Tigray (actually, to remain united, as the Italians had annexed Tigray to Eritrea in 1936). The idea was best formulated by Brigadier S. Longrigg,[11] the chief administrator of Eritrea. In reports he prepared for his superiors at the Middle East General Headquarters, Longrigg elaborated on the strategic advantages and historical justification of the establishment of a 'Tigrai State.'[12] 'The whole of the Coptic–Christian Tigrinia speaking people on either side of the Ethiopian frontier [will be] united in a Tigrai province under Ethiopian sovereignty but under British protection.' He was convinced that emphasizing the uniqueness of Tigrayanism 'was the right interpretation of history,' and a proper base for shaping the region's future. Longrigg had a low estimation of Haile Selassie as a politician and of Ethiopia as an empire capable of modernizing itself. Like many of his colleagues in uniform, he was clearly for a separate Tigray affiliated to a decentralized Ethiopia.[13] It was in the service of these ideas that the British military were active throughout the period discussed.

Haile Selassie's British advisers and members of the British Legation in Addis Ababa differed most strongly with this line of argument. Their ideas were best reflected in a report written by Colonel Cheesman and almost simultaneously with Longrigg's. It was a blunt attack on the officers who had gained some political experience in distant countries of the Middle and Far East and an attack on their pretense to understand Ethiopian affairs. Cheesman criticized the widely accepted theory that underlay the officers' policy that Ethiopia was dismembered or in the process of becoming so. He himself had no doubt that Ethiopian statehood would prevail and that Haile Selassie was the only one capable of stabilizing her.[14]

Annexing Tigray to Eritrea?

A few weeks prior to Italy's entry into the war, Ras Seyum secretly contacted the British consul general in Addis Ababa to declare his support for an eventual British invasion. When he reached Tigray in early March 1941 it was already in British hands. On 5 April 1941, in Asmara, Seyum met with the officers authorized to conduct policy in the region and made ambivalent statements. He emphasized the fact of his being a grandson of the Tigrayan Emperor Yohannes IV, whose throne he claimed had been usurped by the Shoans. He declared that he had been loyal to Haile Selassie, but the emperor betrayed Tigray in 1935, when he planned the major defensive battles to be fought south of the province. Yet he was all for Ethiopian unity and was ready to make peace with the emperor, provided he was treated properly and his daughter's divorce from the crown prince was abolished. The British officers concluded that Seyum was primarily in favor of a separate Tigray, although he might compromise on a united Ethiopia.

There and then, Seyum was appointed governor of Tigray, to be financed and advised by the British. He was promised nothing with regard to his political status once hostilities ceased. Tigray, governed by Seyum, was to remain under the supervision of the political officers of Eritrea (and not of Ethiopia), and Seyum's allegiance to Haile Selassie had to be as ambiguous as possible.

The next day, 8 April 1941, Seyum sent a letter to the emperor (still in Gojjam on his way to Addis Ababa). He greeted Haile Selassie as his emperor and said he was bowing before the restorer of Ethiopia's independence. Yet he signed the letter as Seyum Mangasha Yohannes, adding, most significantly, the name of his grandfather the emperor. Following British policy, he made no mention whatsoever of his appointment by Asmara as governor of Tigray.

While Seyum was doing his best to remain uncommitted, the next week's developments brought about the clearest step towards the separation of Tigray from Ethiopia. On 17 April 1941, Haileselassie Gugsa appeared in Asmara and was told by the British there that he was to be financed and appointed over his territories in eastern Tigray. Seyum's appointment, previously announced as over the whole of Tigray, was reinterpreted as pertaining only to western Tigray. The road from Asmara to Addis Ababa ran through eastern Tigray, and *Amba* Alaje, still garrisoned by the Italians, was also located there. Haileselassie Gugsa was considered by the British to be a good administrator with considerable influence over the Oromo of the Azebo and the Rayya inhabiting southeastern Tigray, who were notorious raiders and robbers. A very lively discussion followed in Asmara in which the Tigrayan was addressed by the British as ras, a title which had been awarded by the Italians.

Haileselassie Gugsa, for his part, promised to be grateful and of good service to his new masters. He was not ambivalent in his opinion of the emperor, and advocated Tigrayan separatism in a speech quite similar to the one he had delivered in 1935 prior to his treason.

The last part of the conversation was to become important in the long run. Haileselassie Gugsa's request for British protection, should Tigray be transferred to the emperor, was denied. The British hinted that the good service on his part would be recognized in due course, but otherwise made no promise regarding the personal future of the Tigrayan.[15]

The appointment of the Ethiopian traitor and Tigrayan separatist Haileselassie Gugsa by Asmara was the clearest possible sign that on the issue of Tigray the British military was ready to confront the emperor. Meanwhile, they refrained from notifying the emperor about their appointments in Tigray. Emperor Haile Selassie learned of them from a letter he received from Haileselassie Gugsa one day after the emperor reentered Addis Ababa. Referring to himself as ras, the Tigrayan avoided recognizing the emperor. He only emphasized his restored mastery over eastern Tigray and the fact that the British were all-powerful across the region.

Haile Selassie's British advisers, headed by Sandford and Cheesman, were also kept uninformed by Asmara of the appointment of Haileselassie Gugsa. They were only told in the second week of April about Seyum's appointment and the decision to control Tigray from Asmara. Their immediate reaction was bitter. They considered the combined effect of the two steps as a break from the Eden statement and as preparatory towards the severance of Tigray from Ethiopia. They reported that in their opinion the military were deliberately exaggerating Seyum's animosity towards the emperor and the whole exercise would result in nothing better than instability and unrest in Tigray. Sandford eschewed informing the emperor and demanded from Asmara that Seyum be flown immediately to make his submission in Addis Ababa. 'The Emperor will shortly be left to rule his country,' he wrote. 'His task will be a formidable one ... I would very strongly urge that we put our fingers in the political pie as little as possible. The Emperor's record shows him to be extremely astute in handling his own people and he is not vindictive. Left to himself he will soon have all the important chiefs eating out of his hand—a result very much to be desired.'

The demand to fly Seyum to the capital of Ethiopia was made also by the Deputy Chief Political Officer for Ethiopia posted in Addis Ababa, Brigadier M. S. Lush. He was against putting Asmara in charge of Tigray and especially angered by Seyum's nomination, as he had personally assured the emperor—in the spirit of Eden's statement—that no such nomination would be made without prior consultation with him.

Chief Political Officer, Major-General P. Mitchell, remained loyal to the military's policy. From Nairobi, he gave orders not to send Seyum to the emperor, then flew to Addis Ababa to receive Haile Selassie reentering his capital. He met with his deputy Lush and instructed him not to interfere in Tigray's affairs, which were to be dealt with from Eritrea. Following what were probably blunt discussions with Sandford, Mitchell wrote to his War Office superiors condemning Haile Selassie's British advisers. They were blamed for distorting the meaning of Eden's statement by working to make Haile Selassie 'an uncontrolled autocratic ruler,' while the British statement contained 'no clear idea of what the nature of the throne may be to which the claim of the emperor will be recognized by HMG at the proper time.' He said he hoped Tigray would be included in Ethiopia, but this was a matter to be decided by Seyum and the people of Tigray.[16]

In May and June 1941, the emperor, aided by his British advisers, started laying the foundations for organizing a modern Ministry of the Interior to serve as the focus of his centralization effort. Without notifying even his British advisers, he made an appointment over Agame, a district in Haileselassie Gugsa's territory. The nominee was none other than the district's traditional chief, Dajazmach Kasa Sebhat (son of Ras Sebhat Aregawi and descendant of Sabagadis of Agame). He was sent northward early in June along with an imperial personal envoy assigned to summon Seyum to make obeisance in the capital.

Meanwhile, the last battle in eastern Tigray against the Italians took place, and it was also Haileselassie Gugsa's first and last test of loyalty to the British. However, he hardly tried to control the Azebo and Rayya Oromos who raided British units on the main road. He was consequently put under house arrest in Asmara. Ras Seyum, in contrast, proved to be useful and was rewarded by the British with the government of the whole of Tigray.

On 4 June, it was learned in Asmara that Kasa Sebhat and the emperor's envoy to Seyum had arrived with seventy followers in southern Tigray. They were disarmed and taken as prisoners to Adwa to report to Seyum. On 8 June 1941, a proclamation was issued in the name of the British army appointing Seyum governor of the whole of Tigray. It did not mention the emperor. Kasa Sebhat was told he could go on to rule Agame, but only in the name of Seyum. The British then sent word to inform the emperor in Addis Ababa that Seyum, the governor of Tigray, was unable and unauthorized to leave his province and travel to the Ethiopian capital. In early June 1941, Tigray seemed to be more than halfway to practical and official separation from Ethiopia.

Tigray back to Haile Selassie

Seyum's appointment by Asmara over Tigray without the ras submitting to the emperor was regarded by Haile Selassie as a disaster. It was, as he saw it, not only a threat to the territorial integrity of Ethiopia but also to his plan to modernize the country through centralization. On 20 June 1941, Haile Selassie directly approached the British War Cabinet. In a bitterly phrased letter addressed to Churchill himself, he demanded, in the spirit of Eden's statement, the transfer of Tigray to Ethiopian administration.[17]

No great breadth of imagination is necessary to visualize the British War Cabinet in the third week of June, when Hitler surprisingly invaded the USSR (on 22 June), discussing the issue. It is safe to assume that Churchill and his advisers brushed aside matters related to the Horn of Africa without concerning themselves unduly with the strategic ideas of brigadiers. By early

July, instructions were issued from London to transfer Tigray from Eritrean to Ethiopian control.

As a result of this development, Seyum Mangasha, a month after obtaining the Eritrean nomination over Tigray, made his decision. On 8 July 1941, he left Adwa and went to Addis Ababa, where he ceremonially pledged allegiance to the emperor of Ethiopia.

What motivated Seyum's decision to finally go to make obeisance in Addis Ababa? As we do not have Seyum's own evidence, we are left only with assumptions. Was he making an ideological decision between Tigrayan and Ethiopian nationalism? Such a choice existed apparently in the minds of foreigners (previously Italians, now the British). In the centuries-old Ethiopian set of cultural and political values, Tigrayan self-awareness was inseparable from Ethiopiawinet; Ethiopianism.

Seyum's decision was a political one and made in accordance with the developing political reality. It stemmed from the trivial calculation of which way to orient himself—the British in Asmara, or Haile Selassie—in order to fulfill his aim of becoming the effective ruler of an Ethiopian Tigray. His previous hesitations and double game were a reflection of the fluid situation. Now that the emperor had proved his determination to regain control of Tigray, and London had decreed accordingly, Seyum must have realized that in the long run his chances lay in Addis Ababa and not in Asmara. His decision in July 1941 was quite analogous to that of his father, Ras Mangasha, half a century before. By going to Addis Ababa and submitting to Haile Selassie in the second week of July 1941, Seyum concluded the first chapter in the story of this struggle over Tigray. It ended with diplomatic victory for Haile Selassie: the province returned to his reviving empire. However, in 1941, it was still a war situation, and the British army and political officers still remained in the entire Horn of Africa. The future of Tigray was not yet determined.

9

UNDER HAILE SELASSIE

TO WOYANE AND BACK

In previous chapters, we followed three major players: the imperial center—Haile Selassie; foreign powers—Italy, then Britain; and Tigray's traditional leading families. The latter were entrenched in their positions of power in the sixteenth century (or earlier). They were united under Yohannes IV and managed, though with some difficulty, to maintain local autonomy and internal rivalries—Seyum Mangasha, Haileselassie Gugsa. The following chapter continues to discuss this triple game, but it also leads to a rare and short moment; the entering into the scene, in 1943, of a fourth factor: a popular Tigrayan protest movement called the Woyane. Though it was soon quelled, and the old tripartite game was quickly resumed, Woyane would prove significant in later years.

Haile Selassie's 'new administration'

The British military went on trying to keep the Tigrayan hereditary chiefs alive on the political map while Haile Selassie was working to promote centralization. Achieving centralism and absolute imperial power through the building of the machinery of a modern state was facilitated as a result of the war. Ethiopia's military defeat of 1935–6 was, to a large extent, the defeat of the old 'feudal' and provincial order, as well as a blow to the older generation's anti-western chauvinistic pride. The need for change and reform according to modern patterns of administration and government was now better seen by Ethiopians as a precondition for national restoration. It was indeed the historic achievement of Haile Selassie that he managed to execute the necessary change by building, in the early 1940s, a modern bureaucracy and armed forces.

From today's perspective, and somewhat outside the scope of this book, it may be added that unfortunately, this modernization of the state machinery was not achieved through proper political modernization. In the long run, the new military and administrative branches served to strengthen the medieval concept of absolute emperorship, a phenomenon for which Ethiopia, in the 1970s, paid the price in a brutal revolution. In the 1940s, this was still in the remote future. Haile Selassie and his planned centralization around the institution of Ethiopian emperorship were the only valid options at the time to lead the country to national modernization.

One main aspect of the 1940s modernization was the establishment of a Ministry of Interior as a body coordinating the centralization of provincial administration.[1] This started immediately upon the emperor's return and was carried out most energetically with the help of British advisers in Addis Ababa. It was quite an effective campaign, as reflected in the 1942 annual report of the British minister: 'In the short space of eighteen months an organized administration has been installed in every province and district, courts have been established, markets have been reopened and traffic is in general free and unmolested. Tranquility has in fact been achieved ...'[2]

In Tigray, however, this was not the case. The centuries-old entrenched power of the leading families, combined as it was with the British military's involvement, saw to it that Haile Selassie's 'new administration' faced, in Tigray, the stiffest resistance than anywhere in the country.

The return of Seyum to Tigray

In spite of the emperor's diplomatic victory due to London's support, the British military in Asmara did not retreat from their plan to eventually annex Tigray to Eritrea—quite the opposite. The idea of encouraging an all-Tigrayan political identity and entity was of growing importance to the British in Asmara. More than half of Eritrea's population, its more advanced urban sector, were Christian Tigrayans. Asmara officers desired a future strategic arrangement dividing a greater Eritrea along ethnic-religious lines. In their vision, a future inclusion of Tigray in a Tigrayan entity was the best solution.

In late 1941, the struggle over Tigray began to revolve around the future regime in the province. The British in Asmara considered it vital to maintain an option of Tigrayan separatism, and to do so by supporting the autonomy of local chiefs. It was for this purpose that they tried to force the emperor to reinstall Seyum over Tigray, and at the same time they refrained from surrendering the traitor Haileselassie Gugsa to Ethiopia.

Ras Seyum remained in Addis Ababa throughout July–September 1941 doing nothing noteworthy except reporting to the emperor on Haileselassie Gugsa's activities in the service of the British. The latter was now confined to his house in Asmara, but his men and nominees were in control of, or had influence over, eastern Tigray. It was indeed over developments in the east that the issue of Tigray came back to the fore in September 1941.[3]

What made matters urgent was security along the Addis Ababa-Asmara road. This line of communication was of immediate military importance as Gondar was still in Italian hands (it fell in November). The road was constantly raided by the Oromo tribesmen of Azebo[4] and Rayya, who turned the whole region of southeastern Tigray into rebel country. The British officers in the province, answerable now to Brigadier Lush in Addis Ababa, started pressing for the return of Seyum to Tigray. In late September 1941, Brigadier Lush started exerting pressure on Haile Selassie to send Seyum back to Tigray as the province's governor-general. In response to this pressure, the brigadier was given a long lesson in the Ethiopian art of diplomatic temporization.

Throughout October 1941, the emperor, suspecting Seyum to be collaborating with the British, did nothing about him. Haile Selassie also claimed—not entirely erroneously—that troubles were fomented by Haileselassie Gugsa's men in the field and demanded the immediate surrender of the traitor. He was refused. The British military, for their part, were not prepared to play it softly and slowly. On 20 October 1941, Lush presented Haile Selassie with an aide-memoire demanding again, this time very strongly, 'to send Seyum with full powers to establish law and order in Eastern and Western Tigray.' The message ended with an ultimatum: 'I am directed to state that the Commander in Chief will regard any further delay to dispatch Ras Seyum as a deliberate refusal on Your Majesty's part to cooperate in matters affecting military operations, and that such refusal will be reported to His Britannic Majesty's Government, with the recommendation that the whole of the territory North of Wallo province be placed under complete and direct British military administration.'[5]

The emperor was not impressed. In fact, in the third week of October, he made nominations of governors of Tigray's sub-provinces. All were people of proven loyalty to the emperor.

On 2 November 1941, Brigadier Lush met again with the emperor. To his frustration he was lectured at length on centralism, democracy, and progress. 'Seyum,' Haile Selassie said, 'like many of the leading chiefs in the country ... [is] a main obstacle to reform.... He had refused to accept the new regime and wished to carry on in the old way... [6]' The emperor was ready to send another official as governor. Lush refused. He himself and his men were having frequent discussions with Seyum, trying to persuade him to go to Tigray and come to terms with Haile Selassie's new regime. The ras was most reluctant. 'He said [to Lush] that he realized that reform was necessary, but that it should be done with the good will of and not against the advice of the older men. His chief complaint was that young upstarts had been placed by the Emperor into positions of responsibility which should be occupied by their fathers.' Nevertheless, Seyum agreed to go on the emperor's terms.

On 3 and 4 November 1941, imperial proclamations were issued announcing the establishment of a new regime in Tigray: 'People, Dignitaries and chiefs of Tigray. You are aware that we have been exerting ourselves since a long time to give the people of Tigray a good administration.... Before we could complete our general plans for the benefit of our beloved people of Tigray, which loves us, the aggressor enemy [the Italians] suddenly arrived and interrupted our work. People of Tigray! ... I know your deep love and loyalty to your emperor, flag and independence. Appreciating your losses in the past I have established a new administrative plan for you....'[7]

The new administrative plan amounted to abolition of the 'feudal' traditional order in the province. Politically, although Seyum was proclaimed governor-general, real power was given to governors of the sub-provinces, who were known to be Seyum's rivals and loyal to the emperor. These were Dajazmach Gabra-Heiwot Mashasha in Adwa, Dajazmach Abbay Kasa in Maqale, and Dajazmach Kasa Sebhat in Agame. The proclamations made no secret of the fact that these chiefs—not Seyum—were intended to be the real masters. Lush felt betrayed and cheated by an emperor he now described as 'the greatest of all intriguers.'[8]

Asmara's card—Haileselassie Gugsa

While the emperor was winning the fight over Seyum's return to Tigray, another issue relevant to the future of the province was developing over the surrender to Ethiopia of Dajazmach Haileselassie Gugsa.

For emperor Haile Selassie, the surrender of Haileselassie Gugsa was of great importance. Putting the traitor on trial in Addis Ababa was a precondition for a successful assertion of the new regime in eastern Tigray. Yet the British military authorities in Asmara, who kept Haileselassie Gugsa in their hands, preferred to avoid surrendering him. They now claimed that they had made a commitment to him upon his surrender to them in April 1941.

Promise or no, Haile Selassie insisted on the traitor's surrender. On 30 July 1941, Haile Selassie submitted an official extradition request. Asmara, however, was determined not to lose its card. All they were willing to do was to let 'Ras Haileselassie Gugsa' decide if he was ready to take the emperor's word that he would not be executed and go to trial in Addis Ababa. Finally, the matter was put before the War Cabinet in London. It was decided that Haileselassie Gugsa was a political refugee, who had been given a promise not to be surrendered. As a result of this decision, Haileselassie Gugsa, together with his family retainers and two of his loyal vassals, was removed to a comfortable life in the Seychelles for the next six years. He was allowed to maintain a small political staff, and to correspond with the outside world. He was apparently doing so with his devotees in Tigray. Eastern Tigray, Haileselassie Gugsa's ex-territory, remained a political vacuum. Neither Seyum nor the representatives of Haile Selassie's new regime were able to pacify it.[9]

As for the personal fate of Dajazmach Haileselassie Gugsa, he was finally surrendered in September 1946 when the issue of Tigrayanism was long considered a dead letter. From February to August 1947, a public trial was conducted. The traitor was sentenced to death, but this was commuted by the emperor to life imprisonment. He was later released and died in house arrest in 1985.[10]

Vacuum in eastern Tigray

The imperial proclamations to the people of Tigray issued on 3 and 4 November 1941, on the eve of Seyum's return, summarized the centralization plans the emperor had for the province. In addition to the appointment of the sub-provincial governors mentioned above, they contained administrative announcements and promises of significance. In essence, they amounted to: (a) the abolition of the traditional 'feudal' tax system that existed prior to Italian occupation, and the introduction of a new system based on cash payments according to progressive criteria; (b) the establishment of a judicial system independent of the new, local administration; (c) the establishment of a provincial 'territorial army' paid by and answerable to the central government, replacing the private armies of the various chiefs.

In western Tigray, the implementation of this new administration seemed throughout 1942 to be going forward with relative success. Even the British military in Asmara had to report (in April) that 'lively commerce with Eritrea is keeping this area quiet,' and that the emperor 'is disarming many of Seyum's men and at the same time profiting by the stability to which the latter's nominal rule contributes. Seyum appears to be resigning himself to this state of affairs.'[11]

However, the picture in the province as a whole was quite different. Eastern Tigray, the former territory of Haileselassie Gugsa, and especially the regions of southern Endarta, remained unpacified. Many of the local chiefs were still loyal to Haileselassie Gugsa; with some of them he most probably corresponded. The Azebo and Rayya Oromos, previously barely obedient even to Haileselassie Gugsa, were absolutely fearless of Seyum or the representatives of the 'new administration.' This strategically important region, through which ran the Asmara-Addis Ababa road, turned into a no-man's-land, with the tribesmen raiding the British convoys and radiating a spirit of anarchy all throughout eastern Tigray. In the April–July period, a large-scale campaign to pacify the region was conducted by Ethiopian units of the new army and by the Tigrayan 'territorials' led by both Crown Prince Asfa-Wossen and Seyum. Despite some initial successes, it proved ineffective.

The failure to pacify eastern Tigray was used in Addis Ababa against Seyum. Palace circles spread propaganda portraying him as incapable of governing Tigray. The ras, back in Adwa from southern Endarta in July 1942, was frustrated. As Lush had expected, Seyum could not deal with the fact that the sub-governors and the various functionaries were not in fact answerable to him. In September 1942, he left Tigray and returned to the capital. There in Addis Ababa, emperor Haile Selassie would see fit to spoil him with the pleasures of money and honors. In imperial ceremonies, he was positioned as ranking second only to Ras Kasa Hailu. He would not be back in Tigray again until 1947.

The road to Woyane

With the hereditary chiefs of Tigray living in Addis Ababa and the Seychelles, the 'new administration' of Haile Selassie was confronted directly with Tigray's people and problems. No smooth process of mutual adjustment emerged. Throughout 1942 and the first half of 1943, Haile Selassie's men were trying to assert themselves over Tigray. They failed. Even without their exiled hereditary chiefs, the people of Tigray, displaying popular protest, resisted Shoan centralism. The policy of the British Eritrean authorities, which had damaged the prestige and power of the emperor, contributed to the creation of this situation. It was especially true of eastern Tigray, which was the center of growing unrest. It was led by various Tigrayan sectors and individuals, as well as by the Oromos of southern Endarta, and threatened to spread from the former territories of Haileselassie Gugsa to the whole province. The main towns along the road from Asmara to Addis Ababa were captured by the British army, much to the alarm of the British officers in Addis Ababa.

Tension between the representatives of the 'new administration' and various sectors and individuals in Tigray was mounting beneath the surface throughout 1942–3. The majority of the new functionaries were Amhara Shoans. In September 1942, Ras Seyum resigned as governor-general and was replaced by his teenage son Mangasha. Real power, however, was vested with the new post of director-general. In November 1942, this was entrusted to an ambitious member of a leading Shoan clan: the Fitawrari Kifle Dadi. Kifle's men put the new tax system to work. Though progressive, it cost the peasants five times more than they had paid under the Italians. The new administrators at the various levels were, for the first time, deprived by the new definition of political and military power. In practice, they naturally inclined to compensate themselves by resorting to bribery and corruption. The 'territorial army,' planned to be salaried and 'non-feudal,' was often used in the traditional manner—i.e., to force 'non-cooperative' villages to play host to the soldiers, who for their part helped themselves to everything removable.[12]

Woyane

With this kind of centralism being identified with the Amhara of Shoa, the situation was ripe for the emergence of a popular protest movement in Tigray. The movement consisted of various factors: protesting peasants, who organized themselves in popular committees; chiefs deprived of power (some seeking to restore the old order, others to make a name so as to be called later to join a new order); bandits, and the like. Such circumstances and factors existed at that time in nearly every Ethiopian province. In Tigray, however, it turned into an active revolt. One other major factor which sparked this development was the continuous raids on the main road by the Oromos of southern Endarta, the Azebo, Rayya, and Wadjrat.

The leadership of the revolt was assumed by intermediate Tigrayan chiefs. Prominent among them was *Belatta* Haila-Mariam Redda. He was a strong-willed member of a leading family who had been promoted by the Italians to the position of a *chikka shum*, a village chief, but reduced by Seyum. In late 1941, he went to Addis Ababa hoping to obtain a prominent position in Tigray's new administration, but was rejected, returned to Tigray, and turned a *shifta*.[13] Other major leaders in the revolt were known to be Haileselassie Gugsa's men. These were the Dajazmachs Yekunu-Amlak Tasfai, Araya Dagala, Tafari Tedla and Kenful.

In August 1943, the revolt was openly on its way. The rebels occupied the towns of Wokru and Quiha along the Addis Ababa-Asmara road, while the Oromos to the south intensified their raids. The 'territorials' and the regular units sent from Shoa were defeated, and unrest spread to the western province. In the middle of September, the rebels captured Maqale, the capital of eastern Tigray.

The revolt was known by the name of Woyane, meaning 'revolt.'[14] (The term became widespread, especially after 1991, when the Tigrayans regained the leadership of Ethiopia). The social aspects of the name have been presented thoroughly and competently by Gabru Tareke and Mamoka Maki.[15]

Two of the points made by Gabru Tareke are of direct relevance to our subject. First is the clearly established conclusion (supported strongly also by the War Office and Foreign Office documents) that the Woyane was a revolt of eastern Tigray and not of the whole of Tigray as conveniently believed. Simultaneous disturbances in western Tigray were but a distant echo of the overt hostilities in the east. Mangasha, the young son of Seyum, who was alleged to have sided with the rebels, took no active part in the revolt. It can be concluded that the British military, by treating Haileselassie Gugsa the way they did, contributed to fomenting the revolt.

The second conclusion made by Gabru Tareke was that the revolt had its various social, political, and even cultural backgrounds, and its ideological manifestations were couched in slogans advocating Tigrayanism. However, in the final analysis, Tigrayanism was more of a rallying slogan than a program to fulfill. M. Perham's summary of this point, written not long after the events, is still valid: '... the revolt ... [was] one more expression of the ancient dualism, a gesture of discontent on the part of Tigray against imperial control ... [It] should be interpreted not as a desire on the part of Tigrayans to break away from the empire, but rather as a demand, especially among the *shums* [local chiefs], for further integration and larger share of attention of government and of the fruits of office.'[16]

Indeed, according to oral evidence, Haila-Mariam Reda made extensive use of Ethiopian patriotic slogans and songs. Entering Maqale, he was quoted as singing: 'Our ruler is Jesus Christ/ Our flag—that of Ethiopia.'[17] Yet the Woyane was a threat not only to the new centralization that Haile Selassie strove to impose, but also to Ethiopia's integrity. Questions of ideology and nationalism aside, if the revolt was to be exploited by the British military in Asmara to promote their strategic ideas (as some rebels hoped and Haile Selassie feared), the revolt could well have been a major step towards Tigray's separatism.

The end of Woyane—Haile Selassie and Tigray

It was just before the beginning of the Woyane revolt that the British military raised officially the idea of creating a separate Tigrayan state. In May 1943, this plan was supported by no lesser figures than Lieutenant General W. Platt (Chief of the East Africa Command) and Lieutenant General W. Lindsell (of the Middle East Forces). It was to be presented to the emperor in the framework of diplomatic negotiations. Their idea was to trade Tigray for the Eritrean coast south to Massawa. In August 1943, when the revolt was well on its way, Brigadier Longrigg, Eritrea's British administrator and the living spirit of the *Politica Tigrina,* presented a long report to this effect.[18] He and his associates regretted the 1941 return of Tigray to Ethiopia. Facing the opening of negotiations which led in December 1944 to a new British–Ethiopian agreement, they set as their main strategic goal the undoing of Tigray's re-annexation to Ethiopia.

To promote his idea of a Tigrayan state, Longrigg emphasized the existence of what he regarded as Tigrayan nationalism. He would pursue this line in an Eritrean context till after the mid-1940s. Meanwhile, the outbreak of the revolt in Tigray seemed providential for the British military. The actions and slogans of the rebels could most suitably serve their purposes. An official and long summary of the revolt made by the British Military Mission in Addis Ababa presented it as stemming from a call by Tigrayan nationalists to reinstall Seyum over their country. In practice, however, what happened was that the British army itself helped crush the revolt.

In late August, Haile Selassie sent to the area units from the new modern army he was constructing.[19] These units were trained, equipped, and advised by the British military mission. The head of the mission in Ethiopia, Brigadier A. Cottam, went himself to supervise the action. Cottam was well aware of his superiors' attitude to Tigrayanism, but at the same time he was familiar with the opinion of the Addis Ababa-based British diplomats that a failure on the part of Haile Selassie to quell the Tigray revolt may well spread anarchy all across the Horn of Africa. This presented him with a dilemma. His reports from the scene of the action leave the strong impression that as a practical officer he decided to react to the developing crisis in accordance with events.

In the situation that arose, the ideal solution from the British military's point of view could have been some sort of settlement reached through negotiations between the Tigrayans and the Ethiopian army. Such negotiations did take place during the first half of September when the Shoan Ras Ababe Aregai,[20] commander of the Ethiopian units (and previously the famous anti-Italian guerrilla leader), met with several rebel chiefs. It was a futile effort. Yet the British, aiming at promoting this line, were ready to make a further contribution. British planes were used to drop leaflets signed by the emperor over rebel territories and all over Tigray. Five different proclamations written in Amharic, not in Tigrinya, were dropped between 15 September and 6 October. These proclamations were masterpieces of political and religious propaganda. They reminded the people of Tigray of their centuries-long attachment to Ethiopia, made clear to them that the powerful British were with the emperor, and emphasized that Haile Selassie meant well towards able Tigrayans and intended to introduce modernization. The leaflets called on the inhabitants of western Tigray to fight the eastern Tigrayan rebels. The last one, written in the name of the *echage*—the premier monk of Ethiopia—threatened the rebels with religious excommunication.[21]

The leaflets proved ineffective. In fact, during the period they were dropped, the rebels went from strength to strength and captured Maqale. The regular Ethiopian units, though successful in some operations, proved unable to decide the struggle. It was the first test of the very young army. On 7 October, Ras Ababe Aregai was suddenly confronted by a force of 5,000 armed rebels. He urgently, almost desperately, called Addis Ababa for help.

The only option left was to bomb the rebels. In early October, Brigadier Cottam recommended this step. After dropping the leaflets on behalf of Haile Selassie, the British army was identified in Tigray with the emperor. It could not afford the continuous situation of unrest in Tigray.

On 6 October 1943, following a request by Haile Selassie, British bombers went into action. 'Leaflets proved ineffective, while bombing was most effective,' their action was summarized.[22] It was indeed a swiftly decisive blow to the rebels, and on 14

October 1943, the Ethiopian regular units recaptured Maqale. The rest was merely a mopping-up operation.

The RAF action ended the struggle over Tigray in two respects. First, the question of Tigray's territorial affiliation to Ethiopia was decided. During the discussions leading to the signing of the new Anglo-Ethiopian agreement of December 1944, the plan of Longrigg and his associates to negotiate with Haile Selassie over Tigray was not even raised. Tigray remained an integral part of Ethiopia, and the 1944 agreement, to a large extent because of British Tigrayan policy, became a landmark in Haile Selassie's reorientation from Britain to the United States.

Second, the struggle ended with the defeat of those sectors in Tigrayan society that had actively resisted the emperor's centralization. In the short run, Haile Selassie tried to exploit this success, and tightened Shoan centralism. Young Mangasha Seyum, suspected of supporting the rebels, was sentenced to death[23] and replaced as governor-general of the province by the army commander, the Shoan Ras Ababe Aregai. Yet, as in the past, Haile Selassie could not carry the issue of centralism too far in the Tigrayan context. He was fully conscious of Tigray's special position in the history and strategy of the region, and of the Tigrayans' strong sense of self-awareness. Not long after the end of the mopping-up operations, the central army was removed from Tigray, and Seyum Mangasha was pardoned and freed. In 1947, he returned to Tigray as governor-general to hold office until 1960 (he was then murdered during the aborted December coup against Haile Selassie). Seyum was succeeded by his son Ras Mangasha Seyum, who, in January 1949, had married Haile-Selassie's granddaughter, Princess Aida. Ras Mangasha Seyum governed Tigray until the 1974 revolution.

In the post-war period, Tigray was the only Ethiopian province to remain governed by members of the historically local leading family. Unlike the rest of the country, it was not subjected to complete Haile Selassie centralism. In local appointments, taxation, and administration, Haile Selassie's regime compromised realistically with traditional Tigrayanism. Tigray would not experience an internal revolution prior to the 1970s, when a new generation in the province would remove the ancient local elite. The Tigrayan People Liberation Front (TPLF) would lead Ethiopia in 1991, proud of their nickname: 'Woyane.'

10

HAILE SELASSIE'S IMPERIAL CENTRALISM

In the introduction, 'Cradle, Gate, Wall, Legacy,' we presented one of the main dimensions of this book. Namely, the tension between two concepts competing over Ethiopia's system. In the most simplistic terms, it was between the 'Amhara' and the 'Tigrayan' visions. The Amhara strove to create a full unity, a supra-ethnic melting pot supporting a centralized imperial political system. The Tigrinya speakers strove to maintain their ethnic-linguistic identity within a more diverse Ethiopia.

Humiliated Tigray

The Tigrayans, though weakened by internal rivalries, remained proud of their identity, and went on keeping the gate of the country. In the late nineteenth century, they returned to lead Ethiopia in a formative time. Marginalized again, and divided by the Italian occupation of Eritrea, they still played a major role in the drama of the war with Mussolini. After liberation, Haile Selassie managed to build a centralizing system around his absolute emperorship. It was applied all over the country and lasted effectively till 1974. It was only in Tigray that he compromised with local, old, traditional leadership: the province remained administered by the descendants of Yohannes. They intermarried with the royal family, identified with the imperial absolute system, and never really challenged it. For Haile Selassie, it was quite convenient. The mighty Tigray of the past was neglected and deserted—nearly stagnant and clearly underdeveloped. Its elite collaborated, its youth (those educated) joined the state system, which revolved around Addis Ababa.

On top of that, mother nature proved cruel, especially in Tigray. Deadly famines occurred, the most devastating in 1958–9, 1965–6, 1972–4, and 1983–4.[1] They created utter destitution. The population of Tigray in the 1960s was estimated at nearly two million, some 90 per cent of whom were peasants. In the densely populated highlands, because land was privately owned for generations (the *Rest* system), land fragmentation forced the bulk of the peasantry to live far below subsistence levels. The recurring famines claimed the lives of tens of thousands of peasants, while the central government continued to levy numerous taxes. During these periods, millions of people died, and more were displaced from their homes. Ras Mangasha Seyum, the last hereditary governor of Tigray, made some attempts to introduce industry to the region, but without success.

The urban dwellers and the educated youth suffered from another dimension of Haile Selassie's centralization, namely his Amharization policy. More than 75 per cent of the population of Tigray speak Tigrigna, which, since the 1940s, was forbidden for use in official institutions such as law courts. It was estimated that in the mid-1970s, only 12.3 per cent of males claimed to speak Amharic, and only 7.7 per cent could read it.

Aregawi Berhe expressed the humiliation: 'Thousands of peasants abandoned their villages, some even seeking shelter in churches and mosques and begging for food in the streets… Tigrayans were obliged to migrate to the former Italian colony, Eritrea, or to Addis Ababa and other cities in southern Ethiopia in search of work, as conditions were relatively better there. It earned them a number of derogatory names that wounded their pride. Tigrayans' mobility was sarcastically compared to that of a Land Rover jeep, to describe how they roamed over large areas of the country. It was said that Tigray was condemned to 'growing rocks' instead of grain. Generations of Tigrayans grew up with deep feelings of desperation. The neglect of Tigray in the 1900s up to the revolution of 1975 was generally perceived by them as a deliberate and systematic policy of the Showa–Amhara ruling class in order to weaken and demoralize the Tigrayans.'[2]

Perhaps no less humiliating for Tigrayans at that time was their experience in Eritrea among fellow Eritrean Tigrayans. Professor David Shinn explained later: 'There was, and perhaps still is a negative psychological element to the relationship, at least for Ethiopia's Tigrayans who live on the other side of the Eritrean border. Many Tigrayans believed that the more highly educated Eritreans, with their experience of Italian colonialism, looked down on Tigrayans. Some Ethiopians perceived that Eritreans saw them as fodder for filling low level positions in an Eritrea that would become the industrial center of the region.'[3]

Tigrayans went on trying to retain their identity.[4] In the Tigray of the 1950s and 1960s, there were some sporadic attempts to re-enliven the spirit of the 1943 Woyane. Gessesew Ayele, a veteran of the Woyane and a representative of Tigray in the Addis Ababa parliament, tried to lead some action in the province. Various local associations emerged, but no significant political action was recorded. In the 1950s, Tigray had only four high schools, their students engaged in cultural activities to promote Tigrayan awareness, with little political effect.

In the Haile Selassie I University, the political atmosphere was much more vibrant. On the all-Ethiopian campus in Addis Ababa, students from Tigray could tell their friends of the glory of their ancestors but also compare the poverty and misery of their parents to those in other regions of Ethiopia. Revolutionary change in Tigray would begin there.

Eritrea under the British—politicization

In the period that Tigray was depoliticized, it was quite the opposite in Eritrea. Under the British administration, Eritrean society underwent a quick process of politicization.[5] The British occupation was, by definition, temporary. The political future of the ex-Italian colony was to be decided by the parties concerned, including the

Eritreans. Conflicting ideas and interests promoted Eritreans' political awareness and the formation of political groupings.[6]

The British officers and administrators encouraged politicization. They considered dividing Eritrea and annexing its western regions to Sudan. They gave special attention to those western regions, encouraging Islam and the learning of Arabic, even bringing books from Egypt for this purpose. In the center of Eritrea, the British encouraged Tigrayanism.[7] They did so through the promotion of Tigrinya and through relations with the neighboring Ethiopian province of Tigray. Even as late as the end of the 1940s, British administrators toyed with the idea of creating a British-influenced and British-protected Tigrayan entity federated with Ethiopia.[8] Consequently, a free Eritrean press was allowed, even subsidized, as was political organization.

An economic crisis contributed to the politicization process. The end of the Italian buildup and the later exodus of Italians resulted in both urban unemployment and inflation. Under the British, Eritrean workers were allowed to unionize, and they formed a syndicate numbering 3,500–5,000 members. In the western and coastal regions, Muslim nomads and villagers were encouraged to organize against their previously Italian-supported chiefs and feudal lords. The bureaucracy was gradually Eritreanized as both old leaders and members of a new generation were promoted to positions of administrative responsibility.

Other external factors contributed to the process of politicization. Some Italian policymakers tried to promote the idea of Italian trusteeship over the ex-colony. Emperor Haile Selassie, for his part, once back on his throne, started working for the restoration of Eritrea to Ethiopia. His emissaries joined hands with the Eritrean priesthood in an effort to organize supporters of a reunification.

This intensive process of politicization did not stimulate an all-Eritrean movement. In the 1940s, the Eritrean intelligentsia was still too small and too isolated to be influenced by nationalist struggles in the neighboring Middle East and Africa. Whatever Eritrean modern self-awareness then existed, it was apparently too weak to overcome the old and now encouraged sectarian differences. In fact, at that time, only a slight majority, at best, of politically active Eritreans were for independence, and many of them favored a trusteeship regime.

The overwhelming majority of Christian Tigrayans, inhabitants of the core highlands, wanted reunification with Ethiopia. Indeed, rather than encouraging the emergence of Eritrean nationalism—which was to emerge more vividly in the 1960s—the processes at work in the 1940s resulted in the politicization of Eritrean ethnic, religious, and regional diversity. A further catalyst in this process was visits by various UN commissions charged with assessing the situation in the ex-colony in order to decide Eritrea's future. Political parties and organizations expressing the interests of various sectors were established, and most of them remained active throughout the period.[9]

The Unionist Party (UP), established in 1944, consisted primarily of Christian highlanders and some Muslims, and advocated reunification with Ethiopia under Haile Selassie as an act of national liberation.[10]

Most members of the Muslim League (ML), established 1946, were Muslim advocates of independence. After the establishment in 1947 of another party named the National Muslim Party of Massawa, the ML represented mainly the Muslims of western Eritrea.[11]

The Liberal Progressive Party (LPP) was established in 1948. It was comprised of Christians and some Muslims advocating independence, preferably with the annexation of Tigray province to Eritrea. Although Eritrean Christians were Tigrinya speakers, only a minority raised the issue of Tigrayanism and followed the LPP in the 1940s. The majority supported the UP, and many perceived Haile Selassie as a national hero.[12]

Finally, there were the new Eritrean Pro-Italian Party, composed of many of mixed Italian-Eritrean origin, and a number of other minor parties.[13]

In 1948–9 the Muslim-dominated parties and the majority of the LPP joined forces to form the Independence Bloc. This organization soon split up, with some factions joining the UP and others forming new parties, including the Muslim League of the

Western Province, the Eritrean Democratic Bloc, the Independent Muslim League, and the renewed LPP.[14]

From Federation to Annexation

It was at this stage in their history that the issues of politically centralizing Ethiopia, and politically diversifying Eritrea, were federated.

From 1947–51, the future of Eritrea was debated in the forums of international diplomacy. At the end of the process, there emerged among the Great Powers and in the United Nations a compromise. The idea of a federation was adopted in December 1950. On 15 September 1952, the British flag was lowered from the Government House in Asmara, and the federation came into being. It remained in existence for ten years, a period characterized by an uneven contest between Ethiopia's imperial absolutism and Eritrea's political diversity.[15]

In retrospect, it is clear that the federation was doomed because of the nature of the Ethiopian political system. First, absolute emperorship could not coexist with political pluralism. Second, Ethiopia was no less diverse than Eritrea in terms of ethnic, linguistic, religious, and regional groups, and Eritrea's unique status would inevitably encourage the emergence of separatist movements throughout the empire. And third, the neighboring Muslim and Arab countries were gaining independence (Sudan in January 1956), which would inevitably affect Eritrea's Muslims and fan Ethiopian Christians' centuries-old fears of Islamic encirclement, encroachment, and penetration.

The UN resolution concerning the federation stipulated that 'Eritrea shall constitute an autonomous unit federated with Ethiopia under the sovereignty of the Ethiopian crown.' On paper, the functional structure of the federation as laid down in its constitution seemed to be clear: the federal government—in fact, the emperor—was to control foreign affairs, defense, finance, commerce, and the ports. An Eritrean Executive answerable to an Eritrean Assembly was to have full internal power over all functions not vested in the federal government.

The initial assembly was to be elected on the basis of existing political parties.[16]

The first assembly,[17] in 1952–6, elected while Eritrea was still under British administration, contained thirty-two members of the UP, eighteen of the Eritrean Democratic Bloc, fifteen of the Muslim League of the Western Province, one of the Nationalist Party, and one independent member. Bairu Tedla[18] of the Unionist Party became the first chief executive of Eritrea along with Ali Radai[19] of the Muslim League, who became president of the new Eritrean Assembly. These results showed that the UN formula suggesting the settlement of Eritrean politics in accord with the wishes of the majority of the population was good in theory. In reality, it was unworkable—Eritrea's fragmented society had no majority.

In Addis Ababa, the federation was conceived from the start as just a temporary obstacle on the road to full reunification. The federation arrangement and constitution were openly ignored and, in time, practically destroyed.

When Haile Selassie enacted the revised 1955 constitution for his people, no mention was made of Eritrea's special status.[20] In practice, the federation was fictitious almost from the start. The federal government—the emperor—controlled defense and finances. By taking advantage of the presence of an overwhelmingly pro-Ethiopian Christian community, it had no difficulty in taking over all positions of real power. Systematic terrorism and other measures against individuals who failed to see the light of reunification proved effective.[21] In the constitutional sphere, however, the process was more visible, and therefore much slower. The tactics pursued by the emperor in this respect were to destroy the federation through the function of his personal representative in Eritrea and to persuade the Eritrean assembly to exercise its constitutional right to vote itself out of existence.

The federal constitution defined the emperor's representative, *enderase*, in Eritrea as the link between the crown, at the head of the federation, and Eritrean institutions. However, for all practical purposes, the emperor's representative—the first one—was Ras Andergachaw Masai. The emperor's son-in-law, was the ruler of the territory. The *enderase*'s speech to the Eritrean assembly in March 1953 left no doubts regarding his understanding of the functional structure of the federation: 'There are no internal nor external affairs as far as the office of His Imperial Majesty's Representative is concerned, and there will be none in future.'[22] In 1954, there started a process of forceful acceptance and assimilation of the Amharic language and culture, as Amhara governors and other political office holders were appointed to administrative posts.

This approach, accompanied by a campaign of riots, left the assembly no alternative but to sanction the systematic depoliticization of Eritrean society. Well before the 1956 elections, all political parties had been banned and dismembered, with the exception of the UP, the continued existence of which was permitted for propaganda reasons. Many prominent opponents of annexation had to go into exile. The trade unions were destroyed, and the press came under federal control. The office of chief executive, held until 1955 by the leader of the UP, was transferred to the representative's deputy. In December 1958, the assembly unanimously abrogated the Eritrean flag, and from September 1959, Ethiopian law was introduced. In May 1960, the assembly changed the name of the Eritrean Executive to 'Eritrean Administration under Haile Selassie, the emperor of Ethiopia.' On 15 November 1962, the assembly voted for its own dissolution and Eritrea's full unification with Ethiopia.

Ethiopia's re-annexation of Eritrea and the ensuing chapter in its history must be seen also in a regional context. The late 1950s and early 1960s were marked by rising Pan-Arabism sweeping the area. Egypt, under Gammal Abd al-Nasser, united with Syria in 1958 and was renamed the United Arab Republic. In the same year, Sudan turned to revolutionary Nasserism. In July 1960, the Republic of Somali was born. Backed by Nasser and other Arab leaders, it claimed a third of Ethiopia's territory. In September 1962, following a revolution in neighboring Yemen, a fratricidal war began there. The Yemen War was in fact an all-Arab conflict between conservative states and revolutionary ones. Ethiopia felt on the defensive, especially when the regime was beginning to be challenged also from within, as an abortive coup d'état led by young officers in December 1960 demonstrated.

The emperor, however, for his part did not remain passive. He worked to strengthen relations with the USA, with Israel, and with others in the Middle East. His main response was to turn to Africa. He managed to maneuver between revolutionaries and conservatives in the emancipating continent and bring about the establishment of the Organization of African Unity in May 1963. The OAU's charter sanctioned the territorial integrity of the member states, Addis Ababa became its permanent center, and the emperor became the senior statement of the continent.[23] The aging monarch secured his absolutism at home for the next ten years.

Eritrean Liberation Front and 'Arabism'

As early as 1955, young Eritrean Muslims began fleeing through Sudan and settling in Cairo. The Egyptian capital, already the center of revolutionary, secular pan-Arabism, radiated the spirit of inevitable victory for a uniting Arab nation, from the Atlantic Ocean to the Persian Gulf. In Cairo, the young Eritreans were given scholarships to study in Al-Azhar University. In a new 'Eritrea House,' many of them were transforming into Arab revolutionaries. Some Eritrean young Christians, angry at the imperial system imposed by Addis Ababa, soon followed. Cairo's 'Voice of the Arabs' began broadcasting to Eritrea in Arabic and in Tigrinya, campaigning against Haile Selassie as a reactionary and a Zionist. Many of the young Eritreans in the Egyptian capital adopted the concept that liberating Eritrea from imperial Ethiopia was part of the greater Nasserite struggle for Arab unity and freedom. In July 1960, their 'Eritrean Liberation Front'[24] was declared in Cairo, and in November 1961 there began actual fighting on Eritrean soil.

The Eritrean Liberation Front (ELF) developed an Eritrean-Arab ideology, and its forces grew from 900 guerilla fighters in 1962 to around 2000 in 1967. It expanded throughout most parts of the province, established regional commands, and obtained assistance and funding first from the Egyptians, then, from 1964 onwards, from the Syrians and Iraqis. As the imperial Ethiopian government introduced full Amharization, banning the use of local languages, it gradually alienated young Christian Tigrayans of the Eritrean mountain region. Hundreds of them joined the ranks of the ELF, strengthening the revolt and transforming it into an all-Eritrean movement.[25]

The 1967 Six Day War in the Middle East dealt a blow to pan-Arabism, and in 1969–70, a new all-regional chapter began to take shape. Each Arab state began solidifying separately around new dictatorships. Here, we shall only mention developments relevant to our story.

On 25 May 1969, Colonel Ja'far al-Numayri captured power in Sudan. He built a military regime oriented on the Soviets and survived till the mid-1980s. In September 1969, Colonel Muammar Qaddafi came to power in Libya and survived till 2011. He developed an ambition to become an all-African leader and in his early years targeted Haile Selassie and his leadership in the OAU. In Libya, he opened a training base for the Eritrean rebels and financed their movement. In October 1969, General Siyad Barre took control of Somalia. He abolished the parliamentarian system which existed from 1960, rebuilt the national army, and held power up to 1991. Siyad Barre allied with the Soviets and adopted Marxist ideology, further strengthening the hostility toward Haile Selassie and the Somali old claim to the Ethiopian Ogaden. In that same year, the PLO, under Yasser Arafat, solidified its position in Jordan as practically a state within a state. It had a direct impact on the conflict in Eritrea, as the PLO adopted the Ba'athist doctrine, which considered Eritrea to be an Arab land. 'The Arabs should realize'—wrote a PLO spokesman in 1969—'that the struggle in Eritrea is an Arab revolution… A revolution which is inseparable from the Arabs' struggle for liberation in any other Arab country,' and that Haile Selassie, the 'Lion of Judah' and an ally of Israel, was a Zionist enemy.[26] The PLO now succeeded Syria as the main host and trainer of Eritrean fighters. They underwent training in Palestinian camps in Jordan, Lebanon, Syria, and South Yemen. A training camp was built in Eritrea, in the desert of Afar, in which Palestinian experts instructed the locals how to upgrade their methods and munitions. Qaddafi was the main financier of this effort. The Libyan and Palestinian aid to the Eritreans was shipped from Aden, and thus the Red Sea became the main channel to Arab support for the Eritreans. This change, from Sudan to the Red Sea, had far reaching implications on the history of the Eritreans' movement, and, in fact, on the history of Eritrea till now.

After the 1967 war in the Middle East, internal tensions mounted in the Eritrean movement, both in Arab capitals as well as in the field. The main division was between fighters and leaders from western Eritrea and those from the Red Sea coast and the central highlands. Those from the west enjoyed hegemony in the 1960s. They were closer to Sudan and the town of Kassala, the source of supplies in those years. Also the leadership in exile, the ELF activists in Cairo, Damascus, Khartoum, and Baghdad were mostly from western areas, notably Idris Adam.[27] A prominent exception was Uthman Salih Sabbe,[28] a native of Massawa. Sabbe was a schoolmaster fluent in Arabic who became the ideologue and chief promoter of the concept of Eritrea's Arabism. 'Eritrea is a part of the Arab world'—he wrote—[29] 'her future is inseparable from that of the Arab homeland... and it is the duty of the Arabs to stand by that sister in her effort to realize her just demands.' Initially chairman of the 'foreign relation mission' of the ELF, he was gradually pushed aside by his rivals, especially in 1967. Expelled from Damascus, Sabbe joined Yasser Arafat in Jordan, and in November 1969, in a PLO camp, he declared the establishment of the Peoples' Liberation Front (PLF), a rival to the ELF. Sabbe managed to befriend Qaddafi as well as the new leaders in Aden and oversaw the change from Sudan to the Red Sea as the channel for arms, training, and finance. Moreover, in 1970, he managed to build relations with the emerging core of Tigrayan-Christian Eritreans in the central highlands, led now by the young Isayas Afawarqi. His PLF was declared the EPLF, the Eritrean Peoples' Liberation Front,[30] a bitter rival of the ELF, which would beat its Eritrean rivals in the 1980s and eventually lead Eritrea to independence.

Tigrayan Eritreans in Addis Ababa

Not many Eritrean Christians moved to Arab capitals. Among those who did was Woldeab Woldemariam.[31] Born in 1905, Woldeab was an editor for the Tigrinya language newspaper initiated by British military administrators in 1942 in Asmara. A founding leader of the Liberal Progressive Party, he was elected to the Eritrean Assembly, attacked by pro-unity agents, hospitalized, and sought asylum in Cairo. From Cairo, Woldeab broadcasted to Eritrea in Tigrinya and helped the cause of the ELF struggle. However, never identifying with the Arab orientation of the ELF, he had little influence on the fighters in the field. He was too old when the Tigrayan Christians took over the EPLF, and would rather become a symbol of Eritrean nationalism.

Younger Eritrean Tigrayans went to Addis Ababa rather than Cairo. Many of the schooled ones found themselves serving an Amhara-dominated authoritarian system. They were managers and functionaries in various economic companies, such as Ethiopian Airlines, in the private sector, etc. In the new campus of Haile Selassie University, for example, in the 1960s, a group of young Eritrean lecturers was meeting secretly. Among them were Abraham Demoz, Bereket Habta-Selassie, and Asmarom Leggese. Together with some non-Eritreans, like Duri Muhammad and Mesfin Wolda-Mariam, they dreamt of conspiring against the emperor and secretly met with young army officers.[32] However, they were unable to do more, and in any case, the Eritrean cause was still overly identified with Muslims and Arabism. After the fall of Haile Selassie, some of them ended as leading professors in western universities. Some, notably Bereket Habta-Selassie, became active supporters of Eritrean nationalism in exile.

The most prominent young Eritrean Tigrayan who unhappily found himself serving Haile Selassie was General Aman Andom.[33] Aman was born in 1924 in the village of Tsazegga, which, as mentioned previously, had for centuries been the headquarters of a local Christian family that succeeded in maintaining local autonomy. Educated in Khartoum, Aman returned to Ethiopia in 1941 with the British forces. In the restored Ethiopia, he proceeded to distinguish himself with a brilliant military career, commanding Ethiopian UN contingents in Korea and Congo. In the Ogaden battles against the Somalis in the early 1960s, General Aman willfully ignored Haile Selassie's orders by penetrating Somali territory. He was consequently 'exiled' to the Senate in 1965, as was the practice with overly independent political figures. Aman continued to cultivate relations with the army's generals, was among the few high-ranking officers admired by the rank and file, and was also in close touch with the academics mentioned above. Aman, as mentioned below, would be a major figure in the 1974 revolution in Ethiopia and in determining its Eritrean dimension.

Haile Selassie's last chance

Aman was also in secret touch with Ras Asrate Kasa,[34] prominent among the Amhara nobility and a key figure in the discussed years. As much as one could oppose Haile Selassie, he was sober enough to see where the emperor's absolutism and centralization would lead Ethiopia. In July 1963, he poured his heart out to a foreign diplomat:

> 'Ethiopia is in crisis and on the eve of a revolution which will destroy the system. The public is of the opinion that there should be a change, either by peaceful means or by violence. Till recently this was what the educated ones thought, now it is also the mood among the masses… There are three foci of tension. One is the army, in which the rank and file hate the high officers. The junior and intermediate officers, lieutenants and majors are clearly revolutionary. The higher officers are rivalry-torn, they hate each other. The other focus is the intelligentsia. Its members can render support to the young officers, but not lead a change by themselves. The third focus are the masses in the peripheral provinces. They want their regional autonomy back, and they are capable of challenging the imperial system. Indeed, we must go back to some decentralization. This is a precondition to further reforms…The emperor knows all this and knows he should delegate some power to the people and its representatives. But after forty years in absolute power, it is difficult for him to make the right choice…'[35]

These were prophetic words. The lieutenants of 1963 would lead the bloody revolution of 1974 and obliterate Ethiopia's elites. They would be supported initially by the intelligentsia, but once in power, they would systematically destroy the educated layer. In 1991, liberation fronts representing the peripheral regions would finally destroy the dictatorial military regime of Mangistu Haile Mariam.

Meanwhile, the Eritrean Liberation Front intensified its pro-Arab propaganda and scored successes in the field. In 1964, Haile Selassie appointed Asrate over the province. He also authorized him to change the army's tactics against the rebels. Asrate strengthened relations with local Eritrean Christians and recruited their sons to new anti-guerrilla units. For a while, it worked. It also deepened the rivalry between the Prime Minister of Ethiopia Aklilu Habta-Wold[36] and Asrate. The latter kept telling the emperor that his prime minister diverted his attention from needed reforms. Aklilu, for his part, repeated accusations that Asrate was preparing a private army in Eritrea in order to capture power. Asrate developed a strong bond with Haile Selassie's heir and eldest son, Asfa-Wossen. But on Aklilu's advice, the emperor would not delegate any authority to his designated successor.

At the end of January 1970, Asrate left Asmara to London for a few months. In his absence, the Ethiopian army, answerable to the prime minister, tried to teach the rebels a lesson in its own way. The Eritreans, inspired and trained by PLO experts, turned to spectacular acts of sabotage, which they filmed and publicized. In October, they managed to blow up the Asmara-Massawa railway line on camera, and on 21 November, they ambushed and killed the commander of the Ethiopian 2nd Division. In response, Haile Selassie declared martial law in the province and removed Asrate from Asmara.[37] In retrospect, this was the last chance to preserve whatever remained of Tigrayan Eritreans' identification with Ethiopia.

11

THREE REVOLUTIONS

DERG, EPLF, TPLF

Three revolutions changed our story and shaped it up to the present day.

First, Haile Selassie was toppled in 1974 by young officers headed by Major Mangistu Haile Mariam.

Second, the EPLF grew stronger in 1975, and by 1981, led by Tigrayan speakers, gained dominance in the movement and led it to Eritrean independence in 1991.[1]

Third, a Tigrayan Peoples' Liberation Front (TPLF) emerged in Tigray in the mid-1970s. It did away with the traditional local aristocracy, which led Tigray for centuries. The TPLF would eventually capture Addis Ababa in 1991 and end the dictatorial regime of Mangistu Haile Mariam.

Thus, for quite a while, Tigrayan speakers dominated 'greater Ethiopia.'

Ethiopia's 1974 revolution—the formative year

Much has been written on the 1974 revolution in Ethiopia and the history of the country under Mangistu Haile Mariam. Here, we shall address one issue, which was our focus throughout.

Namely, the built-in tension in Ethiopia between centralization and decentralization.

Haile Selassie, we saw, brought the ethos and practice of political absolutism to its historical climax, much to the disaster of the country. Eritrea was the pivotal issue in question. The toppling of his regime prompted the question again. The young officers in the Derg, the revolutionary committee, chose General Aman Andom as their first chairman, and thus the head of the state when the emperor was deposed in September. Aman, ever proud of his Eritrean background, set as his prime objective a constructive political solution to the Eritrean problem. His dramatic failure paved the way for hardliners, who would lead Ethiopia to a centralizing dictatorship—again, much to her disaster.

On 20 August 1974, the new Prime Minister Mikael Imru made a speech in parliament. It was the first in the history of the Eritrean conflict in which an Ethiopian official admitted that a serious problem existed in Eritrea and that the solution lay in a political dialogue. Similarly, Aman Andom declared that solving the Eritrean problem was the nation's top priority and that he would do his utmost to achieve a solution. The next week, he left for an extensive tour of the province.[2]

During late August and early September, Aman made public appearances all over Eritrea, addressing packed stadiums in Asmara, Keren, and elsewhere. Speaking in Tigrinya and Arabic, the use of which had been officially forbidden by Haile Selassie, he urged his listeners to blame social, economic, and cultural problems on the defunct regime. He admitted that Ethiopian hardliners, by resorting exclusively to military power, had encouraged Eritrean separatism. However, at the same time, he emphasized that 'Eritrea had been historically an integral part of Ethiopia ... that the problem of Eritrea is the problem of the entire Ethiopia ... [and that] we are jealous of our unity.'

On 9 September 1974, back in the capital, Aman presented a detailed nineteen-point plan to solve the problem. It called for 'general reform of the administrative system, removal of all obstacles which had impeded social progress ... amnesty of political prisoners in Eritrea, return of exiles and their resettlement, promotion of foreign investments ... lifting the state of emergency, punishing officials responsible for misconduct in Eritrea,' as well as 'safeguarding Ethiopian unity.'

Beyond the facade of declarations, however, Aman had attempted during his tour to reach an understanding and to cooperate with Christian Tigrayan elements in the EPLF. Eritrean policemen were in touch with EPLF fighters, and Aman himself was personally acquainted with some of the separatist leaders. Aman apparently believed that Christian Tigrayans in the EPLF would be satisfied with a sort of Eritrean autonomy; according to Zawde Gabra-Sellasse, he thought that they would join hands with the Ethiopian army in a common war against the ELF. Using the services of Sudanese President Numayri, Aman conveyed to some of the Eritrean leaders in exile the idea of an autonomous Eritrea linked federally with Ethiopia. As a token of goodwill, for the first time since the days of the federation, a Christian Eritrean was appointed Eritrea's governor-general. This was Amanuel Amda-Mikael, who, on arriving at Asmara later in September, swore to become Eritrea's servant rather than its governor. Another significant appointment made by Aman was the reinstallation of Brigadier General Goitem Gabra-Egzi, also an Eritrean, as commissioner of the Eritrean police, a position he had held until the removal of Ras Asrate Kasa.

But Aman's attempt to persuade Eritrean leaders was unsuccessful. Nor was he able to convince his younger colleagues in the Derg that his political approach was justified. This double failure was soon to lead to his political downfall—and to his death.

The first to reject Aman's proposals were Eritrean leaders in exile. Neither Muslims nor Christians, of either organization, left any room for compromise. 'This is an unacceptable program,' the EPLF spokesman in Rome stated. 'We want our old flag back.' The Beirut-published EPLF *Eritrean Review* made this quite clear in its September issue: 'Let us bring to the notice of the new rulers of Ethiopia that our military operations will be extended to every span of the Eritrean territory. Then we will see what the Ethiopian colonialist army can do.' In the same issue, Muhammad Said Nawud, the EPLF director of central information, reacted to Aman's proposals: 'Aman Andom is an Eritrean traitor and a stooge of the Ethiopian government ... to arrive at a political solution cannot be accomplished by means of sending stooges to Eritrea. This can only be achieved by adopting a clear-cut position recognizing the realities imposed by the Eritrean revolution ... We are ready to sit with the Ethiopians and negotiate with them on the question of full independence for Eritrea, while at the same time holding our arms in our hands.'

Throughout September, Aman faced growing opposition in the Derg. At the same time, his policy suffered another blow in the province itself, where the EPLF and ELF were still engaged in their fratricidal war. A core unit of some 500 EPLF fighters, long besieged near Karora by the ELF, managed to break away and move to the village of Zager, near Asmara, where contact was established with members of the Ethiopian armed forces (who were, most probably, following Aman's instructions in this matter). When the pursuing ELF forces camped at the nearby village of Woki in the first week of October, a major battle ensued between the two Eritrean forces. The battle lasted for a few days and claimed the lives of some 600 fighters. It ended in a most peculiar way, becoming a milestone in the history of the Eritrean nationalist movement. When news of the battle reached Asmara, some 50,000 citizens left the town—possibly at the urging of Aman's men—and made their way to the site of the battle. By that time, many fighters had ceased firing, refusing to shoot at fellow Eritreans. A mass rally was spontaneously organized at Woki, and facing the pressure of this popular demonstration and manifestation of Eritrean patriotism, the warring units reached an agreement. Nothing was concluded in writing concerning actual cooperation between the rival parties, but the rally was a clear demonstration that the majority of Christian Eritreans looked to the separatist organizations for leadership.

The rally at Woki caused deep frustration among Ethiopian officers of the 2nd Division stationed in Eritrea. Their new commander, Brigadier General Tafari Banti,[3] who had been appointed in September 1974, was known as a hardliner on Eritrea. Following the rally, he asked the Derg for authorization to wage open war on the rebels and demanded reinforcements from the capital. His request was favorably received by Major Mangistu Haila-Mariam. In an attempt to save his position and his policy, Aman managed to prevent a decision to send reinforcements to Eritrea; instead, he left for the province on 6 October 1974. In Asmara, he addressed a mass rally in the central stadium, urging the thousands who had just demonstrated their Eritreanism at Woki to consider the opportunities they had been given: 'All of us, from all the fourteen administrative regions of the country, should strive in unity to advance Ethiopia to the standard of other countries.'

Aman returned to Addis Ababa on the same day. The people of Asmara gave him their reply a week later. On 13 October, representatives of the EPLF and ELF, as well as some 20,000–30,000 citizens, attended another rally held just outside the town. The army, though still restrained, started demonstrating its presence in and around the town. Uthman Sabi declared that the separatists, now stronger than ever, were about to initiate a new stage in the war against the Ethiopians. No more hit-and-run operations, he promised. The Eritrean organizations would launch offensives against the army in its own camps and the main towns.

The victory of the uncompromising sectors in the Eritrean camp signaled that Aman's end was approaching and that the Ethiopian hardliners would emerge victorious. Aman's influence in the Derg rested on the support of a few members, mainly the representatives of the Imperial Guard (1st Division) and of the Addis Ababa police; he had not been a real factor in the making of the protest movement or in the establishment of the Derg. Although in close touch with some of the revolutionaries in the early stages, he was chosen as chairman of the Derg essentially because of his popularity. Aman, however, refused to confine himself to being a mere figurehead. He was confident that his charisma could not fail him and that he was the real guide of the youngsters in the Derg. Without bothering too much about his power base in the ruling body, Aman tried to direct the revolution according to his concepts. In his public appearances as acting head of state, Aman tried to restrain expectations of prompt and drastic changes.

He supported gradual land reform and foreign investments and opposed spectacular nationalizations. He resisted both the Marxist-oriented officers, who favored the immediate transfer of rule to civilians, and those who wished to prolong military rule. He also opposed ideas such as instant execution of arrested officials, and stood for holding proper trials. All this created a gap between the patronizing Aman and the core group in the Derg of mid-level officers led by Major Mangistu.

But it was primarily over the Eritrean issue that differences between Aman and the younger officers turned into a violent conflict.

While Tafari Banti in Eritrea was demanding reinforcements for an extensive military campaign, Major Mangistu in the Derg was pushing for a decision to let the army take the initiative against the rebels. Although Aman could offer no proof of success, he firmly resisted the move. An important and related matter was that the troops designated for the Eritrean campaign were some 5,000 members of the 1st Division, known to support Aman's few followers in the Derg. Their removal from Addis Ababa would further undermine Aman's power base.

The struggle between Mangistu and Aman broke into the open in the second week of November, when both leaders were touring army bases making contradictory statements. Mangistu, reverting to the tactic of ignoring the Eritrean situation, referred to 'the few guerrillas who had been maintaining a state of insecurity in the region for the last 13 years, with the collaboration of foreign countries.'

Aman stood no chance of winning the struggle in the Derg. He was an outsider, while Mangistu enjoyed the support of many of the NCOs and some of the officers. Many of these NCOs were of Oromo origin, and they probably suspected Aman of being too tolerant of Eritreanism. Aman's only chance was to mobilize support outside the Derg, mainly units of the Harar-based 3rd Division, but despite his associates' advice, the overconfident Aman refused to start an open war. Instead, on 15 November he confined himself to his Addis Ababa house and waited for the youngsters of the Derg to come and beg him to return. On 23 November, the Derg sent troops to arrest him, and in the ensuing gunfight, he and two of his associates were killed. On the same night, fifty-seven of the officials arrested since the start of the revolution were executed without trial. Amost all among them were important figures in Ethiopian politics (with the exception of the emperor, who was murdered in August 1975), including Asrate and Aklilu. The Derg ordered 5,000 soldiers of the 1st Division to move to Eritrea and reinforce the army there in preparation for a military confrontation with the separatists.

In the Eritrean context, Aman's defeat by Mangistu resembled that of Asrate by Aklilu. Both Aman and Asrate were working for a political solution, pinning their hopes on the Christian Tigrayan community in Eritrea. Asrate failed primarily because as a representative of conservative absolutism he could not attract the emerging generation of educated Christians. Aman, representing a new Ethiopia, came too late in the Eritrean context. By the time he appeared, Ethiopian hardliners had seen to it that Tigrayan Eritreans identified Ethiopia with systematic brutality. 'Twenty years ago,' a prominent Christian leader in Asmara was quoted as saying, 'I favored union. I was one of those shouting 'Unity or Death.' What we got was Ethiopia and death.' Both Aman and Asrate, however, were given little opportunity to implement their policies. In 1974, as in 1970, hardliners on both sides prevented a political solution in the war-torn province.

With the fall of Aman Andom, the outbreak of conventional, open war in Eritrea became inevitable. All hopes that a new regime in Ethiopia would lead to a peaceful solution were shattered. By the time of the Ethiopian revolution of 1974, a nationalist movement had emerged in Eritrea. The revolution in Ethiopia, inasmuch as it weakened the Ethiopian state machinery, raised expectations among Eritrean nationalists. The uncompromising policy that the Derg adopted after Aman died served only to strengthen the rapidly growing Eritrean movement.

EPLF—From Arabism to Eritreanism and Independence

During the same period, beginning in 1974, the Eritrean nationalist movement also underwent a revolution.[4] Since Eritrean nationalists have always referred to their movement as a revolutionary one, the occurrence of a new revolution within their ranks was less noticeable at the time than in Ethiopia. However, the Eritrean movement changed profoundly in two ways.

First, the period between 1975 and 1977 was one of rapid and significant growth in membership. Up to 1974, the number of active Eritrean fighters was estimated at no more than 2,500. For reasons that included the revolution in Ethiopia, the Eritrean camps started to swell. In early 1975, the number of organized Eritrean fighters was estimated at 6,000. By early 1977, estimates varied from 38,500 to 43,000.

Second, Christian Tigrayans, previously grossly outnumbered by Muslims, started to dominate the EPLF. The political weight of members of the urban intelligentsia began to exceed that of warriors from tribal societies. Field commanders gained influence at the expense of leaders in exile and finally displaced them completely. In both the EPLF and the ELF, cadres in the field, representing views expressed in mass meetings of fighters, came to control the supreme commands. Correspondingly, the Eritrean movement underwent a fundamental ideological change. The two leading organizations abandoned Arab and mildly socialist terminology in favor of Marxist terminology. Both organizations abandoned guerrilla tactics for full-scale conventional warfare.

However, the ELF, headed in 1975 by Ahmad Nasir, and despite its growth, gradually began losing in its competition with the EPLF. The latter gained more power due to the mass absorption of young Christian Tigrayans embittered by Mangistu's oppressive centralism. The ELF went on entrenching in the conviction that it was the only legitimate representative of Eritrean identity, but its pretension contrasted with reality. The main arena for the struggle against the Ethiopian forces moved to the Asmara–Keren and the Asmara–Massawa regions, areas controlled by the EPLF, led now by the charismatic fighter Isayas Afaworki. In March 1976, Uthman Salih Sabi and his exiles in Arab countries broke with the EPLF. In January 1977, temporary military coordination between the fronts led to some victories, but soon they proved unable to overcome their differences. In early 1978, a newly Soviet-equipped and

Cuban-trained Ethiopian army pushed the Eritrean back, and the ELF forces retreated to the western regions. In August 1981, the ELF forces were severely beaten in a major clash with the EPLF, and throughout the early 1980s, many of its fighters gradually defected to the rival front.

The demise and subsequent dismemberment of the ELF in the 1980s stemmed from two processes. First, the western Eritrean Muslim population could no longer remain the movement's driving force when, in the mid-1970s, the Christian Tigrayans of the core regions joined the anti-Ethiopian struggle. Second, the ELF thrived on the pan-Arabism of the 1960s, benefitting from its Arab Middle Eastern support. Consequently, when pan-Arabism was losing ground in the Arab Middle East of the 1970s, the ELF also lost support. Thus, the movement that initiated the modern struggle for Eritrean independence was practically no longer in existence when independence finally materialized in 1991.

Yet the historical significance of the ELF should not be downplayed. In borrowing the 'liberation front' concept from the Arab Middle East, and adapting and implementing it in Eritrea, the ELF can be considered the first modern military and political movement in the Ethiopian–Eritrean context. It thus heralded, inspired, and served as a model for all other liberation fronts that were later to defeat the authoritarian politics inherited from imperial Ethiopia by its succeeding military dictatorship.

The EPLF, on the contrary, proved a great success. In the years of struggle against Haile Sclassie's Ethiopia, and more so against Mangistu's regime, the EPLF was embraced by many in the world as an inspiring model for a progressive, national revolutionary movement. Namely, as a liberation front which managed to address the needs of a battling society, to emancipate women, to mobilize masses, to attract intellectuals, and to provide hope. One out of many enthusiastic participants (he would later be bitterly disillusioned), the future professor in exile, Paulos Tesfagiorgis, summarized:

'In the twenty years of its existence as a liberation front (1971–91), the EPLF developed into an effective fighting machine with clear people-centered ideology. It was a unique organization that captured the imagination of practically every Eritrean, an organization that accommodated, brought together and forged solidarity and camaraderie between diverse Eritrean ethnic groups, classes, and gender, rural and urban areas, Eritreans living inside the country as well as outside ... its members came from all walks of Eritrean life—of highly educated in the best universities of the world, including Harvard, Sorbonne, and Oxford, of successful businessmen ... of medical doctors, pharmacists, and engineers. The EPLF fired up the imagination of farmers and people of nomadic background in the rural areas, of ordinary people who lived anywhere inside the country and those inside Ethiopia, and across Africa, the Middle East, Europe and North America and beyond.... The EPLF articulated the Eritrean struggle as part of the anti-colonial African struggles and saw itself as an African liberation movement... This belief, bolstered by an effective organization and commitment to principles of right of self-determination forged over several years became the engine that drove the war of independence. The Tigrayan People's Liberation Front (TPLF), in neighboring Ethiopian province of Tigray, significantly contributed towards the military defeat of the Ethiopian army and the downfall of the regime, the Derg...'[5]

The TPLF—First revolution in Tigray

In retrospect, it was not surprising that the above-mentioned revolutions occurred in Ethiopia and Eritrea. In both, the background was long ready before the mid-1970s.

In Ethiopia, a 1960 coup, led by the bodyguard of Haile Selassie, heralded a decade of political tension. We mentioned the prophetic words of Ras Asrate in 1963. The young army officers, the intellectuals, the students, the various peoples in the vast periphery, were all preparing for a change. If anything, the 1974 toppling of Haile Selassie came too late. The revolution in the making was consequently hijacked by the less qualified among the young officers, who led the country into comprehensive chaos.

In Eritrea, there had emerged a political public already under the British. It was diverse, active, and was supposed to enjoy more liberties under the 1952 autonomy arrangement. The abolition of the autonomy by Haile Selassie injected bitterness into the rising Eritrean national awareness. The ELF, and then the EPLF, also grew against the revolutionary spirit of the 1960s in Africa and the Middle East. They could mobilize schooled fighters as well as experienced tribal warriors to wage war against the Ethiopian forces, as well as against each other. The Eritrean revolution finally led to an independent Eritrean state centered on the capital of Asmara and under Tigrayan leadership.

In comparison, very little was there in the Tigray of the 1960s to herald a revolution—and, more so, to herald the building of a Tigrayan movement, that within a short time would bring Tigrayans back to the leadership of greater Ethiopia, like it had enjoyed a century earlier.

Tigray, to reiterate, seemed to be hopelessly impoverished, humiliated, and humbled. In the early 1970s, it was still governed by Ras Mangasha Seyum, a descendent of local rulers who had controlled Tigray from medieval times. Though quite a progressive man, the ras was a part of the ancient imperial system to which he belonged and which he served. Tigray's peasantry followed their old traditional ways under the same ancient landowning system. The youth of Tigray, the schooled among them, mostly pursued their future elsewhere.

Those of the schooled Tigrayans who left for Addis Ababa to study in Haile Selassie I University were inspired by the political activism on campus and even led it. They were also inspired by the struggle of the Eritreans and by young Tigrayan Eritrean professors like those mentioned above.

The revolution of Tigray—it can safely be said—began in the Addis Ababa campus.

In the 1960s, the Haile Selassie I University became a focal point of political unrest, in tune with the spirit of the young generation in Western Europe, America, and Africa. The Ethiopian students, gathered from all over the country, remained connected to their provincial roots. In the five-year BA program introduced in 1964, students spent their fourth year in distant provinces teaching peasant children and gaining exposure to the problems of the country.

Fifth-year students prepared papers reflecting on the experiences they had in the rural peripheries. In 1967, a rather militant student leadership emerged. The Student Union was renamed the Union of the Students of Addis Ababa University (USUAA), avoiding the name of Haile Selassie I University. It established a new periodical entitled *Struggle* (*Tigil*), the contents of which became overtly radical, including articles like 'Feudalism Must Be Purged,' and pieces analyzing the guerrilla tactics of Ho Chi Minh and Che Guevara. In response to the students' demonstrations, on 29 December 1969, the student leader Tilahun Gizaw,[6] a Tigrayan (born in Maychew), was assassinated near the university, and the regime tightened its oppressive presence on campus.[7]

In the early 1970s, the Tigrayan University Students' Association (TUSA) was formed.[8] Back in Tigray for the winter vacations, the students were still cautious not to antagonize the local conservative peasant society. But in Addis Ababa, TUSA held secret discussions. The main dilemma of the students was in line with the historical options we followed all throughout. Were the young Tigrayans to participate, together with other fellow Ethiopian students, in an all-Ethiopian revolution? Or should they first emancipate Tigray from the imperial-Shoan yoke? They all resorted to Marxist terminology, which for a while helped to bridge the relevant ideas. The rise of the Derg, and the murderous methods it applied, made the dilemma a matter of life and death. On 14 September 1974, two days after the removal of the emperor, and as the officers under Mangistu began showing their brutality, seven of the Tigrayans among the revolutionary students established the Tigrayan National Organization (TNO).[9] They, and members of other new movements which challenged the Derg (EPRP, MEISON), were pursued and murdered in the capital and in areas under the control of the Derg. Those who managed to flee to Tigray survived, and it took them a while to reorganize.[10] On 18 February 1975, in a place called Dedebit in Shire, the TNO changed its name to TPLF. They declared their struggle 'Second Woyane,' namely, the continuation of the 1943 revolt against Haile Selassie, which was—as described above—quelled with the help of the British. The Woyane, to reiterate, was a spontaneous popular revolt in the name of Tigrayan identity led mainly by low-ranking village chiefs and peasants. The choice of the name was to the point, and the TPLF and its members would be known as Woyane to this day. But the practicalities were much more difficult. How to re-enliven the old Tigrayan pride and turn the dispirited and impoverished locals into effective fighters? In essence, there were two ways pursued by the emerging TPLF. Their combination made the movement capable of toppling Mangistu in 1991.

One way was to connect old Tigray to the revolutionaries in Eritrea; to join forces with the fellow Tigrinya speakers of the EPLF.

After the fall of Aman Andom in Addis Ababa, and the failure of his effort to appease the Eritreans (in November 1974), the Eritrean liberation fronts gained momentum. The ELF, however, despite also including many Tigrayan fighters, was reluctant to join hands with the emerging TPLF. The ELF was led mostly by Muslims (notably Ahmad Nasir), who were still oriented on creating an Arab Eritrea. In contrast, the EPLF Christian Tigrayan core, led by Isayas, was happy to host the pioneers of the TPLF, and supply and train them in modern guerrilla. Also, the EPLF acted for the Tigrayans as a model of how to build a 'liberation front.' Already in November 1974, members of the TNO met secretly with EPLF leaders in Asmara, and in January 1975, the first fighters from Tigray began training in Eritrea. No less importantly, the TPLF members clarified to their hosts that they did not oppose the creation of a separate Eritrean state, as the two movements joined hands to defeat the Derg. Old intra-Tigrayan rivalries from the days of Ras Alula and Ras Walda-Mikael were shelved, for a while. In 1984, the TPLF and the EPLF broke relations, but in early 1988, they began to cooperate again. Thus, a combined force of a 'greater Tigray' was created. Yet no 'greater Tigray' would be reconstituted after their common 1991 victory.

The other road for the TPLF victory was in its leading of a comprehensive revolution in Tigray proper.

As mentioned, Tigray in the early 1970s was still not much different in many respects to the Tigray of medieval times. Ras Mangasha Seyum, the great grandson of emperor Yohannes and the governor of Tigray till the 1974 revolution, fled from the Derg-controlled capital to Shire in Tigray, where he helped to found the Ethiopian Democratic Union (EDU). It was a conservative and pro-monarchy movement consisting mainly of heads of old landowning families and high-ranking, displaced army officers, as well as non-Tigrayan monarchists and liberals. The EDU, headquartered in Sudan, had some initial military successes in Western Tigray and Bagemdir. But the old imperial guard of Tigray was no longer able to mobilize the masses. The EDU, also torn by internal splits, withdrew from the anti-Derg armed struggle by 1978. For a while, it stayed active among Ethiopian communities abroad, and Ras Mangasha, in exile, remained the last living monument to Emperor Yohannes. The image of Yohannes, the greatest Tigrayan, would be re-enlivened as a symbol of past glory, but not before the young students of the TPLF, mostly sons of middle-class urban dwellers, would lead a revolution in Tigray.

How did a group of young students, raised on a complex of theoretical ideologies, regarded by the peasantry as educated yet unsophisticated radicals, manage to restore Tigray? To bring life to a destroyed province? To re-enliven its old potential by mobilizing its impoverished peasants, turning them into an effective army just like in Tigray's old days? In June 1975, the TPLF had about 50 fighters, but in May 1991, at the gates of Addis Ababa, it had some 80,000 well-trained and well-armed fighters, and a total number of members of more than 100,000.

A full answer requires a multi-faceted story; we can only mention some of its dimensions.

All throughout those years, there was held an ideological debate in the TPLF leadership, combined with a personal power game. Ideas stretched from an Albanian-style isolationism to a Tigrayan–Ethiopian identity, etc. Discussions, always couched in Marxist terminology, were held in caves and in fighters' conferences. The first such conference, held on 18 February 1976, elected committees and their heads. Aregawi Berhe was elected as chairman, and Meles Zenawi became head of the political cadre school. The first 'TPLF regular congress' was held in February 1979, and in July 1985, in a new congress, a Marxist-Leninist

League of Tigray (MLLT) was declared, which dominated the movement. Consequently, Aregawi Berhe and other co-founders were purged, and Meles Zenawi became the dominant figure.

Alongside the power struggle among the establishers, there developed their dialogue with the masses. In this, the young leaders were inspired much by old Soviet practices, as well as Chinese and Vietnamese models, accommodated with Tigrayan traditions and culture.

Aregawi Berhe, who lost power in 1985, left for Holland, where he produced a Ph.D. thesis published in 2009: 'A Political History of the Tigray People's Liberation Front (1975–1991).' He analyzed four aspects of the revolution led by the TPLF.

First, the establishment of farmers' associations and People's Assemblies to replace traditional rural governance by the village elderly. TPLF members—he wrote—went to churches, funerals, and markets to encourage farmers to join peasant associations and prepare for land reform. They combated suspicion by presenting themselves as the 'sons and daughters of Tigray,' organized an apparatus of cadres and meetings, in which collective pressure was applied to show loyalty through 'self-criticism' and to silence opposition.

Second, the implementation of land reform. On the eve of the revolution, it was estimated that 25 per cent of farmers had little to no land, 45 per cent of farmers had less than 1 hectare, 23 per cent owned between ½–1 hectare, and 21 per cent owned 1–2 hectares. The TPLF abolished the highly disproportionate old system, and also divided land among urban groups, consolidating its political base both in the city and the countryside.

Third, the introduction of youth and women's organizations. In order to arm rural youth, TPLF raised the age of marriage to 26 for men and 22 for women. In traditional Tigray, only married couples could obtain land. Due to the reform, young people were freed from obligations to land and family and became reserves of the new soldiery. In the meetings, they were trained to shout, 'I want to fight for Tigray!' and 'I'm going to join the TPLF army!' Those who remained reluctant were labeled 'opportunists' and consequently marginalized. The TPLF closed state schools in towns and cities and set up its own schools to mobilize more of the youth. Moreover, the TPLF criminalized sexual violence, and as a result, approximately one third of the TPLF fighters were women.

Fourth, the use of religion. The TPLF, in spite of the revolutionary rhetoric, was cautious not to antagonize the Church. It placed religious and social activities under the control of the People's Assembly (*baitos*) but did not undermine the church's grassroots economic base. In a highly traditional society, and considering Tigrayans' strong Christian heritage, the TPLF managed to win the masses based on religious tolerance, which was also exercised towards Tigrayan Muslims.

The three revolutions—in Ethiopia's center, in Eritrea, and in Tigray—resulted with a long war in northern Ethiopia, which lasted till 1991. Global developments had an impact. The Soviets, who, since 1977, had been behind Mangistu, supporting his army and inspiring his methods, were facing demise. In November 1987, in Moscow, they told Mangistu they could no longer finance his endless military campaigns. The following March 1988, at Afabet in Eritrea, the EPLF scored a major victory over the Ethiopian army. In April, the EPLF and TPLF resumed full military cooperation. By February 1989, the whole of Tigray was practically in TPLF hands. Six months later, the Tigrayans, with some help from the Eritreans, penetrated Shoa. They would take Addis Ababa at the end of May 1991.

It was during those years in the late 1980s that the TPLF leadership had to readdress the old Tigrayan dilemma and face the historical questions we have followed throughout this book. Namely, were they fighting for Tigray proper? For a Greater Tigray? For a Greater Ethiopia?

Both practically and theoretically, the answer is clear. It was for Ethiopia.

In January 1989, the Ethiopian People's Revolutionary Democratic Front (EPRDF) was formed by the TPLF. It included other groups: the Ethiopian People's Democratic Movement (EPDM), the Oromo People's Democratic Organization (OPDO), and the Ethiopian Democratic Officers' Revolutionary Movement (EDORM), which consisted largely of captured officers from the

Ethiopian army. In 1991, after the fall of Mangistu, the EPRDF, joined now by more bodies representing more ethnic groups, would lead Ethiopia until December 2019.

Meles Zenawi was the man behind the establishment of this all-Ethiopian movement. He would be the chairman of the ruling party and leader of Ethiopia until his death in 2012. Meles was also the man behind the ideological change from an isolationist Tigrayan, Marxist-Leninist revolution to the all-Ethiopian revolution which he led after 1991.

In April 1990, already in control of Tigray, in cooperation with Isayas' EPLF, and confident he would topple Mangistu, Meles went to Washington. He met there with Paul Henze, formerly a member of the US National Security Council, a senior CIA agent, and a prominent scholar and historian of Ethiopia. Henze left a detailed memorandum of their conversation. He concluded that Meles wanted to shed his image as a devout Marxist and Tigrayan isolationist. That Meles preferred that Eritrea remain associated with Ethiopia but understood and accepted that Isayas would declare independence. That Meles had no sympathy for Arabs and feared their designs on Ethiopia. That Meles was well-informed on what was happening in the world and had no illusions about the crisis into which the Soviet Union, and communist governments supported by it, were falling. Also, that Meles was abandoning Marxist/populist formulas that up until recently seem to have prevailed in TPLF thinking. That they conceived the creation of a decentralized Ethiopian federation rather than what they considered a 'Shoan–Amhara' dictatorial centralism. [11]

12

RESTORED HEGEMONY, INTER-TIGRAYAN WAR

On 28 May 1991, as the Derg's army was collapsing, and a few days after Mangistu fled from the country, the EPRDF units—actually, the TPLF—entered Addis Ababa. For the first time since the death of Emperor Yohannes 102 years earlier, Tigrayans returned to dominate the country. Meles Zenawi would be the strong leader of Ethiopia until his death in 2012, and the EPRDF would be the ruling party till 2019. In the same year (1991), Eritrea was fully liberated from the remnants of Mangistu's army, and the new state of Eritrea was officially declared in 1993. Isayas Afaworqi, the leader of the victorious EPLF (later PFDJ) would rule Eritrea to this day (2023). Thus, Tigrinya speakers, the representatives of the historic 'greater Tigray,' again led the greater Horn of Africa, and did so for the next three decades. It was a period of rising expectations and some major achievements for Ethiopia, albeit much less for Eritrea. Also, in line with long history, this period saw rising inter-Tigrayan animosity and a costly war.

Meles Zenawi—Back to the 'Tigrayan thesis'

The year 1991 was marked by the collapse of the Soviet bloc and the heralding of global changes. In Ethiopia, in late May, TPLF forces entered Addis Ababa and Meles Zenawi was declared president, then prime minister in 1995. Until his death in 2012 (of cancer, at fifty-seven years old), he led what can be defined as one of the deepest transformations Ethiopia ever experienced. In a way, he was guided by the historical 'Tigrayan thesis,' in a renewed version. Meles and his people challenged the old Amhara concept of a centralized unity, and rebuilt Ethiopia—like in the days of Yohannes—as a federation. Under Yohannes, to reiterate, Shoa and Gojjam were kingdoms, while Eritrea was practically ruled by Ras Alula. This time, Ethiopia was reconstructed as a federation of nine 'ethnic states.'

The new leaders of the EPRDF claimed to open politics, lead a multi-party system, and allow an active press. They also claimed to open culture to local traditions, and to open economy to market rules mixed with governmental involvement. The changes they introduced, and arguably enforced, were exposed to various oppositional forces, occasional crises, and inevitable failures. One of the controversial changes, for example, was the annexation in 1991 of the strategically important region of Walqait to the 'Tigray State,' a change that has been widely criticized ever since.

Ethiopia was also exposed to the social pains of quick economic growth. Population expanded quickly throughout those decades, and ambitious politicians followed the long Ethiopian tradition of protest, often more aggressive in their words than in their deeds. Under Meles, Ethiopia also opened up to the West, the USA, Europe, China, other Asian countries of dynamic economies, and the Middle East and Africa.

All of these points must be taken in relative terms, and against the background of the past; distant and near. In 1991, Ethiopia was one of the world's poorest and most miserable countries, and her people were oppressed beyond hope.

Like many personalities who left a mark on their time, Meles Zenawi was and would remain controversial. He surely had an impact on major developments, and aroused mixed feelings. On the one hand, Meles was extremely talented individual. While leading complex political changes, he had the time to obtain a master's degree in business administration from the British Open University (1995), along with another master's in economy from a Dutch university (2004). He was a tireless reader of scholarly books including on the history of Egypt and wrote all sorts of programs and platforms. Meles had endless hours of discussions with academicians from all over the world, among whom he remained controversial.[1] Meles was ever ready to demonstrate his intellectual superiority over others, especially fellow Ethiopians. He was tough, sometime merciless, showing little grace to those he considered corrupt and inefficient. Meles was not graceful enough to enable a state funeral to arguably one of the greatest Ethiopians, Emperor Haile Selassie, who had been murdered by Mangistu in 1975 (his bones were found and exhumed in 1992). Only a religious ceremony was held in a modest funeral in 2000.[2] Meles' strong personality was perhaps needed to lead Ethiopia into a hopeful future. We shall turn below to his courage to conceive the Grand Ethiopian Renaissance Dam (GERD) on the Blue Nile— arguably his major achievement.

Meles' sudden death in August 2012 left Ethiopia different than the country he and his colleagues had freed from Mangistu in 1991. After centuries of the imperial ethos of divine rulers, and after seventeen years of brutal communist centralism, Ethiopia was rebuilt on the principles of ethnic diversity and the politics of a federation. It was divided into nine 'states,' each with autonomous authority in cultural, educational, linguistic, and local administrative spheres. The new federalism was also introduced because the various regional liberation fronts, which fought against Mangistu and developed all along the struggle as vital movements, had spontaneously emerged along ethnic lines.[3] But the concept of federalism was well entrenched in Tigrayan history and culture, as interpreted by the youngsters of the TPLF during their 1980s revolution in Tigray.

Meles and his men did not follow the legacy of Tigray's old aristocracy. Rather, they were inspired by Ras Alula,[4] Alula, to reiterate, was (like most of them) a son of a common Tigrayan family. He was an ambitious kid from a remote village who managed to become Yohannes' right hand in defending Ethiopia during 1875–96. Alula defeated the invading Egyptians in 1875–6, then the Sudanese Mahdists and the Italians. He turned Asmara into his capital and controlled Eritrea (then the Mareb Melash), thus enabling the restoration of a Greater Tigray for a while. However, as political power shifted to the Amharic speakers, as Tigray was marginalized, and as Eritrea was colonized, so faded the memory of Alula. But young Meles Zenawi did not forget and made Alula his hero. He and the leadership of the TPLF recounted Alula's story around bonfires at nights. They named the units which finally entered Addis Ababa and caused Mangistu to flee, 'the Ras Alula Division.' Alula, in his time, had little respect for the Egyptians, as did Meles. While Haile Selassie was fearful of Nasser, and while Mangistu resorted to empty threats when referring to Sadat, Meles Zenawi never hesitated to confront Mubarak. In their meetings, the Egyptian president avoided speaking about the Nile. Meles, for his part, advised him angrily to study relevant history.[5]

Meles' supporters maintained that for the first time in history, Ethiopia was led by a leader, not ruled by a ruler, and that Meles enabled the ethnic diversity to express itself in a new representative politics. His opponents countered by saying that the whole system he introduced rested on the dictatorial power of a small and armed ethnic minority—the Tigrayans. Moreover, they argued that the Tigrayans only pretended to safeguard a parliamentarian regime while resorting to terrorist methods. They spoke about the frequent arrests of journalists, proved or alleged corruption, forging elections, and especially what they observed as the failure of ethnic federalism to provide stability and democracy. Here we are not in position to discuss all that.[6] Economically, however, what is beyond dispute is that since 1991 the country had made huge steps forward. From the very beginning, Meles declared that the whole new structure would be based on inter-regional economic inter-dependency, and that the federal system would be glued together by a free market economy. Though as a youngster, Meles was a devout Marxist, he matured into a strong believer in emancipating the peasants from the governmental yoke. The government, he maintained, should take care of infrastructure and of supplying water and electricity, not forcing agricultural policy. He was especially committed to the welfare of the northerners and of the dwellers of the periphery, as well as to governmental initiatives regarding the Grand Ethiopian Renaissance Dam (GERD) on the Blue Nile.

The success of the new economy was connected to the growing involvement of Muslims, some one half of the entire population. In the past, Muslims were discriminated against under the Christian imperial domination. Under Mangistu's dictatorship, they were declared officially equal. However, as being mostly traders, entrepreneurs, and owners of small urban businesses, they suffered from the harsh communist system no less than others. The revolution led by Meles made them active partners in nearly everything. Muslims, it can be stated, in spite of die-hard prejudices, became equal citizens and active partners in the economic momentum (Ras Alula, to reiterate, promoted good relations with the Muslim traders of Massawa and Eritrea, in spite of Yohannes' anti-Islamic policy.) It seems that the overwhelming majority of Muslims do identify with Ethiopia, sharing its culture and languages. Yet not a few (especially young) Muslims were influenced by the politicization of Islam in the Middle East. Arabic is being gradually spread, connecting various Islamic communities in Ethiopia and in neighboring countries. On the whole, however, it also seems that the destruction inflicted in Arab countries by Islamic militancy worked to sober up many in Ethiopia. Under Meles, Ethiopia opened up to the Middle East and built relations of mutual benefit with some Arab countries and Israel. She also assumed an important role in combatting terrorism inspired by militant Islam, and for that purpose was not deterred from invading Somalia in 2006. Relations with African states, heavily damaged under Mangistu, were restored, and Meles was regarded in the West as a model for a new kind of African progressive leadership.[7]

Isayas Afafworqi—From liberation hero to refugee exporter

The more Ethiopia opened up to the world and to herself, Eritrea closed to her own diversity. It was one of history's paradoxes. Prior to the 1990s, Eritrea had been the cradle of political modernization in the entire region, while Ethiopia deteriorated from imperial anachronism to Stalinist dictatorship. But as Mangistu's regime began falling apart, Isayas' EPLF was transforming into a totalitarian movement.

After its 1987 Second Congress, the EPLF, hitherto based on volunteers, resorted to forceful general conscription, which directly impacted the democratization process. Following independence, Isayas became the undisputed ruler of Eritrea, practically kidnapping any hope of open politics. In February 1994, the Third Congress of the EPLF renamed itself the People's Front for Democracy and Justice (PFDJ), as if transforming from a military organization into a civilian party. Optimist Eritreans in exile began returning home and tried to contribute to political progress and developing economy. Professor Bereket Habta-Selassie worked on drafting a new constitution. Others returned from their campuses in the West to the new Asmara University. But by the mid-1990s they were all practically silenced. Isayas, it became apparent, refused to transform from a national hero into a leader of a poor, developing state. He did not tolerate those who were schooled in the west, when he and his men fought in the bush. He rather cultivated his personal cult as a soldier in sandals. For keeping a mobilized society, Isayas did his best to pick all sorts of conflicts with neighbors: with Egypt on fishing rights, with Sudan, Saudi Arabia, and Jibouti on hosting his former ELF exiled enemies, with Yemen on islands in the Red Sea.

With Ethiopia, now under the TPLF, it first seemed to be better. The two Tigrayan-led states began enjoying reasonably good relations. Meles and Isayas conducted a sober dialogue, and it was even rumored that they had some family connection. In Addis Ababa, as an observer, Isayas attended the process towards the establishment of the Ethiopian federation. In May 1993, following the official declaration of Eritrea's independence, Meles was invited to Asmara as a guest of honor. The two states established diplomatic relations, opened embassies, and agreed on mutually beneficial economic ties. The Ethiopian Birr remained the currency in Eritrea, and the Eritrean port of Assab remained a gate for Ethiopia. Ethiopian embassies throughout the world hosted Eritrean diplomats. Some observers even believed that one day Eritrea would rejoin federal Ethiopia in one form or another. It was not to be.

After independence, Isayas insisted on the separation of the Eritrean church from the Ethiopian one. In the past, the churches remained united, even under the Fascist conquest and the British administration in Eritrea. In September 1993, with Meles' acceptance, the heads of the Ethiopian church agreed with the bishop of Eritrea on separation, and in September 1994, five Eritrean monks were ordained as bishops by the Coptic patriarch in Cairo. In May 1998, they elected the first patriarch of the new independent Eritrean church.

Meanwhile, at Isayas initiative, the economic relations deteriorated. Ethiopia's coffee export through the Eritrean port of Assab was controlled by Asmara. At first, the Eritreans paid for the Ethiopian coffee, packed it anew, and exported it under their name. The Ethiopian government swallowed the insult until late 1997, when the Eritreans issued their own currency, the Nakfa, and insisted paying Ethiopia with it. Amid the negotiations of what was still an isolated issue, in May 1998, the Eritrean army invaded the town of Badame and claimed it was an Eritrean territory during the time of the Italian colony (1890–1941). New studies on old maps show a complex picture, but it was never an issue prior to the sudden invasion. UN investigation committees would rule that it was a matter of one-sided unprovoked aggression. The ensuing war lasted two years, till June 2000, and it was cruel throughout. At first it was like a World War I trench war, but gradually Ethiopian quantitative advantage tipped the scale. The Ethiopians penetrated Eritrean territory on 12 May 2000 and then pulled back. Estimates of casualties on both sides exceeded 70,000. After a December 2000 agreement, a UN observers force was stationed in the disputed area, on the Eritrean side. In April 2002, a UN committee ruled that the Eritreans were the aggressors, but Badame should return to Eritrea. Ethiopia refused to accept this ruling and blamed Eritrea in subverting Ethiopia and helping terrorists, Muslims and others, in Ethiopia and in Somalia.

By the time the 1998–2000 war broke out, the Eritreans, naturally, were long cementing their nationalism by invoking old historical chapters. Some of the history we narrated above was interpreted by the ELF leaders as an ancient struggle between Muslim Arabs and Ethiopian Christians. For the Tigrayans of the EPLF, their modern Eritreanism was anchored in the medieval periods of Medri Bahri and the autonomy which had been enjoyed by Hamasen, Seray, and Akkle Guzay. As the TPLF embraced Ras Alula, the EPLF embraced Ras Walda Mikael, the last leader of Hamasen, whom Alula deposed and destroyed in 1879 when assuming control of the future Eritrea. It was narrated above (chapter 5) and is now readdressed.

The first to reintroduce Ras Alula to the new war in Eritrea was Mangistu. For the Ethiopian dictator, Alula was a warrior against imperialism in Eritrea. Mangistu named the airport in Maqale after Alula, and in Dogali he built a monument in the site of Alula's 1887 victory over the Italians. For the EPLF, however, Alula was rather a brutal colonialist, who exploited the poor locals while reaping glory for himself. They remembered Alula for the massacre of the Kunama and the Baria and quoted popular poems on his cruelty. Most of all, they remembered him for tricking Ras Walda Mikael and sending him in chains to a prison in Tigray. When, in 1989, the fighters of the EPLF liberated Dogali, they blasted the monument of Alula.[8]

In November 1999, in the midst of the renewed war, now against a TPLF-led Ethiopia, Isayas saw into the republication and distributing in Eritrea of a Tigrinya language book, 'The History of Ras Walda Mikael,' by Yishak Yosief. The Eritrean journalist Mebrahtu Asfaha summarized its message: to bring 'numerous examples ... of the vices, meanness, dishonesties, hypocrisies and trickery in the life of Tigray...' And that, 'the grandiose of all tricksters is none other than [Ras] Alula, who through his sweet tongue of peace deceived the hero of Mareb Melash – Ras Walda-Mikael ... the Hero of Mareb Melash [Eritrea], Ras Walda-Mikael ... was a man of faith, integrity, and promise, whereas, Alula of Tigray was a dishonest and disloyal man... It is only in light of this deceitful attitude practiced from south of the Mareb River can we understand why Eritreans are apprehensive of a dialogue [with Tigrayans]... Therefore, most Eritreans will say we will judge our neighbors from the south of Mareb River not simply in the basis of what they say ... given their long history of deceit...'[9]

As of 1998, Meles became in Eritrea like the villain Ras Alula, and Isayas, the redeemer of the conquered Walda Mikael, the faithful final leader of nineteenth-century Eritrea. Indeed, after the 1998–2000 war, it seemed that there would hardly be some reconciliation between the Tigrayans of Eritrea and their fellow Tigrayans of Tigray.

A frustrated Eritrean in exile described in 2015 the consequences in Eritrea of the 1998–2000 war with Ethiopia.[10]

'This was the President's war [Isayas'] with the anticipation of great victory therefore great honor for the President; but the defeat, the loss – human and material – and shame was every Eritreans'; it was national... The President's action and inaction in regard to the renewed war with Ethiopia set Eritrea in an uncontrollable motion of catastrophic paralysis and indefinite suspension of all the initial steps taken towards democratization ... reducing the country into ultimately a primary producer of refugees in Africa and number two world-wide only surpassed by Syria, a country in a full fledged civil war. Complete and absolute dictatorship reigned since, with any person suspected of harboring sympathy with the reformers or showing any political opposition arrested and left to rot in the prisons that mushroomed too fast for such a small nation.'

13

THE GRAND DAM

THE LEGACY OF MELES ZENAWI

Meles Zenawi emerged stronger at home from the 1998–2000 war with Eritrea. He would emerge even stronger from the Ethiopian 2006 preemptive invasion of the Islamic militant Somalia, a war which ended in 2008. Meles became an authoritative leader and a disputed figure. Many admired him for pushing the country momentously forward. Others criticized him for being arrogant, and for his general policy, notably the ethnic federalism. Amhara-centrists blamed him as a dictator whose influence rested on fixing elections and on the power of an armed minority. His supporters argued that he was actually the first leader of Ethiopia, not her ruler, and that his achievements in all fields—economic, education, freedoms, openness to the world—were by far greater than his failures.

It is beyond our scope here to address all related issues. However, we can focus on one important aspect: laying the foundations for the Grand Ethiopian Renaissance Dam (GERD). As of 2023, this enterprise is still not entirely finished. It was envisioned and carried out in the spirit of Tigray's tradition of courage and defiance at home as well as in external affairs.

If the GERD fulfils its promise, we may state, it would be a historical turning point comparable to that of the 1896 victory of Adwa. Adwa—the result of Menelik's unification, solidification, and early modernization—introduced Ethiopia to the twentieth century as an independent state. The GERD, once completed, would potentially introduce the country to the twenty-first. If it does, it would be the legacy of the years under Meles Zenawi.

Menelik, Haile Selassie, Mangistu—Negligence

Even though, as asserted by the World Bank in 1997, 'the waters of the Blue Nile probably constitute Ethiopia's greatest asset for development,'[1] until Meles, nothing in Ethiopia's long history was actually done about it.

The Blue Nile is the main tributary of the greater Nile River. It contributes nearly four fifths of the waters that give life to downstream Egypt. A long story of mutual dependency between the two countries has developed from medieval times. Ethiopia was the source of Egypt's water. Egypt was the source of patriarchal legitimacy for Ethiopia's Christian political system. By tradition, the Church of Ethiopia was a bishopric of the Egyptian Coptic Church. The *Abuna*, the head of the Ethiopian Church, was for sixteen centuries an Egyptian monk appointed and anointed by the Coptic patriarch and sent to Ethiopia. Thus, each side had a leverage on the other. The Egyptians feared that the Ethiopians would block the Nile, while the Ethiopians feared that the Egyptians would deny them their bishop. A balance of futile threats was created, resulting in the Ethiopians doing practically nothing to use the Blue Nile's waters. The great Emperor Menelik II had talks with the British, who, after they conquered Egypt in 1882 and Sudan in 1898, planned an all-Nile water system. In 1902, the British built what was called later the 'small' Aswan Dam in Egypt, intended to regulate Egypt's annual needs. For the whole Nile basin, they envisioned, Ethiopia was to have the central role. The British hoped that the Nile basin's biggest water reservoir would be in Lake Tana, where water could be stored behind a new dam to secure a multi-annual supply. In the heights of Ethiopia, there was little evaporation, little siltation, and potential to produce hydroelectricity for all. In the same year, they approached Emperor Menelik and secured his commitment 'not to construct, or allow to be constructed, any work across the Blue Nile, Lake Tsana, or the Sobat, which would arrest the flow of their waters into the Nile, except in agreement with His Britannic Majesty's Government and the Government of the Soudan.'[2]

However, Haile Selassie did not allow the British to build a dam in Lake Tana. For a permission to build and manage the Tana Dam, London was ready to give Ethiopia a generous annual subsidy, free electricity, and free port in Somaliland. But the Ethiopians had their reasons to believe that once the British set foot in western Ethiopia, they would never leave. When the British left the Nile region in the 1950s and 1960s, no all-Nile water system existed. Rather, a new leadership of young military officers in Egypt hurried to build a super-dam in Egypt, and not for the benefit of all the river's African riparian countries.

The High Dam of Aswan, inaugurated in 1971, was to provide Egypt and Sudan with multi-annual water control. The rest of the Africans, notably Ethiopia, were ignored.[3] Haile Selassie responded by cutting the historical relation between the churches of Ethiopia and Egypt. On 28 June 1959, he attended a ceremony in Cairo's main church, during which the Coptic patriarch recognized the Ethiopian *abuna* as a patriarch, his equal. Thus, the Ethiopian Church became fully independent.

Instead of confronting Nasser, the emperor invited various American experts to survey the Blue Nile. They submitted reports from 1957. The US Bureau of Reclamation performed a thorough investigation of the hydrology of the upper Blue Nile basin. The American study contained a list of twenty-six potential projects within Ethiopia, including preliminary designs of four dams for irrigation and hydroelectric power along the Blue Nile and Atbara River.[4] The detailed survey, in a dozen volumes presented in 1964, was shelved somewhere in the imperial palace. It remained untouched for forty years.[5]

The military dictator Mangistu Haila-Mariam (1974–91) used the idea of an Ethiopian dam to threaten Egypt. But as he turned

Ethiopia into a theater of endless fratricidal wars, he could build nothing. Egypt's president, in 1970, Anwar Sadat, was for Mangistu an 'imperialist aggressor,' who wanted to conquer Lake Tana. The Ethiopian ruler exchanged threats with Egypt and promised that the Soviets, 'the people who built the Aswan dam for the Egyptian fellahin, they will assist the Ethiopian masses in the same way they assisted the Egyptian masses nearly a generation ago.'[6] By 1991, after both Mangistu and the USSR had collapsed, nothing had been done about the Blue Nile.

Mubarak and Toshka

Meles Zenawi and President Husni Mubarak of Egypt (1981–2011) shared the same international orientation, along with similar interests in regional stability. Their dialogue about the Nile, however, was leading nowhere. Mubarak remained convinced that the great river belongs only to Egypt. In January 1997, his government announced a new ambitious enterprise, the Toshka Canal, 'the greatest engineering project in the Arab world.' It included digging a 240-kilometer canal from Lake Nasser in a northwestern direction to the oases of Farafra and Kharj. 'The biggest water pump in the world' was to pump water for eighteen new towns and hundreds of small new settlements in the desert. 'The New Valley' or the 'New Civilization,' as Mubarak liked to call it, was to populate some 7 million inhabitants by 2017, and then develop to be the home of some one fifth of Egypt's population. The total cost was estimated at 88 billion USD. Mubarak recruited investors from the Gulf Emirates, and the canal was to be named after Shaykh Zayd of Abu Dhabi.

However, the greater the challenge, the greater the failure. The planners were overly optimistic about the engineering problems, the heat of the desert, the quality of the soil, and the financial cost. In 2005, it was announced that fulfillment of the first stage would be delayed until 2022. Then, in 2012, following the fall of Mubarak, the whole enterprise was shelved. At that time, Shaykh Zayd Canal was sixty kilometers short of its goal, and only a few thousand acres were reclaimed (the declared goal was 2 million).[7]

The 'Death of the Nile'?

By the time the Toshka project was shelved, the Nile River could no longer fulfill such expectations. In the great basin of the African river, riparian populations grew, and the river's waters subsided. Due to climate changes, the Nile was losing its vitality. Global warming led to increased evaporation of water into the atmosphere and changed the patterns of airstreams and ocean currents. This in turn altered the distribution of precipitation. Some regions in the river's basin had begun experiencing greater rainfall and flooding, while others became more prone to droughts. Climate change is affecting livelihoods in many parts of the world, and is expected to continue to do so in the future. In parts of the Middle East and Africa, social and political structures were directly affected, and so too were the children of the greater Nile basin.

According to various studies, the all-Nile rate of flow has been falling consistently since 1967. A British journalist who toured the river in 2017 published an alarming article titled: 'Death of the Nile: The world's longest river is sick – and getting sicker.'[8] It provides perhaps an overly alarming photo-finish of the all-Nile situation before the GERD enters the picture. The journalist traveled along the Blue Nile, then from Khartoum to the Mediterranean. He described human suffering, managerial neglect of the river, and deteriorating ecology. Booming populations have dirtied and drained the river, while climate change threatens to cut its flow. The Blue Nile, he concluded, is still vigorous, but as for the White Nile, the picture he paints is far gloomier: 'Though slightly longer, the White Nile carries a fraction of the volume. ... [in Khartoum] the Blue Nile, swollen and colored brown by the Ethiopian rains, roars into the confluence, pushing back for miles its insipid and slightly yellow counterpart...'

Meles Turns to Africa

The first decade of the new millennium was marked by growing Ethiopian anger at what was conceived as Egypt's contempt for the other Nile countries. Some issues were discussed in The Nile Basin

Initiative meetings, but the Egyptians and the Sudanese would not discuss Toshka, nor their 1959 water agreement. The Ethiopians responded by initiating 175 local water projects in the ninety tributaries of the Blue Nile and Lake Tana. Some of these plans did materialize,[9] but they all were of a modest scale that did not really influence the Nile system. Meetings between Meles and Mubarak proved unhelpful. The Ethiopian tried to lecture his host on the history of the Nile, but Mubarak was not interested.[10]

Responding to Mubarak's policy, Meles Zenawi returned to the all-African sphere. On 26 May 2001, the African Union (AU) was established in Addis Ababa, replacing the old OAU and consisting of all fifty-five countries on the continent. The Ethiopian capital hosted now close to 500 embassies, diplomatic missions, and international organizations from all over the world, and became one of the five biggest diplomatic concentrations in the world.[11] Meles and his men also became the living spirit of the Intergovernmental Authority on Development (IGAD), a multinational body founded in 1986 by Djibouti, Ethiopia, Somalia, Sudan, Uganda, and Kenya, with Eritrea joining after gaining her independence in 1993. In 1996, the heads of those states assembled in Addis Ababa to amend the IGAD charter and revitalize the organization. From our point of view, IGAD consisted of many Nile Basin countries (excluding Egypt). In practice, Meles Zenawi acted as de facto chairman of IGAD and the AU.[12]

Deliberations in the Nile Basin Initiative continued, but this time Ethiopia took the lead. In 2007, Ethiopia, Kenya, Uganda, Rwanda, Burundi, and Tanzania agreed on the principle of 'equitable share.' But the Egyptians, insisting on their 'historical rights,'[13] delayed signing the document. In May 2009, a meeting of heads of states was held in Kinshasa. It was decided that no full consensus was necessary to endorse a binding resolution— namely, Egypt and Sudan could not veto a majority decision. The signing of the document was delayed to 14 April 2010, to the next meeting in Sharm el-Sheikh, Egypt. However, in that meeting, Egypt and Sudan opposed three of the articles, notably the one on a binding majority decision. The Egyptians insisted on the validity of the 1959 agreement between them and Sudan, and on their right to veto any decision aimed at changing the status quo.

The meeting in Sharm el-Sheikh created a tense atmosphere. The Egyptian minister Mufid Shihab declared that the Nile issue was a matter of national security; of life and death. Dr. Nasr al-Din Alam, the minister of water resources and irrigation, said that Egypt had 'historical rights' which she maintained for centuries, and would not sign any document undermining them. If other countries would sign a separate agreement, he declared, Egypt would do all that was necessary to safeguard her rights. The Egyptian media followed that line, in some cases even more aggressively. There were also other voices in the Egyptian media calling for restraint: to stop ignoring Egypt's African sisters and turn to water-saving options at home. A month later, on 14 May 2010, in Entebbe, other members of the Nile Basin Initiative, namely Ethiopia, Kenya, Uganda, Rwanda, Burundi, Tanzania, and Congo signed a 'Cooperative Framework Agreement,' which endorsed the principle of 'equitable share.' A spokesman for the Egyptian government responded that Egypt would not join nor sign any agreement harming her 'historical rights.'

In the footsteps of Ras Alula?—*Confronting Egypt*

In July 2010, Meles Zenawi was interviewed by an Egyptian journalist for Egyptian TV. It was a long interview in which Meles was asked to speak to the Egyptian public. The Ethiopian leader made no effort to be nice. At times, he betrayed a touch of anger. Meles spoke with full determination as the Egyptian interviewer seemed almost embarrassed. [14]

The Ethiopian prime minister referred to Egypt's insistence on the status quo, based on her 1929 and 1959 water agreements with Sudan. Egypt, said Meles, is telling Ethiopia to accept them. But these were colonial documents, he stated, reflecting nineteenth-century colonial injustice. At that time, the British imperialists forced upon Africans their ideas of boundaries and their tailored agreements. Today, Meles stated, with a hardly concealed rage, Africans accept the boundaries, not the agreements. The upper

Nile countries, said Meles, will never agree to be excluded from mutual ownership of the river. They will not be ignored any more like beggars. Ethiopia, he went on, was never colonized, and she did not sign off on the colonial agreements about the Nile. Kenya and Uganda now oppose the agreements imposed on them by imperialism. The 1959 agreement is based on the premise that Egypt and Sudan own all the waters of the river, but this is no longer acceptable. Ethiopia, the source of some 85 per cent of the water, is entitled to nothing by that agreement. All riparian countries, Meles reiterated, should create together a new situation from which all would benefit. Egypt still insists on an unfair solution, he said, by which she gets all, even though she contributes nothing.

The main point that Meles repeatedly made was that a 'win-win situation' can be created by building new dams in the upper river. A new Nile system would be beneficial also for the Egyptians and the Sudanese. Meles described it as a no zero-sum game. Storing water in highland Ethiopia, in the deep gorge of the Blue Nile, will increase its quantity by three milliard cubic meters a year. The upper Nile countries' need for irrigation water is little. The flow of water to Egypt and Sudan will not be reduced. Egypt is indeed the gift of the Nile, but Ethiopia also has the right to benefit from the river. She was exposed to horrible famine; more and more Ethiopians are hungry. The Egyptians should recognize the needs of these Ethiopians. The Aswan High Dam exhausted its potential as an electricity producer, while the Blue Nile has an enormous potential at generating electric power. Ethiopia knows that Egypt needs more water for irrigation than herself. She can use the Nile water without harming Egypt.

Meles went on to criticize Egypt's water strategy and the role of the Egyptian media. Alluding to the Toshka Project, he said that Egypt wastes water while Ethiopians die of hunger. Egyptian politicians and journalists, he said, irresponsibly tell the Egyptian public that dams in Ethiopia would hurt Egypt. They exert pressure on international bodies to avoid financing Ethiopian projects. They spread lies and hurt Ethiopia as well as Egypt. No project in Ethiopia is planned to hurt Egypt.

Meles made no effort to resort to diplomatic niceties. The interview lasted forty minutes, during which he did not volunteer even a small smile. The note of optimism was in stating, time and again, that an agreement was inevitable: 'The relations between Egypt and Ethiopia is like a very old marriage, with no possibility of divorce. Like all marriages … it has its ups and downs but it is very solid… Sometime we quarrel sometime we agree … this has been the case for five thousand years … the Nile connected the two countries together. It is impossible to break them apart… Egypt and Ethiopia can eat together, on the basis of the Nile.'

In the modern era, no Ethiopian leader spoke to the Egyptians on the Nile in such self-assured, even blunt language. Meles, to reiterate, was a self-assured Tigrayan, a successor in his eyes of Ras Alula, the man who—as described above—defeated the Egyptians in battles throughout 1875–84 and had little respect for them.

The inauguration of the GERD

The interview with Egyptian television reflected a new reality and opened a new chapter in history. The timing was significant. A year earlier, in October 2009, a group of Ethiopian experts surveyed the Blue Nile area, where the Americans in 1964 had marked as the right place for an all-Nile dam. In July–August 2010, at the time of the interview, more advanced surveys were made in that spot, and in November, a detailed plan was submitted to the prime minister. Meles said nothing of it in the interview. It was all kept in secret till 30 March 2011, a day before a contract was signed with the Italian construction company Salini Costruttori, and three days before the ceremony inaugurating the works on the new dam.

Sometime after assuming leadership, Meles ordered the old American surveys of the Blue Nile be put on a shelf in his office. According to his close adviser, Meles would occasionally spend hours at night with these volumes. These were the surveys done in 1927, 1956–64, and a survey by a German firm presented in 1962. Meles then initiated a secret series of surveys code named 'Operation X.' It resulted with choosing a site some forty kilometers from the Sudanese border. After more studies, he confirmed the choice in 2008. In October 2009 and July–August 2010, more surveys were conducted, and the plan was adopted by the Ethiopian government in November. It remained secret until a month prior to the laying the foundation stone ceremony.[15]

On 2 April 2011, a ceremony was held inaugurating the works on a new Blue Nile Dam. Unlike the Aswan ceremony held fifty years earlier, this was a most modest event. Meles made a dry speech of an appeasing nature to the land of the High Dam. He stated that the whole enterprise would be financed by Ethiopia and would be beneficial to all Nile countries. It would fulfill the principle of 'equitable share,' rescue Ethiopians from a future of hunger, and create a win-win situation to all children of the Nile.'[16]

The Ethiopians planned to complete the enterprise in 2017. The dam was to be 1,800 meters long and 170 meters high, creating Renaissance Lake (*Hedas Hayq*), which would store 63 billion cubic meters of water. An electric station would produce 6,000 megawatts. It would be the biggest station in Africa, capable of also supplying other Nile countries with cheaper electricity.[17] The area around the site was developed. New roads, a new airport, a cement factory, and more. On 28 May 2013, the infrastructure necessary to divert the Blue Nile to enable further progress on the dam was completed.

The GERD and Ethiopia's future

In the early stages, the Ethiopians hoped to finance the whole enterprise, estimated initially at 5 billion USD. By 2013, only 15 per cent of this sum was collected. In April of that year, Ethiopia and the Bank of China signed a billion USD contract to build two power stations which would transfer electricity from the dam to the rest of the country.[18]

By 2018, Ethiopia had begun developing economically in an astonishing pace, enjoying foreign investments and preparing herself to use the electronic revolution which the GERD promised. The country's population, estimated at around 90 million when the project was launched, is predicted to reach 270 million by 2050.

Meles did not survive to see the completion of the dam. In the last years prior to his death, he toyed with the idea of retiring. He said that under his guidance, Ethiopia built solid political institutions, and his authority was needed no more. Indeed, the sudden death of Meles put the new system to test. In Ethiopia's modern times, whenever a ruler died, the political structure he had built collapsed. This was the case with the emperors Tewodros, Yohannes, Menelik, and Haile Selassie. They never managed to transfer power to a designated heir. Mangistu managed to flee, and his entire regime disappeared. Meles was succeeded by Hailemariam Dasalegn, who served as a prime minster until 2018. However, Hailemariam was not an authoritarian leader, but rather a front figure representing the political establishment of the EPRDF. In April 2018, Dr. Abiy Ahmed was elected by the ruling EPRDF as Ethiopia's prime minister. The fact that his father was a Muslim, and his mother was a Christian—he himself a protestant—was hardly an issue. Much more important was the fact that he was an Oromo by ethnicity. In a few months, Abiy made it clear he was not a mere front-figure, but a strong young leader, seeking yet another redefinition of Ethiopia. In a series of daring moves, Abiy made peace with Eritrea, mended fences with other neighbors, released prisoners, and enabled political exiles to return. Moreover, he pushed aside the prominent veterans of the 1991 revolution, including the leading Tigrayans. They returned to their old Tigray to struggle for its old autonomy. The all-out war which consequently began in November 2020—a new chapter in the ancient Ethiopian tension between the ethos of centralization and the reality of diversity—is still raging (2023).

The GERD is the inheritance of the Tigrayan revolutionary Meles Zenawi. It is one enterprise around which there is an all-Ethiopian consensus. Any transformation of Ethiopia, any new kind of political system, any hope for economic progress, can hardly succeed and be fulfilled if it fails. The GERD is not only a dam—it is the cornerstone of twenty-first-century Ethiopia.

NON-CONCLUSION

'THE THEORY OF DISINTEGRATION' AND THE 'GRAND DAM'

Approaching the end of writing, I had the feeling of composing a requiem. Tigray was again marginalized in 2018, and in November 2020, it was invaded by the central Ethiopian army, as well as by Eritrean forces. Once again, Tigray was devastated, starving, decimated. It all seemed like a tragic end to a two-millennia story. Then, as if rising from the ashes, Tigrayan forces, reorganized in a mountainous corner of the region, launched an offensive. They called it 'Ras Alula Operation.' As these lines are written, the conflict is still raging. Another vicious circle in the history narrated above is being reopened. It seems that the future of Ethiopia, and possibly also of Eritrea, will be shaped once more by the outcome of the current Tigrayan drama.

From the days of ancient Aksum, Tigray has been the gate and the wall. Sometimes, it was the very heart; always an integral part of Ethiopia. In the preface to this book, we mentioned discussion in the 1940s between British political officers.; those in Asmara wanted to tear Tigray from Ethiopia and annex it to Eritrea, and those who opposed it. I quoted Colonel R. E. Cheesman, who thought that Ethiopian integrity—including Tigray—would survive. He explained that 'the crazy structure of the Ethiopian Empire' was 'held together by a mysterious magnetism, which is incomprehensible to one who has no more than a superficial knowledge of Ethiopia.'

Today, some eighty years after Cheesman wrote these wise lines, the question of Ethiopia's integrity is again in the air. But the ancient 'magnetism' he was referring to is hardly there. Gone is the institute of emperorship sanctioned by political Christianity. Gone are the regional feudal hierarchies based on traditional loyalties; the priests who could and would make peace between fellow believers; the shared old sense of uniqueness inspired by ancient cultural heritage and fed by early modern victories. Most of the old 'mysterious' formula was destroyed by the revolution of 1974–91, by Colonel Mangistu and the Derg officers. They worked to replace Ethiopia's traditional world with crude Marxist materialism, and with Leninist-Stalinist brutality. This combination bore no new 'magnetism.'

The period from 1991 to 2018 brought new hopes. Dozens of regional universities created new layers of schooled youth, including young women. Muslims began to participate actively in a quickly developing economy. Local regional identities were revived in a federal all-Ethiopian framework. But the promise was hardly fulfilled. The new system contributed to the re-strengthening of ethnic tensions, rising economic expectations, often illusionary, growing frustrations, and socioeconomic pains. All of these resurfaced strongly in the current crisis.

What indeed would restore the 'magnetism' that may again hold Ethiopia together?

Many scholars address the question. The main issue, of course, is ethnicity and Ethiopianness (Ethiopiawinet). Some offer relevant theoretical discussions on ethnicity and nationalism—others, on ethnic federalism as an experiment in state building. A rich literature combining theoretical aspects with factual observations has been produced.[1] Studying for this book, I did my best to delve into this literature, but I limited my writing to narrating what I understood as the relevant long history. For me, history is the great teacher. She is wiser, especially if she is old like Ethiopia's. I try to be a student of her complex development.

Re-examining a two-millennia story, I went in the footsteps of an old school of Ethiopianists: those who followed what Christopher Clapham called the 'Great Tradition.'[2] Namely, the focusing on the central highlands as the main representative of Ethiopian long history. Surely and admittedly, what I have produced is just one dimension of the all-Ethiopian story, which, especially in the late nineteenth century, is much richer, wider, and more diverse.[3]

Against the background of what is narrated above, it can be stated that ethnic politics in Ethiopia is not an 'experiment.' Ethnic identities—ever combined with power politics, regional traditions, linguistic and cultural heritages, and sociopolitical dynamism—have been an inseparable dimension of a country defined as a 'museum of peoples.' They were ever co-existing and competing with an imperial ethos of religiously sanctioned centralism. For Tigrayans, to generalize and reiterate, ethnicity was a basic concept of Ethiopianness. For Amharic speakers, an all-Ethiopian imperial centralizing unity seemed more natural. But even the greatest of the 'Amhara' emperors knew how to somehow compromise with the country's diversity. The Solomonians with Medri Bahri; Menelik and Haile Selassie with semi-autonomous Tigray (mainly when Tigray was weakened). Where Haile Selassie failed in the ultimate test of compromising—namely, in the case of the 1952–62 federal arrangement with Eritrea—he and his regime paid dearly. Emperor Tewodros, and to distinguish, Colonel Mangistu, ended in disaster by trying to impose centralization.

The opposition movements that failed tried to topple Mangsitu in the name of all-Ethiopian and universal ideologies (EPRP, MUESON, EDU). Those that succeeded represented regional-ethnic forces and ideas: the liberation fronts of Tigray, Oromo, Afar, Somali, etc. They were the products of long histories not necessarily contradictory to Ethiopianness. Ethnicity, combined with class struggles, religious grievances, regional awareness, and more, proved to be a pivotal pillar of Ethiopian history. Ethnicity has been divisive, but also the basis for constructive cooperation. Ethnicity in Ethiopia was never 'an experiment.'

Tigrayans were the flag bearers of decentralism and ethnic federalism. They had their big moments in 1872–89 and 1991–2018. A minority of tough, strong people, who often also fell victim to their own divisiveness, endless rivalries, jealousies, and treacheries. In the days of Yohannes, they lost Asmara and avoided urban development. In the days of Meles Zenawi, they failed to win the hearts of many other groups in Ethiopia. They often proved arrogant and over-ambitious.[4] They could hardly keep power following the sudden death of Meles in 2012.

Still, in my opinion, the key to a restoration of the all-Ethiopian 'magnetism' is the Renaissance Dam. Will it be completed? Will it be the hub of an all-Ethiopian effort? If the gigantic structure on the Blue Nile, the great promise for a better future, will not be the new 'magnet,' what else could hold Ethiopia together?

pp. [3–5]

NOTES

1. PREFACE

   1. FO 371/35626, 'Memorandum on Internal Situation in Ethiopia' by Colonel Cheesman, 17 June 1943.
   2. H. Erlich, *Ethiopia and Eritrea, Ras Alula, 1875–1897*, Michigan State University Press, 1982. Reprint, new preface, Red Sea Press, New Jersey and Asmara 1997. Hereafter: *ER1982*; idem, *The Struggle Over Eritrea, 1962–1978*, Hoover Institution, Stanford, 1983. Hereafter *ER1983*; idem, *Ethiopia and The Challenge of Independence*, Lynne Rienner Press, Boulder, 1986. Hereafter *ER1986*; idem, *Ethiopia and the Middle East*, Lynne Rienner Press, Boulder, 1994. Hereafter *ER1994*; H. Erlich and I. Gershoni (eds.) *The Nile–Histories, Cultures, Myths,* Lynne Rienner Publishes, Boulder 2000; H. Erlich, *The Cross and the River – Ethiopia, Egypt and the Nile*, Lynne Rienner Publishers, Boulder, 2002. Hereafter *ER2002*; Idem, *Ethiopia and Saudi Arabia–Christianity, Islam, and Politics Entwined*, Lynne Rienner Publishers, 2007. Hereafter *ER2007*; Idem, *Islam and Christianity in the Horn of Africa, Somalia, Ethiopia, Sudan*, Lynne Rienner Publishers, 2010. Hereafter *ER2010*; idem, *Alliance and Alienation–Ethiopia and Israel in the Days of Haile Selassie,* Red Sea Press, New Jersey, 2014. Hereafter *ER2014*; idem, *The Crisis of the Nile–Egypt and Ethiopia from Aswan to the Renaissance*, Dayan Center, (in Hebrew) 2016. Hereafter *ER2016*; idem, *Haile Selassie–His Rise His Fall,* Magnes Press, Jerusalem (in Hebrew) Lynne Rienner Publishers, 2019. Hereafter *ER2019* (Amharic version, Eclipse Publishers, Addis Ababa, 2021).

2. INTRODUCTION

   1. For general background and essential data, see W. Smidt, 'Tigray,' S. Uhlig (ed). *Encyclopaedia Aethiopica*, 4, pp. 888–95.

      The five volumes of S. Uhlig (ed). *Encyclopaedia Aethiopica*, Hamburg—vol. 1, 2003 (843pp.); vol. 2, 2006 (1082pp.); vol. 3, 2008 (1211pp.); vol. 4,

2010 (1198pp.); vol. 5, 2014 (1279pp.)—are the result of a collective effort by nearly all members of the relevant academic community. Each article also contains an updated bibliography. An irreplaceable fountain of knowledge.

Hereafter: *EAE 1; EAE 2; EAE 3; EAE 4; EAE 5*.

See also: D. Appleyard, W. Smidt, 'Tegray,' in David Appleyard, Alessandro Bausi, Steven Kaplan, Siegbert Uhlig, Wolfgang Hahn (eds.) *Ethiopia – History, Culture and Challenges*, Hamburg, 2017, pp, 46–50.

2. W. Smidt, 'Hamasen,' *EAE 2*, pp. 987–90; A. Bausi, 'Saraye,' *EAE 4*, pp. 537–9; W. Smidt, 'Akkala Guzay,' *EAE 1*, pp. 166–8; Tsegay Berhe, 'Agame,' *EAE 1*, pp. 137–8; Merid Walda-Aregay, 'Adwa,' *EAE 1*, pp. 105–7; W. Smidt, D. Nosnitsin, 'Sera' [Shire], *EAE 4*, pp. 626–8; Tsegay Berhe, 'Adyabo' *EAE 1*, p. 110; A. Bausi, 'Tamben,' *EAE 4*, pp. 852–3; Sevir Chernestov, 'Endarta,' *EAE 2*, pp. 297–8; Tarekegn Gebreyesus, 'Wajarat,' *EAE 4*, pp. 1,075–6.
3. For a detailed and scholarly analysis see: Sergew Hable Sellassie, *Ancient and Medieval Ethiopian History*, Addis Ababa 1972, Ch. I, 'Ethiopia and the Civilized World,' Ch. II 'The Emergence of the Aksumite Civilization,' Ch. III, 'Turning Points of Ethiopian History' pp. 21–115; Stuart Munro-Hay, 'Aksum,' *EAE 1*, pp. 173–9.
4. For more see also, Alessandro Bausi, H. Erlich, Gianfranco Fiaccadori, Alessandro Gori, 'Red Sea,' *EAE 4*, pp. 345–52.
5. Rainer Voigt, 'Ethio-Semitic,' *EAE 2*, 440–4.
6. E. Ullendorff, *The Ethiopians*, Oxford 1966, p. 36.
7. D. Levine, *Greater Ethiopia*, Chicago 1974, ch. 7.

    Tigrinya speakers call their region Tigray; Amharic speakers refer to it as Tigre. Until 1991 the Amharic version was the official one and was used by most scholars. Today the name of Tigray is adopted by all.
8. On the concept of Zion [the biblical Jerusalem] in Ethiopian Christian thought, and on the identification of Aksum with Zion, see: S. Kaplan, 'Zion,' *EAE 5*, pp. 189–92.

3. 'MEDRI BAHRI'

1. R. Pankhurst, 'Debarwa,' *EAE 2*, pp. 122–3.
2. Taddesse Tamrat, *Church and State in Ethiopia, 1,270–1,527*, Oxford, 1972.
3. See: *ER2002*, ch. 3.
4. Sevir Chernestov, 'Baher Negas,' *EAE 1*, p. 444.
5. A revised translation of Alvares account: C. F. Beckingham and G. W. B. Huntingford, *The Prester John of the Indies*, Cambridge, 1961.
6. D. Nosnitsin, 'Yeshaq, Baher Negas,' *EAE 5*, pp. 60–61.
7. Chihab ed-Din Ahmed Ben Abd el-Qader ('Arab Faqih), *Futuh al-habasha*, Translated and edited by René Basset, Paris, 1897; Takla-Tsadiq Maquriya, *Yagran Ahmad Warara*, Addis Abba 1974; Franz-Christoph Muth, 'Ahmad b. Ibrahim al-Gazi,' *EAE 1*, pp. 155–58.

8. The description of Miguel de Castanhoso was translated and edited by in R.S. Whiteway, *The Portuguese Expedition to Abyssinia*, London, 1902.
9. Gengiz Orhonlu, *Habesh Eyaleti*, Istanbul 1974; Oliver Schulten, *The Ottoman Time in Africa–Habes Eyalety and Turkiyya, 1500–1884*, A Bibliography, Wuppertal, 2017; Salih Özbaran, *The Ottoman response to European expansion: studies on Ottoman-Portuguese relations in the Indian Ocean and Ottoman administration in the Arab lands during the sixteenth century*, Istanbul, 1994. The following is based also on ER1994, pp. 21–40.
10. W. Smidt, 'Habes,' *EAE 2*, pp. 950–52.
11. J. Miran, E. van Donzel, 'Naib,' *EAE 3*, pp. 1,116–8.
12. W. Smidt: 'Law: Traditional Law Books,' in: *EAE 3*, pp. 516–8. See also the article on the law of Ḥamasen: W. Smidt: 'Ḥəggi Habsəllus Gäräkəstos,' *EAE 3*, p. 10–11; W. Smidt, 'Hamasen,' *EAE 2*, 987–90.
13. H. Erlich, W. Smidt, 'Marab Mellas,' *EAE 3*, pp. 773–5.
14. Bairu Tafla, 'Walda Mikael Salomon,' *EAE 4*, pp. 1105–7.
15. See also: Richard Reid, 'The Trans-Mereb Experience: Perceptions of the Historical Relationship between Eritrea and Ethiopia,' *Journal of Eastern African Studies*, 1, 2007, pp. 238–55.

4. THE ERA OF THE JUDGES

1. E. Ficquet, 'Understanding *Lij* Iyasu through his Forefathers: The Mammedoch *Imam*-s of Wello,' in E. Ficquet and W. Smidt, (eds.) *The Life and Times of Lij Iyasu of Ethiopia, New Insights*, Zurich, 2014, pp. 5–29; E. Ficquet, Hussein Ahmed, 'Wallo,' *EAE*, pp. 1,119–22.
2. E. Ficquet, 'Mammadoch dynasty,' *EAE 3*, pp. 715–7.
3. Tarekegn Gebreyesus Kaba, 'Rayyaa,' *EAE 4*, pp. 341–3.
4. 'Aksum,' UNESCO World Heritage Centre.
5. D. Crummey, 'Rist,' *EAE 4*, pp. 381–2.
6. P. Gilkes, 'The *Restegna* of Tigrai,' Paper delivered to the Conference on Feudalism, Addis Ababa University, May 1976.
7. Zewde Gabre-Sellassie, *Yohannes IV of Ethiopia: A political biography*, Oxford, 1975, pp. 2–3.
8. W. Smidt, 'Salt,' *EAE 4*, pp. 500–3.
9. R. Caulk, 'Firearms and Princely Power in Ethiopia in the Nineteenth Century,' *Journal of African History*, XIII, 4, 1972, pp. 609–30; R. Pankhurst, 'Fire-arms,' *EAE 2*, pp. 547–9.
10. Zewde Gabre-Sellassie, *Yohannes IV*, p. 19.
11. See: Mordechai Abir, *Ethiopia: the Era of the Princes*, London, 1968; Shiferaw Bekele, 'Reflections on the Power Elite of the Wärä Seh Mäsfenate (1786–1853),' *Annales d'Ethiopie*, vol. XV, 1990, pp. 157–79; Idem, 'The State in the Zamana Masafent' in Taddese Beyene, R. Pankhurst, Shiferaw Bekele, *Kasa and Kasa: papers on the lives, times and images of Tewodros II and Yohannes IV (1855–*

1889), Addis Ababa University, 1990; D. Crummey, 'Society and Ethnicity in the Politics of Christian Ethiopia during the Zamana Masafint,' *International Journal of African Historical Studies*, VIII, 2, 1975, pp. 266–78.
12. Bairu Tafla, 'Dajjazmch,' *EAE* 2, pp. 62–3.
13. D. Nosnitsin, 'Ras,' *EAE* 4, pp. 330–1, For Ethiopian titles see: 'Titles, ranks, functions,' *EAE* 5, pp. 580–90.
14. C. C. Rossini, *Canti Popolari Tigrai*, Trübner, 1903, p. 288.
15. J. Abbink, 'Mikael Sehul,' *EAE* 3, pp. 962–4. See also: M. Kropp, 'La théologie au service de la rebellion Chroniques inédites du *ras* Mika'el,' *Orientalia Suecana*, 1992–1993, pp. 126–38.
16. D. Crummey, 'Walda Selasse,' *EAE* 4, pp. 1108–10.
17. Tsegai Berhe, 'Sabagadis Waldu,' *EAE* 4, pp. 430–1.
18. D. Nosnitsin, 'Wube Hayla Maryam,' *EAE* 4. pp. 1169–72.
19. S. Gobat, *Journal of Three Years' Residence in Abyssinia*, London MDCCCXLVII, p. 236.

5. THEIR FINEST HOUR

1. See R. Caulk, 'Bad Men of the Borders: Shum and Shefta in Northern Ethiopia in the 19th Century,' *The International Journal of African Historical Studies*, 1984, pp. 2027; T. Fernyhough, 'Social mobility and dissident elites in northern Ethiopia: the role of banditry, 1900–1969,' in D. Crummey (ed.), *Banditry, Rebellion and Social Protest in Africa*, London, 1986, pp. 151–72.
2. For the whole story, see (among others): Taddese Beyene, R. Pankhurst, Shiferaw Bekele (eds.), *Kasa and Kasa : papers on the lives, times and images of Tēwodros II and Yohannes IV (1855–1889)*, Addis Ababa 1990; Crummey, D., *Priests and Politicians: Protestant and Catholic Missions in Orthodox Ethiopia, 1830–1868,* Oxford 1972; P. Henze, *Layers of Time: A History of Ethiopia*, London, 2000; H. Marcus, *The life and times of Menelik II,* Red Sea Press, 1995; S. Rubenson, *King of Kings, Tewodros of Ethiopia*, Addis Ababa 1966; Bahru Zewde, *A History of Modern Ethiopia, 1855–1991*, London, 2002, pp. 27–42.
3. Zewde Gabre-Sellassie, 'Araya Selasse Demsu,' *EAE 1*, p. 314.
4. I. Orlowska, 'Mircha Walda Kidan,' *EAE* 3. pp. 932–3. See genealogy in Bairu Tafla (ed.), *A Chronicle of Emperor Yohannes IV (1872–1889)*, Wiesbaden, 1977, Introduction, p. 31.
5. E. Sohier, 'Takla-Giyorgis II,' *EAE* 4, pp. 827–9.
6. R. Pankhurst, 'Kirkham, John,' *EAE* 3, p. 409.
7. For more and bibliography, see: Bairu Tafla, 'Yohannes IV,' *EAE* 5, pp. 73–80.
8. Ch. 5 and ch. 6 below are based extensively on *ER1982*: my book, *Ethiopia and Eritrea, Ras Alula, 1875–1897*, Michigan State University Press, 1982, reprint, new preface, Red Sea Press, New Jersey and Asmara, 1997. This book is essentially my London University, School of Oriental and African Studies (SOAS) Ph.D. dissertation, 1973. I had spent 1971–2 studying various primary

sources. They included Ethiopian, Egyptian, Sudanese, British, French, and Italian archival materials. Their list is in said book, pp. 207–9. The references are too numerous and too detailed to be presented in the notes below, but they can easily be traced in the 1982 (1997) book. For the chapters here, I also derived from my articles in *EAE*: 'Alula Engeda,' *EAE 1*, pp 211–23; 'Isma'il,' *EAE 3*, pp. 216–7; 'Mareb Melash', p. 3, pp. 773–5 (with W. Smidt); 'pre-Colonial Eritrea,' *EAE 2*, pp. 358–9; 'Egypt, relations with,' *EAE 2*, pp. 240–6; 'Muhammad Ratib,' *EAE 3*, pp. 1,055–6; 'Mahdists,' *EAE 3*, pp. 657–9; 'Uthman b. Abi Bakr Diqna,' *EAE*, *4*, pp. 1,046–7; 'Kufit, battle of,' *EAE 3*, p. 446; 'Dogali, battle of,' *EAE 2*, pp. 186–7, 'Adwa, Battle of,' *EAE 1*, pp. 107–9.

9. I. Orlowska, 'Re-imagining Empire: Ethiopian Political Culture under Yohannis IV (1872–89),' *Ph.D. thesis at the School of Oriental and African Studies, University of London*, January 2006.
10. The passage on Yohannes' coronation is based on the above-mentioned Ph.D. thesis by Izabela Orlowska, who worked in Tigray in 2002–3. Her study relied in particular on a chronicle commemorating Yohannes that was housed in the church of Dabra Berhan Sellase in Adwa, [see: Marilyn Heldman, 'Dabra Berhan Sellase,' *EAE 2*, pp. 14–15]. This chronicle was most probably composed by the priests who were the architects of the occasion.
11. On the identification of Aksum with Zion, Jerusalem, see: S. Kaplan, 'Zion,' *EAE 5*, pp. 189–92.
12. S. Rubenson, 'Atnatewos,' *EAE 1*, pp. 393–4.
13. *ER2002*, p. 76.
14. See: H. Erlich, A. Gori, A. Bausi, G. Piaccadori, 'Red Sea,' *EAE 4*, pp. 345–53.
15. G. Douin, *Histoire du Règne du Khédive Ismail*, Cairo, 1933–41; D. Landes, *Bankers and Pashas: International Finance and Economic Imperialism in Egypt*, Cambridge [Mass.], 1958 (rep., 1979); A. Ben-Dror, *Emirate, Egyptian, Ethiopian: Colonial Experiences in Late Nineteenth-Century Harar*, Syracuse University Press, 2018.
16. This paragraph and the following ones are based on *ER1982*, pp. 9–57; *ER2002*, pp. 53–63: 'Yohannes, Ismail, and the Ethio-Egyptian Conflict.'
17. W. Smidt and D. Nosnitsin, 'Gura,' *EAE 2*, pp. 922–4.
18. A. Bayumi, *Mawsuat al-tarikh al-askari al-misri fi al-ahd al-hadith*, vol. 3, Cairo, N. D., p. 147.
19. See *ER1982*, ch. 3. See more on the spirit of the time in Tigray against the defeated Egyptians in W. Smidt, 'A War-song on Yohannes IV Against the Egyptians,' *Studies of the Department of African Languages and Cultures*, no. 41, 2007, pp. 105–28.
20. In his memoirs, Ahmad Urabi described the chain of events: the beginning of his protest movement (considered by many as the first manifestation of Egyptian modern nationalism), the exiling of Ismail by the powers, the ensuing deepening crisis, and the fall of Egypt into British hands–all in one long chapter titled 'the War in Ethiopia.' A. Urabi, *Kashf al-sitar an sir al-asrar*, Cairo, 1929, pp. 30–50.

NOTES

21. See *ER2002*, pp. 101–19.
22. S. Rubenson, *The Survival of Ethiopian Independence*, London, 1977, pp. 335–46.
23. R. Pankhurst, 'Alga,' *EAE 1*, p. 197.
24. Guebre Sellassie, *Chronique du Règne de Ménélik II, Roi des Rois d'Éthiopie*, Paris, 1930–32, ch. XXIV.
25. H. Rubinkowska, W. Smidt, 'Mikael Ali,' *EAE 3*, pp. 957–9.
26. H. Marcus, *The Life and Times*, pp. 50–4; See also Zewde Gabre-Sellassie, *Yohannes IV*, pp. 94–100; Guebre Sellassie, *Chronique*, ch. XXIV–XXV.
27. E. Ficquet, 'Boru Meda,' *EAE 1*, p. 609.
28. H. Marcus, *Life and Times of Menelik II*, pp. 53–5.
29. Shiferaw Bekele, 'Petros, Abuna,' *EAE 4*, pp. 139–40.
30. *ER2002*, pp. 75–6.
31. Bairu Tafla (ed.), *A Chronicle of Emperor Yohannes IV*, p. 91.
32. Zewde Gabre-Sellassie, 'Araya Sellase Yohannes,' *EAE 1*, p. 314.
33. See *ER2002*, pp. 41–2.
34. The quotes above are from R. Caulk, 'Religion and State in Nineteenth-Century Ethiopia,' *Journal of Ethiopian Studies*, vol. 10, 1972, pp. 23–41; *ER2002*, pp. 71–7, 'Yohannes IV and Islam.'
35. Bahru Zewde, *A History of Modern Ethiopia*, p. 48.
36. Bairu Tafla, 'Takla Haymanot,' *EAE 4*, pp. 837–9.
37. H. Marcus, *The Life and Times*, pp. 68–71; Zewde Gabre-Sellassie, *Yohannes*, p. 234, quoting Heruy, 'History of Ethiopia,' p. 60; Guebre Sellassie, op.cit., p. 185.; G. Branchi, *Missione in Abissinia (1883)*, Rome, 1889, p. 20.
38. Bairu Tafla, 'Walda Mikael Salomon,' *EAE 4*, pp. 1105–7.
39. The passages below are based on *ER1982*, pp. 11–13, 20–6.
40. J. Kolmodin, *Traditions de Tsazzega et Hazzega*, Uppsala, 1912, no. 261.
41. The passage is based on *ER1982*, ch. 8: 'Asmara.'
42. R. Pankhurst, 'Asmara, pre-colonial history of Asmara,' *EAE 1*, pp. 373–4; R. Pankhurst, *Economic History of Ethiopia*, Addis Ababa, 1968, pp. 573, 693.
43. See: J. Miran, *Red Sea Citizens: Cosmopolitan Society and Cultural Change in Massawa*, Indiana, 2009; G. Talhami, *Suakin and Massawa under the Khedive Ismai'l 1865–1879*, University of America Press, 1979; W. Smidt, 'Massawa' *EAE 3*, pp. 849–57.
44. R. Pankhurst, *Economic History*, p. 693.
45. A. Wylde, 'A Journey to the Court of King John,' *The Daily News*, 16.5.84.
46. For Eritrean tribes and Islam, see J. Miran, 'A Historical overview of Islam in Eritrea,' *Die Welt des Islams*, 2005, pp. 177–215. Also: W. Smidt, 'Habab,' *EAE 2*, pp. 946–7; D. Morin, 'Beni Amer,' *EAE 1*, 527–9; K. Volker-Saad, 'Mansa,' *EAE 3*, pp. 735–7; A. Mohammad, 'Asaorta,' *EAE 1*, pp. 361–2.
47. The following passages are based also on *ER1982*, ch. 7: 'The Year in Which the Dervishes were Cut Down,' ch. 9: 'The Italians in Massawa,' and ch. 10: 'Dogali.'
48. S. Chernetsov, 'Fitawrari,' *EAE 2*, p. 552.

49. Zewde Gabre Sellassie, 'Dabbab Araya,' *EAE 2*, p. 4.
50. The passage below is based on *ER2010*, ch. 2: 'From Disastrous Confrontation to Pragmatic Friendship: Ethiopia and Sudan, 1884–1898,' pp. 11–42.
51. The full text is in Muhammad Abu Salim, *Al-A'thar al-kamila lil-imam al-mahdi*, Khartoum 1990–1994, vol. 5, pp. 234–6.
52. Bairu Tafla, *A Chronicle of Emperor Yohannes IV*, Introduction, p. 15.
53. Bairu Tafla, *Chronicle*, p. 65.
54. Bairu Tafla, *Chronicle*, p. 149.
55. Bairu Tafla, *Chronicle*, p. 149.
56. Zewde Gabre Sellassie, 'Araya Sellase Yohannes,' *EAE 1*, 314.
57. G. Vernetto, 'Naretti, Giacomo,' *EAE 3*, pp. 1147–8.
58. Bairu Tafla, *Chronicle*, p. 149.
59. C. Giglio, *Ethiopia e Mar Rosso*, V, no. 115, p. 140; Yohaness to Menelik in A.S.MAI, (Archivio Storico dell sopresso Ministero dell'Africa Italiana, Italian Foreign Office) 36/3-28, Antonelli to Robilant, 26.11.85.
60. FO 95/747, Yohaness to Victoria, 12 Miyazia 1878 E.C. (19.4.1886).
61. A. Polera, *I Baria e Cunama*, Rome 1913; *ER1982*, pp. 10002.
62. The following derives from *ER1982*, ch. 11: '1887: The End of Alula's Government in the Mareb Melash,' pp. 110–26; Ch. 12: ' 1888–1889: The End of the Tigrean Emperor,' pp. 127–39.
63. A. Salimbeni, 'Diario d'un pioniere africano,' *Nuova Antologia*, 1936.
64. G. Portal, *My Mission to Abyssinia*, London 1892, pp. 158–72, 217; Yohannes to Victoria, 12.12.87 in FO 95/748.
65. FO 403/90, Portal to Baring, 25.12.87.
66. The following derives from *ER2010*, ch. 2, pp. 11–42.
67. See Hussein Ahmad, 'Talha b. Ja'far,' *EAE 4*, pp. 847–8. Hussein Ahmad, 'The Life and Career of Shaykh Talha,' *Journal of Ethiopian Studies*, vol. 22, 1989, pp. 13–30; Hussein Ahmad, *Islam in nineteenth century Wollo*, Leiden: Boston University, 2001; Zewde Gabre Sellassie, *Yohannes*, pp. 195–18. (According to Ethiopian historian Takla Sadiq Makuriya, Ethiopian Muslims helped the 'darbush' to penetrate and destroy Gondar, in a later raid, August 1889. *Yaityopya tarik*, Addis Ababa, 1968, p. 61).
68. Heruy Walda Selasse, *Ityopyana Matamma*, Addis Ababa, 1909, Ch. 1, pp. 5–6; CO 106/224, Intelligence Report 182, Memorandum by Major Wingate, 21–27 April 1889.
69. Isma'il bin 'Abd *al*-Qadir al-Kordofani, *Al-Tiraz al-manqush bibushra qatl Yuhanna malik al-hubush* [The Embroidery Embellished with the Good News of the Death of Yohannes the King of the Ethiopians]. This manuscript was published by Muhammad Ibrahim Abu Salim and Muhammad Said al-Qaddal, (eds.), *Al-Harb al-Habashiyya al-Sudaniyya: 1885–1888*, Beirut: 1991, pp. 59–60. See also: Iris Seri-Hersch, 'Confronting a Christian Neighbor: Sudanese Representations of Ethiopia in the Early Mahdist Period, 1885–89,' *International Journal of Middle East Studies*, Vol. 41, 2009, pp. 247–267.

70. See Zewde Gabre Sellassie, *Yohannes*, pp. 238–40.
71. Zewde Gabre Sellassie, *Yohannes IV*, p. 243; For background, consult H. Marcus, *The Life and Times*, pp. 102–4.
72. See Zewde Gabre Sellassie, *Yohannes IV*, pp. 542–4, as quoted from Heruy Walda Selasse MS, *History of Ethiopia*, pp. 81–85.
73. N. Shuqayr, *Ta'rikh al-Sudan wa-Jughrafiyat*uha, Cairo, 1903, pp. 1,073–5.
74. N. Shuqayr, *Ta'rikh al-Sudan*, pp. 1,076–17.
75. The following episode exemplifies the cultural barrier. In his appeasing letter to Hamdan Abu 'Anja, the Ethiopian emperor called him 'the admired *Dajjach* Abu 'Anja,' and went on to wish him good health. *Dajazmach*—literally 'commander of the gate—was the Ethiopian rank equivalent to the Mahdist/Arabic *Amir*; a general, a prince. It was customary in Ethiopia to abbreviate it to *dajjach*. No doubt, Yohannes meant to honor Abu 'Anja, but his translator—we know from Abu 'Anja's reply that the letter was sent in both Amharic and Arabic—innocently wrote *dajjach* in Arabic letters. [See also Zewde Gabre Sellassie, *Yohannes*, p. 248.] Unfortunately, *dajaj* in Arabic means a chicken, and one can only imagine Abu 'Anja's expression on reading that he was 'an admired chicken.' The insult, in itself bad enough, came at a very inappropriate time. Abu 'Anja had suddenly fallen ill and was to die, probably of cholera or typhoid fever, later in the same month. Whatever health Abu 'Anja still enjoyed, it helped little, as can be understood from his aggressive response. 'As to you calling me a chicken in the beginning of your letter,' Abu 'Anja wrote in his reply to Yohannes, 'know that I am not a chicken. You are a chicken, because you are an infidel who repeatedly angers God.' To set the record straight, Abu 'Anja presented himself rather as 'the commander of the armies of Islam prepared to annihilate the cursed unbelievers.' See *ER2010*, pp. 26–30: 'The trap of demonization: are you calling me a chicken?'
76. Takla-Sadiq Makuriya, *Yaityopya tarik*, Addis Ababa, 1968, pp. 63–64.
77. Heruy Walda Selasse, *Ityopyana matamma*, Addis Ababa, 1909, Ch. 3, pp. 11–15; see also Takla-Sadiq Makuriya, *Yaityopya tarik*, p. 63.
78. Zewde Gabre Sellassie, *Chronique du Regne*, p. 248.
79. *ER1982*, pp. 133–4.
80. Tsegay Berhe, 'Mangasha Yohannes,' *EAE 3*, pp. 728–9.
81. *ER1982*, p. 134–6; Also: C. C. Rossini, *Italia ed Etiopia dal trattato d'Uccialli alia battaglia di Adua*, (Rome 1935), pp. 46–2; For Mangasha being the son of Gugsa, Yohannes's brother, see Takla-Sadiq Makuriya, *Yatiopya Tarik*, p. 63; A. Wylde, 'Unofficial,' MG, 10.5.97; A. Wylde, 'Modern,' p. 41.
82. J. Ohrwalder, *Ten Years: Captivity in the Mahdi's Camp* (by F. R. Wingate), London, 1892, p. 250. The Mahdia also paid the battle of Matamma. Later in the same year, on 3 August 1889, the Mahdists, venturing toward Egypt, were defeated in the battle of Tushki. The combined effect of Tushki and Matamma proved a turning point. It marked the end of the Mahdists' visional drive to export their revolution through jihad along the Nile and to the entire Islamic

pp. [57–73]

NOTES

world. 'From 1889 to 1896, although the old ideological pretensions were not abandoned ... the Mahdist state ... was reduced to a Sudanese sultanate.' See the chapter 'The Mahdia and the Outside World,' in P. M. Holt, *The Mahdist State of the Sudan,* Oxford, 1970.

6. COLLAPSE

1. The following chapter is based on *ER1982*, pp. 140–96.
2. For ensuing developments, also consult C. C. Rossini, *Italia ed Etiopia*.
3. R. Pankhurst, 'Kefu Qan,' *EAE 3*, pp. 376–7.
4. Tsegay Berhe, 'Sibhat Aregawi,' *EAE 4*, pp. 587–8.
5. K. Pedersen, 'Mashasha Warqe,' *EAE 3*, pp. 831–2.
6. Tsegay Berhe, 'Sebhat Aregawi,' *EAE 4*, pp. 587–9.
7. S. Dege, 'Tewoflos,' *EAE 4*, pp. 937–8.
8. C. C. Rossini, *Italia ed Etiopia*, p. 99.
9. D. Nosnitsin, 'Nebura id,' *EAE 3*, pp. 1,161–2.
10. *ER1982*, pp. 186–7.
11. See H. Marcus, *The Life and Times*, pp. 158–60.
12. See G. C. Novati, 'Italian War, 1895–96,' *EAE 3*, pp. 226–8; H. Erlich, 'Adwa, Battle of,' *EAE 1*, pp 107–9.
13. Zewde Gabre Sellassie, 'A Glimpse of History Power, Treachery, Diplomacy and War in Ethiopia 1889–1906,' *A Paper Presented to The Second International Littmann Conference,* Axum, January 6–12 2006.
14. A. Wylde, 'An unofficial mission to Abyssinia,' *The Manchester Guardian,* 14 May 1897.
15. For events in Northern Ethiopia after the battle of Adwa, see F. Martini, *Il Diario Eritreo,* Rome. N.D.
16. I. Orlowska, 'Gabra Selasse Barya Gabar,' *EAE 2*, p. 628.
17. Gebre-Hiwet Baykedagne, *Emperor Menelik and Ethiopia,* Asmara, 1912, p. 12, quoted in A. Berhe, 'The Origins of the Tigray People's Liberation Front,' *African Affairs* (2004), 569–92.
18. Mussie Tesfagiorgis, 'Bahta Hagos,' *EAE 1*, pp. 448–9.
19. J. Miran, 'A Historical overview of Islam in Eritrea,' *Die Welt des Islams,* 2005, pp. 177–215.
20. See: Tekeste Negash, *No Medicine for the Bite of a White Snake: Notes on Nationalism and Resistance in Eritrea, 1890–1940,* Uppsala, 1986, pp. 40–54; R. Caulk "Black snake, white snake': Bahta Hagos and his revolt against Italian overrule in Eritrea, 1894.' in D. Crummey (ed.), *Banditry, Rebellion, and Social Protest in Africa,* London, 1986.
21. See *ER1983*, pp. 2–3:

    Geographical Differences

189

NOTES

The Central Highlands. This core area is centered on Eritrea's capital, Asmara and its environs, and comprises about a quarter of Eritrea's territory and about half its population. Most of the inhabitants are Tigrinya-speaking Christians, but there is also a significant Muslim population—both peasants and town-dwellers.

The Southern Coastal Area. This area extends southward from Massawa. It is mainly a desert and contains one-fifth of the territory and one-tenth of the population; the overwhelming majority are Muslim (mostly nomads, but some peasants).

The Sahil, Northern Eritrea. This area includes the northern coastal strip along the Red Sea and the regions lying between it and the Sudanese border. It is inhabited mostly by Tigre-speaking Muslim nomads.

The Western Plateau. This region lies between the Gash and Setit rivers and is inhabited by Muslims (with some Christians and animists).

Ethnolinguistic Differences

Tigrinya Speakers. Tigrinya, a Semitic language, is spoken by the inhabitants of the highlands (the districts of Hamasen, Sarai, and Akalla-Guzai), Keren, and Massawa. It is also spoken in the province of Tigre in Ethiopia proper. According to British estimates made in 1952, the number of Tigrinya speakers in Eritrea was 524,000—some 487,000 Christians, and the rest, Muslims.

Tigre Speakers. [See: J. Miran, 'History and language of the Tigre-speaking peoples,' *'Studi Africanistici. Serie Etiopica'* 8, Napoli: Università di Napoli *'L'Orientale,'* 2010: 33–50].

The Tigre language (not to be confused with the Ethiopian province of Tigre or the Tigrinya language) is spoken by the majority of the inhabitants of the Sahil and the western plateau–members of the Bani Amir tribes and the various Sahil clans, as well as urban dwellers and others. In 1952, the number of Tigre speakers was estimated at 329,000, of whom 322,000 were Muslims.

Afar and Sabo Speakers. These languages are spoken by members of the Afar clans, the Assawurta, and other Muslims, estimated to number 99,000 in 1952.

Arabic Speakers. The number of Arabs in Eritrea is small, and all are concentrated in the coastal towns. Many Muslims speak and write Arabic due to the influence of Islam in the modern period.

Amharic Speakers. Many Eritreans use Amharic because of the Ethiopian policy of Amharization following the 1962 annexation.

Other Groups. This includes several small communities, including the Baria and Kunama, the Belain clans, and others, estimated in 1952 to number 79,000—58,000 Muslims, 14,000 Christians, and 7,000 Kunama animists.

Religious Differences

Christians. The majority of the highlanders and some western Eritrean tribesmen are Ethiopian Christians. There are also Protestant and Catholic communities, mainly in the highland towns. They were estimated in 1952 to total 510,000, of whom 350,000 were Catholics and 160,000 were Protestants.

Muslims. Almost all the clans and town dwellers of the coast, the Sahil and the west, and many villagers and town dwellers of the highlands are Muslims. The total estimate for 1952 was 514,000.

22. The following section is based on *ER1983*. Detailed studies on the structure and organization of Eritrean society in the Italian period may be found in C. C. Rossini, *Principi di Diritto Conseutudinario dell'Eritrea*, Rome, 1916; R. Perini, *Di Qua Dal Mareb*, Florence, 1905; S.F. Nadel, 'Land Tenure of the Eritrean Plateau,' *Africa 16* (1946) 1–22, 99–109; J. S. Trimingham, *Islam in Ethiopia*, Oxford University Press, 1962; S. H. Longrigg, *A Short History of Ethiopia*, Oxford, 1945; Great Britain, War Office, 'Military Report on Eritrea' WO 33/410, 1909; Tekeste Negash, *No Medicine for the Bite of a White Snake*.
23. For a detailed bibliography on Eritrea, see K. Checole, 'Eritrea: A Preliminary Bibliography,' *Africana Journal 6* (1975): 303–14. For the Italian period, consult, among others: S. H. Longrigg, *Short History of Eritrea*; M. Perham, *The Government of Ethiopia*, 2nd ed. Evanston, 1969; and Zewde Gabre Sellassie, 'Eritrea and Ethiopia.'
24. J. Miran, 'A Historical overview of Islam in Eritrea,' *Die Welt des Islams*, 2005, pp. 177–215.
25. Later, these families regained some of their importance as the British (1941–52) and Haile Selassie took them into their administrations.
26. U. C. Dirar, 'From Warriors to Urban Dwellers: *Ascari* and the Military Factor in the Urban Development of Colonial Eritrea,' *Cahiers d'etudes africaines*, 2004, p. 533–74.

7. BACK TO CENTER STAGE

1. The following is based on *ER1994*, pp. 83–91; *ER2019*, pp. 24–30; H. Erlich, 'From Wello to Harar, Lij Iyasu, the Somali Sayyid and the Ottomans,' in E. Ficquet and W. Smidt, (eds.), *The Life and Times of Lij Iyasu of Ethiopia, New Insights*, Zurich, 2014, pp. 137–45.

2. See E. Ficquet, 'Understanding *Lij* Iyasu through his Forefathers.'
3. For the religious dimensions, see also: S. Kaplan, 'The Exaltation of Holy Cross and the Deposition of the Emperor of Ethiopia: Lej Iyasu a Masqal Drama,' *Northeast African Studies*, 2021, vol. 21, pp. 1–18.
4. G. Haile, 'Religion in Ethiopian Politics,' (Paper presented at the *Michigan State University International Conference of Ethiopian Studies*, April 1992; see the seal on Wikipedia 'The seal of Negus Mikael.'
5. H. Rubinkowska, 'Seyum Mangasha,' *EAE 4*, pp. 646–7.
6. H. Erlich, 'Gugsa Araya,' *EAE 2*, pp. 905 6.
7. For background and more details on Seyum and Gugsa see A.S.MAI 54/9-27: Two long reports by A. Pollera and P. Franca, Addis Ababa, 16 August 1934, and FO 371/27523 "Ras Gugsa and His Forebears" Extracts of FO Reports'.
8. The following sections are based on *ER1986*—the chapter 'Tigrean Politics, 1930–1935, and the Approaching Italo-Ethiopian War,' pp. 135–64. See there for detailed references.
9. M. Alehegne, 'Yishaq, Abuna' *EAE 5*, pp. 61–2.
10. See: C. Zoli, *Ethiopia d'Oggi*, Rome, 1935, p. 216.
11. H. Rubikowska, 'Asfa Wasan Hayla Sellase,' *EAE 1*, pp. 366–7.
12. Gabra-Selassie had persistently opposed Tafari and supported Zawditu and had also been an admirer of the Italians. See also: I. Orlowska, 'Gabra Sellase Barya Gaber,' *EAE 2*, p. 628.
13. H. Erlich, 'Hayla Selasse Gugsa,' *EAE 2*, pp. 1,066–7.
14. For Ras Gugsa and his relations with Asmara and Addis Ababa, see especially A. S. MAI 54/38-159, a long report dated 9 May 1933.
15. A.S.MAI 54/38-159, P. Lecco report, May 1933.
16. On Haile Selassie Gugsa not being the son of Ras Gugsa, see also: G. L., Steer, *Caesar in Abyssinia*, London, 1936, p. 145. It was indeed widely rumored in Tigray that Gugsa was not the son of Ras Araya, the son of Yohannes, and in any case, it was quite apparent that Yohannes had never heard of this grandson of his. Mangasha was in fact not the son of Yohannes, but of his brother Gugsa. See, among many others, a long report by A. Pollera in A. S. MAI 54/9-27, 16 August 1934.
17. *ER1986* p. 146–7, quoting Astuto to De Bono, 9 June 1934, in A.S.MAI 54/58-158.
18. R. Hess, *Italian Colonialism in Somalia*, Chicago, 1968, pp. 172–3.
19. See G. Baer, *The Coming of the Italian–Ethiopian War*, ch. A.
20. *ER1986*, p. 150, quoting A.S.MAI 54/9-27. A translation of a telegram from the King of Kings to Ras Seyum intercepted toward the end of February 1935.
21. T. Konovaloff, *Con le armate del negus*, Bologna, 1938, p. 36.
22. FO 371/19184, 'Report of the Inter-Departmental Committee on British Interests in Ethiopia,' Maffey to Foreign Office, 18.6.1935, and especially FO 371/19194, 'Committee on Territorial Exchanges in Abyssinia,' July 1935.

23. *Foreign Relations of the United States*, [Hereafter *FRUS*] *Diplomatic Papers*, 1936, The Near East and Africa, Vol. III. The Chargé in Ethiopia (Engert) to the Secretary of State, Addis Ababa, January 7, 1936: 'Time is still playing into the hands of the Abyssinians... it looks as if so far things were going more or less according to Ethiopian plans.' See these files in|: https://history.state.gov/search?q=Haile+selssie [Office of the Historian, Search: Haile Selassie].
24. FO 371/ 20934, 'Annual Report 1936,' section B, 'Feudal organization and Generalship.'
25. FO 371/20167, an account by Konovaloff, 31 March 1936.
26. On the battles of the 1935–6 war, see: A. Del-Boca, *The Negus*, Addis Ababa 2012, pp. 153–77; and the most detailed: A. Mockler, *Haile Selassie's War, The Italian–Ethiopian Campaign 1935–1941*, New York, 1984, Part II, pp. 37–173; *The Autobiography of Emperor Haile Sellassie I–1892–1937*, E. Ullendorff, (ed. and trans.), Oxford, 1976, ch. 38–46, pp. 251–90. A. Del Boca, *Gli Italiani in Africa Orientale*, vol. 1, (Roma-Bari, 1976), vol. 2, (Roma-Bari, 1979).

8. FASCISTS, BRITISH

1. *ER2007*, pp. 39–67: 'Camels for Mussolini.'
2. G. C. Novati, 'Africa Orientale Italiana,' *EAE 1*, pp. 129–34.
3. On the role of the Church, see: FO (Foreign Office Files) 371/41498 'The Church of Ethiopia During the Italian Occupation' by A. E. Matthew, 27 October 1943, and 'The Church of Ethiopia 1941–1944,' 21 July 1944.
4. The richest collection of documents on Tigray and Ethiopia under Italian occupation are reports in A.S.MAI, series 54, 35.
5. A. Sbacchi, 'Italy and the Treatment of the Ethiopian Aristocracy, 1937–1940,' *The International Journal of African Historical Studies*, vol. 10, no. 2 (1977), pp. 209–41; A. Sbacchi. 'Ethiopian Opposition to the Italian Rule,' in R. Hess (ed.), *Proceedings of the Fifth International Conference on Ethiopian Studies, Session B*, Chicago, 1978, pp. 583–99.
6. 'FO 371/20934,' [British]Annual Report, 1936,' on Ethiopia.
7. The following section derives extensively from *ER1986*, ch. 8: 'Tigrean Nationalism, British Involvement, and Haile Selassie's Emerging Absolutism—Northern Ethiopia, 1941–1943,' pp. 166–201. See there for detailed references.
8. M. Perham, *The Government of Ethiopia*, Northwestern University Press (second edition), 1969, p. 463.
9. R. Pankhurst, 'Sandford, Daniel Arthur,' *EAE 4*. pp. 523–4.
10. T. Ofcansky, 'Cheesman, Robert Ernest,' *EAE 1*, p. 712.
11. F. Guazzini, 'Longrigg, Stephen-Hemsley,' *EAE 3*, pp. 597–8.
12. War Office, 230/ 168, Longrigg to WO, 12 August 1943, and his report, 21 September 1943; also his book *A Short History of Eritrea*, Oxford 1945.
13. War Office, 230/ 168, 'Committee on Ethiopia, Report on Future Policy towards Ethiopia.' n.d.

14. FO 371/35626, 'Memorandum on Internal Situation in Ethiopia' by Colonel Cheesman, 17 June 1943. Also: FO 371/35626, 'Political Consciousness in Ethiopia' by Colonel Cheesman, 6 July 1943.
15. WO 230/16, 'Record of Interview between the D. C. P. O and Ras Haile Selassie Gogsa, April 1941' in Kennedy-Cooke to Mitchell, 26 April 1941; P. Gilkes, *The Dying Lion,* London, 1975, 277, note 2.
16. WO230/16, CPO to GHQ, Middle East, 14 May 1941.
17. WO 230/16, Telegram from Haile Selassie to W. Churchill, 20 June 1941.

9. UNDER HAILE SELASSIE

1. See M. Perham, The government of Ethiopia, London 1948 (second edition, Northwestern University, 1969); C. Clapham, *Haile-Selassie's Government*, New York, 1969.
2. FO 371/35626, Ministry of Interior—'Annual Report for the Year Ending 10th September 1942'; FO 371/46055, 'Ethiopia's Record of Achievements 1942–1944.'
3. This passage is based on FO 371/35627, 'Annual Report, 1942,' in Howe to Eden, 20 August 1943.
4. A. H. Omer, 'Azaboo,' *EAE 1*, pp. 413–4.
5. WO 230/16 Aide-Memoire by Lieutenant-Colonel T. R. Blackley, 20 October 1941.
6. WO 230/16 Note by Lush, 3 November 1941.
7. WO 230/16 DDPO to CPO, 7 November 1941.
8. WO 230/16 DCPO to CPO, 7 November 1941
9. FO 371/35643 'Gugsa File.'
10. See *ER2019*, pp. 58–64, 83–84.
11. WO 212/313A, Weekly Intelligence Summary.
12. See Gilkes, *Dying Lion*, ch. 4, and the files WO 201/2690; WO 230/16; FO 371/35626, 371/35627.
13. See F. Berhe, 'Studies on the Biography of Haile Mariam Redda' 28 pp., online.
14. The meaning of *woyane* is people exercising a 'republican' sort of democracy without any permanent or hereditary officials. G. Tareke, *Ethiopia: Power and Protest. Peasant Revolts in the Twentieth Century*, Cambridge, 1991, quoting Abba-Yohannes Gabra-Egziabher's Tigrinya-Amharic Dictionary, Asmara 1956, p. 638.
15. G. Tareke, *Ethiopia: Power and Protest*. Gebru's book, based also on the correspondence of Ethiopian officials as well as on other Ethiopian documents, may be regarded as a definitive description of the protest movement and an analysis of its leadership and its organizational structure. Also: M. Maki, 'The wayyane in Tigray and the reconstruction of the Ethiopia government in the 1940s,' *Proceedings of the 16th International Conference of Ethiopian Studies*, edited by S. Ege, H. Aspen, B. Teferra and Shiferaw Bekele, Trondheim, 2009; and M. Momoka, 'Wayyana,' *EAE 4*, 1, 164–6.

16. M. Perham, *The Government of Ethiopia*, p. 357.
17. H. Tasfai, *Ras Seyum Mangasha*, B.A. thesis (Addis Ababa University, 1976), Institute of Ethiopian Studies, Addis Ababa University.
18. WO 230/168, 'Future Disposal of Eritrea,' 12 August 1943.
19. The following is based on: WO 201/2690, 'Tigre Operations.'
20. Bahru Zewde, 'Abbabe Aregay,' *EAE* 1, p. 22.
21. The proclamations are available in FO 371/35607, 95–9.
22. FO 371/35608, WO to FO, 22 October 1943.
23. Details of his trial according to his own evidence in H. Tasfai, *Ras Seyum*.

10. HAILE SELASSIE'S IMPERIAL CENTRALISM

1. J. Young, *Peasant Revolution in Ethiopia: The Tigray People's Liberation Front, 1975–1991*, Cambridge, 1997, p. 49.
2. The passage above and below is based on: A. Berhe, 'The Origins of the Tigray People's Liberation Front,' *African Affairs*, 2004, 569–92.
3. 'Time to Bring Eritrea in from the Cold (But It's Harder than It Sounds) – By David Shinn,' *African Arguments*, 13 January, 2014.
4. See, for example, the analysis by an anthropologist who stayed in Adwa in the early 1970s: C. Rosen, 'Tigrean Political Identity—an Explication of Core Symbols,' in R. Hess (ed.), *Proceedings of the Fifth International Conference on Ethiopian Studies*, Session B, (Chicago, 1978), 259–64.
5. For the Italian and British periods, see: F. Guazzini, 'Colonial History of Eritrea,' *EAE* 2, pp. 359–65.
6. G. Trevaskis, *Eritrea: A Colony in Transition, 1941–1952*, London, 1960; D. C. Cumming, 'The Disposal of Eritrea,' *Middle East Journal* 7, 1953, 18–32; S. and R. Pankhurst, *Ethiopia and Eritrea: The Last Phase of the Reunion Struggle, 1941–1952*, London, 1953.
7. W. Smidt, 'Eritrean Weekly News,' *EAE* 2, pp. 373–4.
8. See *ER1986*, 'Tigrean Nationalism, British Involvement and Haile-Sellasse's Emerging Absolutism, 1941–1943,' pp. 166–201.
9. See L. Ellingson, 'The Emergence of Political Parties in Eritrea, 1941–1950,' *Journal of African History*, 18, 1977, pp. 261–81.
10. T. Ofcansky, 'Unionist Party,' *EAE* 4, pp. 1,021–2.
11. H. Erlich, 'Muslim League,' *EAE* 3, 1,086–8.
12. R. Reid, 'Liberal Progressive Party,' *EAE* 3, pp. 560–1.
13. H. Erlich, 'Pro-Italian Party,' *EAE* 4, pp. 220.
14. H. Erlich, 'Independence Bloc,' *EAE* 3, pp. 141–2.
15. For the federation period, see Gabra-Sellase, 'Eritrea and Ethiopia'; L. Ellingson, 'The Origins and Development of the Eritrean Liberation Movement,' in R. L. Hess, ed., *Proceedings of the Fifth International Conference on Ethiopian Studies*, Chicago, 1978, session B; E. W. Luther, *Ethiopia Today*, Stanford, 1958; and H. Erlich, 'The Eritrean Autonomy, 1952–1962: Its

Failure and Contribution to Further Escalation,' in Y. Dinstein, (ed.), *Models of Autonomy*, Rutgers University Press, 1981, pp. 171–82.
16. For the Eritrean constitution and relevant legal discussions, see United Nations, General Assembly, *Official Records, 7th session: Supplement no. 15*, 1952, pp. 76–89; A. A. Schiller, 'Eritrea: Constitution and Federation with Ethiopia,' *American Journal of Comparative Law 2*, 1953, pp. 375–83.
17. W. Smidt, 'Eritrean Assembly,' *EAE 2*, pp. 369–70.
18. Shumet Sishagne, "Tedla Bayru Oqbit,' *EAE 4*, pp. 813–4.
19. Mussie Tesfagiorgis, 'Ali Musa Raday,' *EAE 1*, pp. 201–2.
20. For full text, see Perham, *Government of Ethiopia*, p. 433.
21. Haile Walda Selasse, 'Man yemasker yanabara–man yarda yaqabara,' *Addis Zaman*, 4–14 October 1979.
22. Luther, *Ethiopia Today*, p. 147.
23. See: *ER2019*, pp. 124–132.
24. H. Erlich, 'Eritrean Liberation Front,' *EAE 2*, pp. 370–2.
25. *ER1983*, ch. 2.
26. *Al-Muharrir*, Beirut, 10 April 1969.
27. H. Erlich, 'Idris Muhammad Adam,' *EAE 3*. pp. 116–7.
28. G. Schroder, 'Uthman Salih Sabi,' *EAE 4*. pp. 1,049–50.
29. Uthman Salih Sabbe, *Ta'rikh Iritriya*, (History of Eritrea), Beirut 1974.
30. H. Erlich, 'Eritrean People's Liberation Front.' *EAE 2*, p. 373.
31. Shumet Sishagne, 'Walda Ab Walda Maryam,' *EAE 4*, pp. 1,095–7.
32. *ER2014*, pp. 158–60.
33. P. Henze, 'Aman Mikael Andom,' *EAE 1*, pp. 216–7.
34. Shiferaw Bekele, 'Asrate Kasa,' *EAE 1*, pp. 384–5.
35. *ER2019*, pp. 131–2.
36. Aberra Jembere, 'Aklilu Habtaold,' *EAE 1*, pp. 170–2.
37. *ER1983*, p. 41.

11. THREE REVOLUTIONS

1. See: R. Iyub, *The Eritrean Struggle for Independence: Domination, Resistance, Nationalism, 1941–1993*, Cambridge, 1995.
2. This section derives from *ER1983*, ch. 4: 'Eritrea and the 1974 Revolution in Ethiopia,' and *ER1986*, ch. 11: 'The Ethiopian Army and the 1974 Revolution.' See there for notes.
3. P. Henze, 'Tafari Banti,' *EAE 4*, pp. 814–5.
4. The following is based on *ER1983*, pp. 55–110; and on *ER1994*, ch. 10 and ch. 12. See there for notes.
5. 'What Went Wrong?: The Eritrean People's Liberation Front from Armed Opposition to State Governance,' A Personal Observation Occasional Paper by Paulos Tesfagiorgis, November 23, 2015 (online). For some of the relevant aspects of the revolution under the EPLF, see: G. Tareke, *The Ethiopian*

Revolution, War in the Horn of Africa, Yale University Press, 2009, ch. 2, 'The Victorious Nationalists: Insurgent Eritrea,' pp. 55–75; J. Gebre-Medhin, *Peasants and Nationalism in Eritrea: A Critique of Ethiopian Studies*, Red Sea Press, 1989; V. Bernal, 'Equality to die For?: Women Guerrilla Fighters and Eritrea's Cultural Revolution.' *Political and Legal Anthropology Review,* 2000, pp. 61–76.

6. R. Balsvik, Tilahun Gizaw,' *EAE 4*, pp. 912–3.
7. *ER2019*, pp. 146–9; ' A New Challenge at Home: The Students.'
8. The passages below are based on: A. Berhe, *A Political History of the Tigray People's Liberation Front (1975–1991): Revolt, Ideology and Mobilization in Ethiopia*, Tsehai Publishers, Los Angeles, 2009; A. Berhe, 'The Origins of the Tigray People's Liberation Front,' *African Affairs* (2004), 569–92; A. Fantahun, 'Aregawi Berhe – The return of a political survivor,' *Ethiopia Observer*, 18 August 2018; J. Young, *Peasant Revolution in Ethiopia*; G. Tareke, *The Ethiopian Revolution*, 2009, ch. 3: 'Insurgent Tigray,' pp. 76–110.
9. These were: Alemseged Mengesha (nom de guerre: Haylu), Ammaha Tsehay (Abbay), Aregawi Berhe (Berhu), Embay Mesfin (Seyoum), Fentahun Zere'atsion (Gidey), Mulugeta Hagos (Asfeha), and Zeru Gesese (Agazi).
10. A group named Tigray Liberation Front, which established contacts with the Eritrean Liberation Front, was destroyed by the TPLF already in 1975.
11. See: 'Meles Zenawi's interview with Paul Henze 1990,' online.

Here are some citations from the record of their conversation:

> Meles: I acknowledge that I myself was a convinced Marxist when I was a student at HSIU in the early 1970s and our movement was inspired by Marxism. But we have learned that dogmatic Marxism-Leninism is not applicable in the field. We do not believe that any foreign system can be imposed on a country. The only way people can be liberated is in their own terms and in accordance with their own traditions and their own situation… We are not trying to apply an Albanian system. We are not trying to apply a Soviet system or a Chinese system. We know the Albanians are also changing some features of their system … I have always found it difficult to understand (especially now, in light of what has been happening in the world) how you could stick to a doctrine as unsuccessful and discredited as Marxism has become.
>
> Meles: Our movement has always been Tigrayan before it has been anything else. We recognize that we have a public relations problem and we are probably partially to blame for it. That is one of the reasons we come here now … Probably a third of all Tigrayans live in other parts of Ethiopia. Tigrayans have always emigrated—some to stay and others as temporary laborers. That was one of the things that alienated Tigrayans from the Derg very early. Land reform did not anger people in Tigray as much as the restrictions on seasonal labor migration. Tigrayans used to go to many other parts of the country to work,

sometimes for more than half the year. They brought their earnings home to support their families or invest in their farms. There was no part of Ethiopia where money earned in this way was more important to the people. The Derg was stupid to forbid this, for it forced our people into poverty and hopelessness and it gave our movement important support from the very beginning.

Henze: How do you see the future of Ethiopia?

Meles: The country will have to be a federation and there will have to be recognition of the right of every people in it to have autonomy. We can no longer have Amhara domination.

Henze: What do you mean by AMHARA domination?

Meles: ...When we talk about Amhara domination, we mean the Amhara of Shoa, and the habit of Shoan supremacy that became established in Addis Abeba during the last hundred years. This system has to change. The people who think they have a right to dominate in Addis Abeba have to change their mentality. This is the mentality the Derg adopted from the very beginning. No people of Ethiopia have the right to dominate any other... In Tigrinya our name means movement—harnet. We use the term Woyane because that has historical meaning in Tigray. It means a popular rebellion against outside oppression—that is what the Woyane Rebellion of 1943. It was against Shoan domination and exploitation of Tigray. The Derg calls us Woyane too. We like that. We [EPRDF] are a united movement politically but we have different currents of opinion. We have freedom of discussion within the movement.

Henze: What is your position on separatism?

Meles: We are not separatists. We want a united Ethiopia. But we do not want a centralized Shoan-dominated Ethiopia. Federation is the only way this can be done. We are in favor of federation. This is the only way the damage the Derg has done can be repaired.

Henze: This brings us to Eritrea and the EPLF. How are your relations with the EPLF? Do you talk to Isaias Afewerki?

Meles: I talk to Isaias often. We have no disagreements now. During the 1970s we worked together and had no serious disagreements with them. In 1984 we broke relations. The break was over different understandings of the Soviet Union. They still believed the Soviet Union offered a model for the future and that it could be reformed. They argued that the Soviets were misled on Ethiopia. They wanted to persuade the Soviets to support them instead of the Derg. They thought the Soviet system was a model they could apply in Eritrea. We thought this was foolish because we had learned in Tigray that we had to develop our own model and apply our own system in accordance with our own conditions and practical experience.

Henze: What are your differences?

Meles: The EPLF has a much more difficult situation than we do. Many of our differences result from that, and we have an understanding and sympathy for their position. In Tigray we have a united people. No more than 10 per cent of our people are Muslims and our Muslims are Tigrayans first and Muslims only second. That is not true in Eritrea. The population is much more divided. The Eritrean Muslims themselves are divided. There are at least three groups among them. They don't see things the same way the Christians do. The EPLF has some of them with it and its policies have been sensible—it is trying to make the Muslims part of a united movement. But that is not possible and the closer the EPLF comes to taking power in Eritrea the more dangerous this issue becomes...

Henze: What would be your preferences?

Meles: We look at this from the viewpoints of the interests of Tigray first, and then Ethiopia as a whole. We would like to see Eritrea continuing to have a relationship with Ethiopia. We know that Tigray needs access to the sea, and the only way is through Eritrea. Whether Eritrea is part of Ethiopia or independent, we need this access and, therefore, must have close ties. There are many Tigrayans in Eritrea. They are concerned. They don't want to be treated as foreigners there. There has always been close connections between Tigray and Eritrea for the highland people are all the same. They have the same history.

Henze: Would you expect the EPLF to participate in a provisional government in Addis Ababa?

Meles: We don't know. We think they could play a constructive role. We would really like to see Eritrea retain a relationship to Ethiopia, but we don't know if Isaias can work out the situation to make this possible. Our own position is very delicate. We have to have good relations with Eritreans, so we recognize their right to self-determination, going as far as independence if they want it... But we really hope that Eritrea can remain part of a federated Ethiopia.

Henze: You say you have set up an effective administration in Tigray. How does it work? Are you providing public services? Are schools operating?

Meles: Everything is done by councils. Local councils decide local level issues. Everybody participates in them... And Muslims have full equality with Christians. The village councils are the most important element in our administration because issues are decided at that level and we do not attempt to interfere. In the TPLF itself things are decided at our annual congress. We are now beginning to open schools. We have opened several clinics. We have some training programs. We need help and will welcome help from abroad.

Henze: What are your relations with the church?

NOTES

Meles: The church is very important in Tigray, as you know. We were never opposed to the church and we wanted its support. There were arguments in the church about accepting the authority of the Patriarch in Addis Abeba. Most of the priests didn't want to accept the patriarch chosen by the Derg after they deposed Abuna Tewoflos [he was arrested in 1976 and murdered in 1979] because they regarded him as having no power of his own. They wanted to go to Alexandria to get authorization for ordination of new priests but it was decided that this was impractical, because the church did not want to put itself under the control of the Egyptian Coptic Church again. That question was settled after World War II [the two churches separated in 1959]. So the bishops worked out rules for creating new priests within Tigray. Then there was an argument about whether priests could carry weapons and serve in the TPLF. The Bishops eventually decided that since the Derg represented the Devil and it was appropriate to fight the Devil with any means available, it was alright for priests and deacons to join the TPLF and fight the Devil. And some of them have done it.

Henze: Do any of the Arab countries give you travel documents?

Meles: We have never received any help from Arabs. They give the Eritreans help because they like to think of them as Arabs and the EPLF makes concessions to them to keep up this feeling, but we cannot do this. We do not sympathize with Arabs.

Henze: How did your movement begin? How did you relate to Ras Mangasha's movement?

Meles: I went to the Wingate School in Addis Abeba and entered HSIU in 1973 [aged 18]. I did not finish the university. In 1974 I joined with Tigrayan friends who had the same ideas I had and we went to Tigray to begin the armed struggle because we did not believe the Derg was going to establish the kind of system that would benefit us. We found peasants in Shire who were sympathetic to us, especially one old man (now dead) who protected and encouraged us [Gessesew Ayele (Sihule)]. We took the Woyane rebellion of 1943 as our model. We saw it as a people's movement. Ras Mangasha's movement [EDU] was based on defending the interests of the prominent landowners. We didn't have much in common. His movement declined and ours grew because we had the confidence of the people... Tigrayans know how to help themselves. All they need is the opportunity... We have issued our [new] program [the EPRDF statement of 10 March 1990] and we believe in it. We want to bring democracy and freedom to Ethiopia. We do not want to establish a dictatorship. Our program is not a Marxist-Leninist program. We state very clearly that we will set up a provisional government that will create a new governmental system and then turn the government over to the people…

12. RESTORED HEGEMONY, INTER-TIGRAYAN WAR

1. See, for example: A. de Waal, 'The theory and practice of Meles Zenawi,' *African Affairs*, vol. 112, issue 446, January 2013, pp. 148–55; Rene Lefort, 'The theory and practice of Meles Zenawi: A response to Alex de Waal,' *African Affairs*, vol. 112, issue 448, July 2013, pp. 460–70: A. de Vaal, 'The theory and practice of Meles Zenawi: A reply to René Lefort,' *African Affairs*, vol. 112, issue 448, July 2013, pp. 471–5.
2. See *ER2019*, pp. 185–6.
3. See: W. Teshome, 'Ethiopian Opposition Political Parties and Rebel Fronts: Past and Present,' *International Journal of Human and Social Sciences*, 4:1 2009, pp. 60–8.
4. In September 1991, I came to Addis Ababa, at the invitation of Meles Zenawi. 'In Tigray, in the general command of our liberation front' Meles said, 'we had only one copy of your Ras Alula book. I told all commanders to read it. Myself, I separated the chapters and saw to their binding as booklets. The separate chapters rotated between the caves. Some got chapter 7 and then chapter 2, others in a reverse order. I think I was the only one who read it from A to Z. But we all read it. At night, around a bonfire, we would learn the history of our Tigrayan ancestors, and admired Ras Alula….'
5. An interview with Meles Zenawi, Addis Ababa, 2009.
6. In his 2011 article: 'Ethnic-based federalism and ethnicity in Ethiopia: reassessing the experiment after 20 years,' *Journal of Eastern African Studies*, vol. 5, no. 4, November 2011, pp. 596–618, Jon Abbink, a leading historian and an anthropologist, defined the TPLF (EPRDF) regime as 'ethnic-based federalism, informed by a neo-Leninist political model called revolutionary democracy.' He stated that 'In this model… ethnic identity was to be the basis of politics. Identities of previously non-dominant groups were constitutionally recognized and the idea of pan Ethiopian identity de-emphasized… After 20 years of TPLF/EPRDF rule, the dominant rhetorical figure in Ethiopian politics is that of ethnicity, which has permeated daily life and overtaken democratic decision-making and shared issue-politics…The federal state, despite according nominal decentralized power to regional and local authorities, is stronger than any previous Ethiopian state and has developed structures of central control and top-down rule that preclude local initiative and autonomy. Ethnic and cultural rights were indeed accorded, and a new economic dynamics is visible. Political liberties, respect for human rights and economic equality are however neglected, and ethnic divisions are on the increase, although repressed. Ethiopia's recent political record thus shows mixed results, with positive elements but also an increasingly authoritarian

governance model recalling the features of the country's traditional hierarchical and autocratic political culture.'

Eight years later, in 2019, after the collapse of the TPLF-EPRDF government, leading historian Bahru Zewde summarized what he observed as the main reasons for its toppling: 'In sum, these were the long-term factors: (1) a lack of inclusive governance and human rights abuses, (2) TPLF hegemony, [which led to...]a general public disgust with the ethnic politics and ethnic economics that the TPLF regime instituted in the country. This disgust arose from a feeling that one segment of the population was gaining political power and economic benefits at the expense of others. (3) Public disgust with patronage politics, and (4) youth unemployment.,' 'Discussing the 2018/19 Changes in Ethiopia: Bahru Zewde,' *NokokoPod*, Institute of African Studies, Carleton University (Ottawa, Canada), 2019 (1): 1–16.

7. In 1998, then US President Bill Clinton said Meles was part of a new generation of African leaders with whom the west could do business along with Paul Kagame of Rwanda and Yoweri Museveni of Uganda.
8. See *ER1982*, Preface to the 1995 edition: 'A Political Biography of Ras Alula – A Generation Later.'
9. M. Asfaha,'Enduring Peace between Ethiopia and Eritrea: The Narrative of Vices, Meanness, Dishonesties, Hypocrisies and Trickeries that Led to the War,' *TesfaNews*, 25 January 2014.
10. 'What Went Wrong?: The Eritrean People's Liberation Front from Armed Opposition to State Governance' A Personal Observation, Occasional Paper by Paulos Tesfagiorgis November 23, 2015. (on Internet). See also H. Erlich, 'Vicissitudes of History and Human Rights – Ethiopia and Eritrea,'Y. Dinstein and J. Lahav (eds,), *Israel Yearbook on Human Rights,* vol. 47, 2017, pp. 221–31.

13. THE GRAND DAM

1. *World Bank*, 'The World Bank, Ethiopia and the Nile: A Strategy for Support to Ethiopia,' in Country Department for Ethiopia, 'Eastern Nile Development Program,: A Draft,' Washington, D.C., June 1998.
2. See more in *ER2002*, pp. 79–84.
3. A. T. Wolf and J. T. Newton, 'Case Study of Trans-coundary Dispute Resolution: the Nile waters Agreement,' http://www.transboundarywaters.orst.edu/research/case_studies/Nile_New.htm
4. R. Collins, 'In Search of the Nile Waters,' in H. Erlich and Israel Gershoni (eds.) *The Nile – Histories, Cultures, Myths,* Boulder, 2000, pp. 245–67; Daniel Kendie, 'Egypt and the Hydro-Politics of the Blue Nile River,' *Northeast African Studies*, 1999, pp. 141–69.
5. On Haile Selassie, Egypt and the Nile, see *ER2002*, pp. 123–63.
6. On Mangistu, Egypt and the Nile, see *ER2002*, pp. 163–77.

7. There is a vast literature on the Toshka project. See *ER2002*, pp. 214–7; Among the latest articles, see also: A. Fecteau, 'On Toshka New Valley Mega Failure,' in www.egyptindependent.com, 26 April 2012.
8. P. Schwartzstein, 'Death of the Nile,'
9. In May 2010, the Beles Hydroelectric Power Plant, sometimes referred to as Beles II or Tana Beles, was inaugurated. The power plant receives water from the lake. Then, after utilizing it to produce electricity, the water is then discharged into the Beles River. The mouth of the Beles in the Blue Nile is located about 40 kilometers above the Grand Ethiopian Renaissance dam. The last generator was operational in February 2012.
10. In 2003, I participated in a conference in Addis Ababa University and was summoned to a conversation with PM Meles Zenawi. He had read my 2002 book, *The Cross and the River: Egypt, Ethiopia, and the Nile*. It was clear that he was studying the historical background thoroughly. He told me: 'Whenever I met with Mubarak, he demonstrated disinterest to talk about the Nile. When I began raising the issue, he began looking at the ceiling.' Somewhat later, the Egyptian ambassador to Israel asked me for a copy of that book. 'For my president,' he smiled.
11. M.T. Maru, 'Ethiopia and the African Union,' *Horn Affairs,* July 2016; https://hornaffairs.com/2016/07/03/paper-ethiopia-and-african-union.
12. See: H. Vershoeven, 'The Titan who Changed the Horn of Africa,' https://www.aljazeera.com/indepth/opinion/2012/08/2012821115259626668.html.
13. For the two concepts, see *ER* 2002, pp. 3–10.
14. http://www.ethiopian.tv PM *Meles Zenawi interview with Egyptian* TV on Nile Sharing (Part 1–4, 19 July, **2010).**
15. An interview with Professor Fasil Nahum, Addis Ababa, 2013. Also: http://www.water-technology.net/projects/grand-ethiopian-renaissance-dam-africa/
16. http://grandmillenniumdam.net/the-dam-speech/
17. http://www.water-technology.net/projects/grand-ethiopian-renaissance-dam-africa/
18. http://dams-ethiopianism.blogspot.co.il/2013/04/afp-ethiopia-and-china-sign-1-billion.html; http://www.survivalinternational.org/news/6079;

NON-CONCLUSION

1. Just a sample: J. Abbink, 'Ethnicity and Conflict Generation in Ethiopia: Some Problems and Prospects of Ethno-Regional Federalism,' *Journal of Contemporary African Studies, 24, 3, Sept. 2006,* pp. 389–413; Lemante, G. Selassie. 'Ethnic Federalism: Its Promise and Pitfalls for Africa,' *Yale Journal of International Law,* 2003, pp. 51–107; Siraw Megibaru Temesgen, 'Weaknesses of Ethnic Federalism in Ethiopia,' *International Journal of Humanities and Social Science,*

2015, pp. 49–54; M. Bassi, 'Federalism and Ethnic Minorities in Ethiopia: Ideology, Territoriality, Human Rights, Policy,' *DADA Rivista di Antropologia postoglobale*, 2014, pp. 45–74; J. Záhořík, 'Reconsidering Ethiopia's ethnic politics in the light of the Addis Ababa Master Plan and anti-governmental protests,' *The Journal of the Middle East and Africa*, 2017, pp. 257–72.

2. C. Clapham., 'Rewriting Ethiopian History,' *Annales d'Éthiopie*, 2002, pp. 37–54.
3. See: J. Markakis, *Ethiopia: The Last Two Frontiers*, Oxford, 2011.
4. In June 2010, the government announced the establishment of METEC (Metal and Engineering Corporation) as a part of her Growth and Transformation Plan–GTP. The proclaimed aimed was to achieve partial industrialization of Ethiopian economy. An ambitious plan to connect to the global market not just as a poor agricultural land. METEC was a combination of fifteen firms and factors which had been established in the previous decade, including a vehicles assembly line and arms production, all under the management of the ministry of defense. The corporation was also charged with overseeing the works on GERD, as well as the connections with foreign firms involved in the construction. The plan clearly reflected the thinking of Meles Zenawi. Namely, the government should initiate and control new steps in new directions, and that the armed forces should be involved and thus be even more interested in political continuity. See: http://www.bloomberg.com/news/2013-02-18/ethiopian-military-run-corporation-seeks-more-foreign-partners.html.

INDEX OF NAMES

Ababe Aregai, Ras, 120, 121
Abbay Kasa, Dajazmach, 113
Abd al-Nasser, Gammal, 130, 167
Abiy Ahmed, 175
Abraha Araya, Dajazmach, 70
Abraha Hagos, Dajazmach, 70
Abraham Demoz, 134
Abu Anja, Hamdan, 49, 52, 53
Adal, Ras, 38, 40, 42, 49, 51, 53, 54, 57
Ahmad Nasir, 144
Ahmet Pasha, 17
Ahrendrup, A., 35
Aida, princess, 121
Aklilu Habta-Wold, 136, 143
Alam, Nasr al-Din, 171
Ali, Ras, Oromo warlord, 27
Alula, Ras, 2, 36, 37, 38, 40, 41, 42, 43–4, 45, 47, 49–50, 51, 52, 53, 54, 55, 59–60, 61, 62, 63, 64, 65, 66, 67, 68, 149, 156, 157–8, 162–3
Alvares, Francisco, 12
Aman Andom, 134–5, 138–43, 149
Amanuel Amda-Mikael, 139

Amedeo, Duke of Aosta, 98
Andergachaw Masai, Ras, 129–30
Antanewos, Abuna, 39
Antonelli, P., 61
Arafat, Yasser, 132, 133
Arakil Bey, 35
Araya Dagala, 117
Araya Selassie Demsu, Ras, 30, 45
Araya Selassie Yohannes, Ras, 39, 40, 41, 47, 51, 52, 53
Araya, Gugsa, 78, 80–1, 83–5
Aregawi Berhe, 124–5, 150–1
Asfa-Wossen, *Maridazmach*, 80, 115, 136
Asmarom Leggese, 134
Asrate Kasa, Ras, 135, 136, 143
Astuto, R., 86, 87–8
Atnatewos, Abuna, 33
Atsada (Ras Seyum's wife), 86
Ayele, Gessesew, 125

Badoglio, Pietro, 92, 97, 99
Bahru Zewde, 40
Bahta Hagos, Dajazmach, 71, 72
Bairu Tafla, 46

205

INDEX OF NAMES

Baldissera, O., 55, 58
Baratieri, O., 63, 64, 67
Barre, Siyad, 132
Beraki, Blatta, 71
Bereket Habta-Selassie, 134

Caulk, Richard, 22
Cheesman, R. E., 3, 102, 103, 105, 177–8
Christopher [Cristóvão] da Gama, 14, 15
Conti-Rossini, C., 65
Cora, G., 82
Cottam, A., 119, 120
Crispi, F., 67
Croce, Benedetto, 1
Cyril V, patriarch, 39

Dabbab Araya, Fitawrari, 45, 49, 54, 55, 58, 60, 62, 70
Dabra Berhan Sellase (Adwa), 33
De Bono, Emilio, 82
Di Manchi, Paterno, 82
Duri Muhammad, 134

Eden, A, 101, 102, 105, 106, 107

Fasiladas, or Fasil, emperor, 20, 21, 23

Gabra-Heiwot Mashasha, Dajazmach, 113
Gabra-Selassie, Dajazmach, 70
Gabru Tareke, 117–18
Galadewos, emperor, 14, 15, 16
Gandolfi, A., 63
Gebrehiwet Baykedagne, 70
Gessesew Ayele, 125, 200
Gilkes, Patrick, 21–2
Gobaze, *Shum* of Wag, 31

Goitem Gabra-Egzi, 139
Gordon, Charles, 36
Gragn, Imam (Ahmad Ibn Ibrahim), 13, 14, 15, 20, 40
Graziani, R., 98–9
Gudit, queen, 11
Guevara, Che, 148
Gugsa Araya Selassie, Ras, 70

Hagos Mircha, Ras, 51, 63, 65, 66, 68–9
Haila-Mariam Gugsa, Ras, 51
Haila-Mariam Redda, *Belatta*, 117
Haileselassie Gugsa, 80, 85–6, 87, 113–14
Hailu Takla-Haymanot, Ras, 81
Hayla-Selasse I, emperor, 76
Henze, Paul, 153
Heruy Walda-Selasse, 54
Hitler, Adolf, 107
Ho Chi Minh, 148
Howe, R. G., 102

Idris Adam, 133
Imru Haile Selassie, Ras, 81
Isayas Afawarqi, 133, 144, 155, 160–1
Ismail, *Khedive*, 34–5, 36, 39
Iyasu, Lij, emperor, 75–7
Iyoas I, emperor, 24

Kasa Hailu, Ras, 115
Kasa Haylu, Ras, 92, 93
Kasa Mircha, Dajazmach, 31. *See* Yohannes IV, emperor
Kasa Sebhat, Dajazmach, 113
Khalifa, Abdallah al-Ta'ishi, 52, 53
Kifle Dadi, Fitawrari, 116
Kifle Iyasus, 25
Kirkham, John, 31

206

INDEX OF NAMES

Konovaloff, T., 91, 93

Lebna Dengel, emperor, 12, 13, 14
Lecco, P., 84–5, 88
Levine, Donald, 8–9
Lindsell, W., 119
Longrigg, S., 102–3, 119
Loring, William, 35
Luqas, Abuna, 39
Lush, M. S., 106, 111–12

Maki, Mamoka, 117
Makonnen, Ras, 63, 66, 69
Mangasha Seyum, Ras, 77–9, 80–1, 108, 121, 124
Mangasha Yohannes, Ras, 55, 59, 60, 60, 61, 62–3, 64–5, 68, 69, 72
and Menelik, 63–4
Mangistu Haile Mariam, 136, 137, 141, 157, 162
fall of, 167–8
Mara Takla-Haymanot, king, 11
Maria Theresa (MT), 91
Markos, Abuna, 39
Marye of Yejju, Ras, 26
Mashasha Warqe, Dajazmach, 61
Matewos, Abuna, 39
Medri Bahri, 12, 16, 17, 72, 162, 179
Meles Zenawi, 150–1, 153, 155–7, 158–9, 172–3
initiated Operation X, 173–4
Mendes, Afonso, 20
Menelik II, emperor, 75–6, 166–7
Menelik, king, later emperor, 6, 19, 32, 37, 38, 49, 51, 52–3, 54, 55, 65
crowning as emperor, 57–8
Tigrayan policy, 60–1, 62
victory of Adwa, 66–8
Mennen, queen, 48
Mentwab, queen, 24, 48
Mesfin Wolda-Mariam, 134
Miguel de Castanhoso, 15
Mikael Imru, 138
Mikael Sehul, Ras, 24–5, 31, 59
Mikael, Ras. *See* Muhammad ʾAli, Imam
Minas, emperor, 16–17
Mitchell, P., 106, 111
Mubarak, Husni, 168
Muhammad ʾAli, Imam, 38, 40, 51, 76, 77–8
Muhammad Ahmad, the "Mahdi", 46
Muhammad bin Abdalla Hassan, "the Mullah", 77
Muhammad, the prophet, 7, 20, 46
Muhammad Said Nawud, 139–40
Mulugeta Yigezu, Ras, 93
Munzinger, Werner, 35
Mussolini, B., 2, 61, 83
returned to *Politica Tigrigna*, 75
summoned his devotees, 89

Napier, R., 30, 31
Naretti, G., 48
al-Numayri, Jaʿfar, 132, 139

Orlowska, Izabela, 32
Ozdemir Pasha, 16

Perham, M., 118
Petros, Abuna, 39
Platt, W., 119

INDEX OF NAMES

Portal, G., 50, 51

Qaddafi, Muammar, 132–3

Radai, Ali, 129
Radwan Pasha, 17
Ratib Pasha, Muhammad, 35, 36, 41
Rayya Oromo, 20
Rubenson, Sven, 37

Sabagadis Woldu, Dajazmach, 26, 27, 31, 59
Sabi, Uthman, 141
Sadat, Anwar al-, 168
Salama, Abuna, 30, 60, 62
Salt, Henry, 25
Sandford, D. A., 101–2, 105
Sbacchi, Alberto, 97
Scotti, Virgilio, 89
Sebhat Aregawi, Dajazmach, 59, 60, 62, 63, 66, 70
Seble Wongel, queen, 14, 15
Serza Dengel, emperor, 17, 22
Seyum Gabra-Kidan, Dajazmach, 60, 61
Seyum Mangasha, Dajazmach, Ras, 51, 69–70
Shihab, Mufid, 171
Shinn, David, 125
Shoaraga, Menelik's daughter, 77
Susenios, emperor, 20
Tafari Banti, 140–1, 142
Tafari Makonnen, Ras, 76, 78
Tafari Tedla, 117
Taitu, queen, 68
Takla Giyorgis II, 31, 33
Takla-Haymanot of Gojjam, king. *See* Adal, Ras
Talha bin Ja'far, Shaykh, 51–2

Taytu (Meneik's wife), 65
Tebaba Sillase, Halima, 39
Tedla Haile, 89
Tedla, Bairu, 129
Tedla Haile, Lij., 89
Tekeste Negash, 71
Tekle Haymanot II, emperor, 24
Tesfa-Mariam, Dajazmach, 71
Tewodros II, emperor, 29–30, 34, 84
Tewoflos, *Echage*, 55, 64
Tilahun Gizaw, 148
Ullendorff, Edward, 8
Umm Durman, 46, 52, 55
Urabi, Ahmad, 36
Uthman Diqna, Amir, 49
Uthman Salih Sabbe, 133

Vasco da Gama, 13
Victoria, queen, 30, 45, 48, 50, 69
Vittorio Emanuel III, 96
Voigt, Rainer, 7

Wadaju Ali, *nagadras*, 91
Walata-Israel, 80
Walda Selassie, Ras, 25, 26, 31, 59
Walda-Mikael, Ras, 18, 41, 42, 63, 65, 71, 149, 162–3
Woldeab Woldemariam, 134
Wube Hailemariam, Dajazmach, 26, 27
Wylde, A., 68

Yekunu-Amlak Tasfai, 117
Yishak, Bahr Negash, 13, 14–15, 16
Yishak Yosief, 162
Yishaq, Abuna, 79

INDEX OF NAMES

Yohaness II, emperor, 24
Yohannes IV, emperor, 9–10, 29, 31–2, 50, 52, 57, 76, 103–4
  arrangement with Menelik, 40–1
  arrangement with Menelik, 40–1
  coronation at Aksum, 31, 32–4
  defeating the Egyptian challenge, 34–7
  dominating the future Eritrea, 41–2
  end of, 55–6

Ethiopia as a federation, 37–9
  and Islam, 39–40
  letter to Abu 'Anja, 53, 54
  Mahdia threats, 45–6
  unhappiness, 46–9

Zanaba-Warq, princess, 80, 83, 84–5
Zara Yaqob, emperor, 12, 39
Zawde Gabra-Sellasse, 139
Zawditu Menelik, 41, 53, 65, 76
Shaykh Zayd, 168
Zion, *Amba*, 60
Zoli, C., 82

209

INDEX

Ababe Aregai, Ras, 120, 121
Abbay Kasa, Dajazmach, 113
Abd al-Nasser, Gammal, 130, 167
Abiy Ahmed, 175
Abraha Araya, Dajazmach, 70
Abraha Hagos, Dajazmach, 70
Abraham Demoz, 134
Abu Anja, Hamdan, 49, 52, 53
Abu Dhabi, 168
Abyssinia, 101
Adal, Ras, 38, 40, 42, 49, 51, 53, 54, 57
Addis Ababa Legation, 83
Addis Ababa, 42, 48, 61, 62, 64, 65, 67, 69, 70, 77, 116, 124–5, 131
   AU establishment in, 170
   fall of Aman, 149
   TPLF entry into, 155–6
Aden, 133
Adigrat, 26
Adulis port, 6
'Adwa Complex', 83
Adwa, 25, 36, 61, 70, 78–9, 86–7, 90, 166
Afar desert, 22, 35, 132–3

Afars, 39
Africa Corpus, 50
'Africa Orientale Italiana', 96–7
African Union (AU), 170
Africans, 167, 171–2
Agame, 26
Agazian tribes, 6
Ahmad Nasir, 144
Ahmet Pasha, 17
Ahrendrup, A., 35
Aida, princess, 121
Aklilu Habta-Wold, 136, 143
Akkele Guzay, 35, 71, 62, 65, 72, 162
Aksum, 39, 59, 79, 90–1, 177
Aksumite Ethiopia, 5–7, 8, 9, 10
Alam, Nasr al-Din, 171
Al-Azhar University, 131
Ali, Ras, Oromo warlord, 27
Ali, Wadaju, 79
all-Ethiopian conference (Boru Meda, Wallo), 38
Alula, Ras, 2, 36, 37, 38, 40, 41, 42, 43–4, 45, 47, 49–50, 51, 52, 53, 54, 55, 59–60, 61, 62, 63, 64, 65, 66, 67, 68, 149, 156, 157–8, 162–3

INDEX

Alvares, Francisco, 12
Aman Andom, 134–5, 138–43, 149
Amanuel Amda-Mikael, 139
Amedeo, Duke of Aosta, 98
Amhara Shoans, 116
Amhara, 8
kings, 9
Amharic language, 7, 20, 124, 130
Andergachaw Masai, Ras, 129–30
Anglo-Ethiopian agreement (1944), 121
Antanewos, Abuna, 39
Antonelli, P., 61
Arab Middle East, 145
Arafat, Yasser, 132, 133
Arakil Bey, 35
Araya Dagala, 117
Araya Selassie Demsu, Ras, 30, 45
Araya Selassie Yohannes, Ras, 39, 40, 41, 47, 51, 52, 53
Araya, Gugsa, 78, 80–1, 83–5
Aregawi Berhe, 124–5, 150–1
Asem valley, 31
Asfa-Wossen, *Maridazmach*, 80, 115, 136
Asmara University, 160
Asmara, 36, 42–4, 49, 54–5, 60, 62–3, 71, 72, 73
Asmarom Leggese, 134
Asrate Kasa, Ras, 135, 136, 143
Astuto, R., 86, 87–8
Aswan Dam, 166, 168
Atbara (River), 167
Atlantic Ocean, 131
Atnatewos, Abuna, 33
Atsada (Ras Seyum's wife), 86
AU. *See* African Union (AU)

Ayele, Gessesew, 125
Azebo, 111, 117

Badame (town), 161
Badoglio, Pietro, 92, 97, 99
Bagemdir, 22, 81, 83
Baghdad, 133
Bahru Zewde, 40
Bahta Hagos, Dajazmach, 71, 72
Bairu Tafla, 46
Baldissera, O., 55, 58
Bank of China, 174
Baratieri, O., 63, 64, 67
Baria, 162
Barre, Siyad, 132
battle of Debra Abbay, 26
battle of Debra Tabor, 27
battle of Gundat, 41
battle of Gura, 35–6, 39, 41
battle of Zantara, 15
Belgium, 44
Beraki, Blatta, 71
Bereket Habta-Selassie, 134
Berhanena Salam (newspaper), 79
Blue Nile Dam, 174
Blue Nile, 12, 23, 157, 159, 166–8
Boru Meda, Wallo, 38, 39, 39, 40
Britain, 30
British Legation, 103
British Military Administration, 102
British Military Mission, 119
British Open University, 156–7
British Tigrayan policy, 121
British War Cabinet, 107
British, 44, 45, 48, 51, 69
Burundi, 170, 171

Catholic Portuguese, 20

212

INDEX

Caulk, Richard, 22
Cheesman, R. E., 3, 102, 103, 105, 177–8
China, 156
Christian kingdom of Amhara, 12–13
Christian Tigrayans, 111, 127, 132, 144–5
Christianity, 6, 12, 13, 20, 37, 38–9
Christopher [Cristóvão] da Gama, 14, 15
Church of Our Lady Mary of Tsiyon [Zion], 9, 20
Churchill, W, 107
Clapham, Christopher, 178–9
Congo, 135, 171
Conti-Rossini, C., 65
'Cooperative Framework Agreement', 171
Coptic Church, 6, 12
Cora, G., 82
Cottam, A., 119, 120
Crispi, F., 67
Croce, Benedetto, 1
Cyril V, patriarch, 39

Dabbab Araya, Fitawrari, 45, 49, 54, 55, 58, 60, 62, 70
Dabra Berhan Sellase (Adwa), 33
Damascus, 133
Dasalegn, Hailemariam, 175
Dayr as-Sultan monastery, 33
De Bono, Emilio, 82
Debarwa, 12, 14, 16, 17
Debra Tabor, 38, 40, 42
Derg, 139–40, 141–3
Di Manchi, Paterno, 82
Djibouti, 170
Dogali, 50–1, 52, 63

Duri Muhammad, 134
Dutch university, 157

eastern Tigray, 107, 111
Eden, A, 101, 102, 105, 106, 107
EDU. *See* Ethiopian Democratic Union (EDU)
Egyptian Coptic Church, 96, 166
Egyptians, 32, 39, 46, 71, 131, 166, 170–1
ELF. *See* Eritrean Liberation Front (ELF)
Endarta, 25
EPLF. *See* Eritrean Peoples' Liberation Front (EPLF) 'the Era of the Judges', 23, 24, 27, 59–60
Eritrea, 12, 32, 35, 41–2, 36, 58, 61, 68
under colonialism, 71–3
Eritrean Assembly, 134
Eritrean Christians, 127, 134–5
Eritrean Democratic Bloc, 128, 129
Eritrean Liberation Front (ELF), 131–2, 136, 144–5
Eritrean Muslims, 131
Eritrean nationalists, 143–4
Eritrean Peoples' Liberation Front (EPLF), 133, 139, 144–6, 160
Eritrean Tigrayans, 125, 134
Eritreanism, 42–4, 142
Eritreans, 97, 136, 161–2
Ethiopian Airlines, 134
Ethiopian Christians, 102, 162
Ethiopian Democratic Officers' Revolutionary Movement (EDORM), 152–3

213

INDEX

Ethiopian Democratic Union (EDU), 150
Ethiopian People's Democratic Movement (EPDM), 152–3
Ethiopian People's Revolutionary Democratic Front (EPRDF), 152–3, 155, 156
Ethiopians, 92, 96, 161, 170
Ethiopian–Sudanese conflict, 46
ethnic federalism, 8
Europe, 83–4, 93, 146, 156

famines, 58
Farafra, 168
Fasiladas, or Fasil, emperor, 20, 21, 23
'Feudalism Must Be Purged', 148
Fitawrari, 45
France, 44, 45, 88, 89, 90, 92

Gabra-Heiwot Mashasha, Dajazmach, 113
Gabra-Selassie, Dajazmach, 70
Gabru Tareke, 117–18
Galadewos, emperor, 14, 15, 16
Gandolfi, A., 63
Ge'ez language, 6, 7, 10
Gebrehiwet Baykedagne, 70
Germany, 44
Gilkes, Patrick, 21–2
Gobaze, *Shum* of Wag, 31
Goitem Gabra-Egzi, 139
Gojjam, 23, 32, 38, 39, 40, 83
Gondar, 21, 23–4, 25, 26, 27, 39, 51–2, 53, 111
Gordon, Charles, 36
Gragn, Imam (Ahmad Ibn Ibrahim), 13, 14, 15, 20, 40
Grand Ethiopian Renaissance Dam (GERD), 157, 159, 165–6, 169, 174–5
Graziani, R., 98–9
'Great Tradition', 178
'Greater Ethiopia' (Levine), 8–9
Gudit, queen, 11
Guevara, Che, 148
Gugsa Araya Selassie, Ras, 70
Gulf Emirates, 168
Gult (landownership system), 21, 22, 43, 65, 69
Gundet, 35, 36

Habashat tribes, 6
Habesh Eyaleti', 16
Hagos Mircha, Ras, 51, 63, 65, 66, 68–9
Haila-Mariam Gugsa, Ras, 51
Haila-Mariam Redda, *Belatta*, 117
Haile Selassie I University, 147–8
Haile Selassie, emperor, 2, 9, 48, 113–14, 157, 167
Haileselassie Gugsa, 80, 85–6, 87, 113–14
Hailu Takla-Haymanot, Ras, 81
Hamasen, 17–18, 35, 41, 44, 162
Harar, 13, 15, 35, 42, 77
Hayla-Selasse I, emperor, 76
Hazzega village, 18, 41
Henze, Paul, 153
Heruy Walda-Selasse, 54
Hewett Treaty (Jun 1884), 36–7, 44, 45, 48
Hitler, Adolf, 107
Ho Chi Minh, 148
Horn of Africa, 75, 95, 107–8, 119, 155
Howe, R. G., 102

Idris Adam, 133

INDEX

Imru Haile Selassie, Ras, 81
Independent Muslim League, 128
Intergovernmental Authority on Development (IGAD), 170
Iraqis, 131
Isayas Afawarqi, 133, 144, 155, 160–1
Islam, rise of, 11
Islamic rulers, 13
Islamic–Christian conflict, 13–14
Islamic–Christian relations, 6–7
Ismail, *Khedive*, 34–5, 36, 39
Israel, 131, 132, 159
Istanbul, 16
Italians, 32, 41, 44–5, 54, 55, 77
   annexed Tigray to Eritrea, 95
   Dogali and, 50–1
   Gugsa relations with, 79
   Menelik signed a treaty with, 58
   Menelik's defiance, 52–3
   took control of Maqale, 92
Italy, 83–5, 87–8, 91–2
   Friendship Agreement between Ethiopia and, 82
   passed new racist laws, 98–9
Iyasu, Lij, emperor, 75–7
Iyoas I, emperor, 24

Jabarti, 39, 40
Jesuits, 20
Jordan, 132

Karora, 140
Kasa Hailu, Ras, 115
Kasa Haylu, Ras, 92, 93
Kasa Mircha, Dajazmach, 31. *See* Yohannes IV, emperor
Kasa Sebhat, Dajazmach, 113
Kassala, 49, 50, 133

Kebra-Nagast, 8–9
Kefu qan, 58
Kenya, 170, 171, 172
Khalifa, Abdallah al-Ta'ishi, 52, 53
Kharj, 168
Khartoum, 46, 133, 169
Kifle Dadi, Fitawrari, 116
Kifle Iyasus, 25
Kinshasa, 170
Kirkham, John, 31
Konovaloff, T., 91, 93
Korea, 135
Kufit, 49
Kunama, 162

Lake Ashange, 15, 50
Lake Tana, 166–8, 170
Lebanon, 132
Lebna Dengel, emperor, 12, 13, 14
Lecco, P., 84–5, 88
Levine, Donald, 8–9
Liberal Progressive Party (LPP), 127–8, 134
Libya, 132
Lindsell, W., 119
London, 101
Longrigg, S., 102–3, 119
Loring, William, 35
Luqas, Abuna, 39
Lush, M. S., 106, 111–12

Mahdia, 44, 45–6, 49, 51–2, 53–4, 55, 57, 80
Maichaw, 93
Makeda, queen, 6
Maki, Mamoka, 117
Makonnen, Ras, 63, 66, 69
Mamluks, 12, 13
Mammedoch dynasty, 20

INDEX

Mangasha Seyum, Ras, 77–9, 80–1, 108, 121, 124
Mangasha Yohannes, Ras, 55, 59, 60, 60, 61, 62–3, 64–5, 68, 69, 72
and Menelik, 63–4
Mangistu Haile Mariam, 136, 137, 141, 157, 162
fall of, 167–8
Maqale, 49, 53, 60, 64, 69, 79, 92
captured by rebels, 117
recaptured by Ethiopian units, 121
Maqdala, 29, 30, 31, 48
Mara Takla-Haymanot, king, 11
Mareb Melash, 39, 41, 42, 43, 44, 54, 55, 63
Mareb River, 22, 91, 97, 162–3
Maria Theresa (MT), 91
Markos, Abuna, 39
Marxist-Leninist League of Tigray (MLLT), 150–1
Marye of Yejju, Ras, 26
Mashasha Warqe, Dajazmach, 61
Massacre of the Baria (Eritrea), 49–50
Massawa port, 22, 26
Massawa, 16, 17, 27, 35, 36, 39, 43, 45, 58, 119
Matamma (Al-Qallabat), 55, 57, 80
Matewos, Abuna, 39
Medri Bahri, 12, 16, 17, 72, 162, 179
Meles Zenawi, 150–1, 153, 155–7, 158–9, 172–3
initiated Operation X, 173–4
Mendes, Afonso, 20

Menelik II, emperor, 75–6, 166–7
Menelik, king, later emperor, 6, 19, 32, 37, 38, 49, 51, 52–3, 54, 55, 65
crowning as emperor, 57–8
Tigrayan policy, 60–1, 62
victory of Adwa, 66–8
Mennen, queen, 48
Mentwab, queen, 24, 48
Mesfin Wolda-Mariam, 134
Middle East, 75, 126, 131, 146, 159
Miguel de Castanhoso, 15
Mikael Imru, 138
Mikael Sehul, Ras, 24–5, 31, 59
Mikael, Ras. *See* Muhammad ʿAli, Imam
Minas, emperor, 16–17
Ministry of Colonies, 82
Ministry of Foreign Affairs, 82
Mitchell, P., 106, 111
ML. *See* Muslim League (ML)
Monophysism, 38–9
Moscow, 152
MT. *See* Maria Theresa (MT)
Mubarak, Husni, 168
Muhammad ʿAli, Imam, 38, 40, 51, 76, 77–8
Muhammad Ahmad, the "Mahdi", 46
Muhammad bin Abdalla Hassan, "the Mullah", 77
Muhammad, the prophet, 7, 20, 46
Muhammad Said Nawud, 139–40
Mulugeta Yigezu, Ras, 93
Munzinger, Werner, 35
Muslim Arabs, 162
Muslim League (ML), 127–8

INDEX

Muslim League of the Western Province, 127–8, 129
Mussolini, B., 2, 61, 83
  returned to *Politica Tigrigna*, 75
  summoned his devotees, 89

Nakfa (currency), 161
Napier, R., 30, 31
Naretti, G., 48
National Muslim Party (Massawa), 127
Nile Basin Initiative, 169–71
Nile River, 34–5, 166–7, 169
North America, 146
northern Ethiopia, 99, 152
al-Numayri, Ja'far, 132, 139

Organization of African Unity (OAU), 131, 170
Orlowska, Izabela, 32
Oromo cavalry, 26, 27, 37
Oromo people, 19, 20
Oromo People's Democratic Organization (OPDO), 152–3
Othman Pasha, 16
Ottomans, 13, 14, 15, 75
  and Bahr Negash, 15–18
Ozdemir Pasha, 16

Perham, M., 118
Persian Gulf, 131
Petros, Abuna, 39
Platt, W., 119
PLO, 132–3
Politica Tigrigna, 61, 62, 81, 102
Portal, G., 50, 51
Portuguese religious challenge, 20

Portuguese–Ethiopian campaign, 14–15

Qaddafi, Muammar, 132–3
Qallabat, 52
Quarram, 87
Quiha (town), 117

Radai, Ali, 129
Radwan Pasha, 17
'Ras Alula Operation', 2, 177
Ratib Pasha, Muhammad, 35, 36, 41
Rayya Oromo, 20
Rayya, 111, 117
Red Sea, 6, 7, 11, 13, 15, 16, 22, 34, 45, 133, 160
  Portuguese raid, 14, 16
Renaissance Lake, 174
Republic of Somali, 130
Rest (landownership system), 21, 43
revolution (1974), 138–43
River Mareb, 17, 18, 58, 64, 71
Rome, 44–5, 61, 63, 66–7, 72, 82, 90
Rubenson, Sven, 37
Rwanda, 170, 171

Saati, 50, 66
Sabagadis family, 26
Sabagadis Woldu, Dajazmach, 26, 27, 31, 59
Sabi, Uthman, 141
Sadat, Anwar al-, 168
Salama, Abuna, 30, 60, 62
Salini Costruttori, 173
Salt, Henry, 25
Sandford, D. A., 101–2, 105
Saraye, 35, 41, 71

INDEX

Sbacchi, Alberto, 97
Scotti, Virgilio, 89
Sebhat Aregawi, Dajazmach, 59, 60, 62, 63, 66, 70
Seble Wongel, queen, 14, 15
Semien, 26, 27
Seray, 162
Serza Dengel, emperor, 17, 22
Seychelles, 116
Seyum Gabra-Kidan, Dajazmach, 60, 61
Seyum Mangasha, Dajazmach, Ras, 51, 69–70
Sharm el-Sheikh, 170–1
Shaykh Zayd Canal, 168
Shihab, Mufid, 171
Shinn, David, 125
Shoa, 22, 23, 32, 38, 39, 40, 68–70, 54, 61
Shoan hegemony, 64–5, 60
Shoaraga, Menelik's daughter, 77
Sidamo, 83
Six Day War (1967), 132
Solomonians, 12–13
Somalia, 92, 132, 159, 170
Somalis, 77, 135
South Yemen, 132
southern Endarta, 115
southern Tigray, 87, 107
Soviet Union, 153
Suakin, 35
Sudan, 35, 45–6, 52, 102, 126, 130, 132–3, 170–1, 172
Suez Canal, 34, 45
Susenios, emperor, 20
Syria/Syrians, 131, 132

Tafari Banti, 140–1, 142
Tafari Makonnen, Ras, 76, 78
Tafari Tedla, 117

Taitu, queen, 68
Takkaze River, 17, 22, 20, 26
Takla Giyorgis II, 31, 33
Takla-Haymanot of Gojjam, king.
    See Adal, Ras
Talha bin Ja'far, Shaykh, 51–2
Tamben, 59, 60, 62
Tana Dam, 167
Tanzania, 170, 171
Taytu (Meneik's wife), 65
Tebaba Sillase, Halima, 39
Tedla Haile, 89
Tedla, Bairu, 129
Tedla Haile, Lij., 89
Tekeste Negash, 71
Tekle Haymanot II, emperor, 24
Tesfa-Mariam, Dajazmach, 71
Tewodros II, emperor, 29–30, 34, 84
Tewoflos, *Echage*, 55, 64
'the *theory of disintegration*', 3
Tilahun Gizaw, 148
Tigray
    fall of, 68
    firearms adoption, 22–3
    landownership system, 21–2
Tigrayan Muslims, 152
Tigrayan Peoples' Liberation Front (TPLF), 122, 137, 148–9
Tigrayan University Students' Association (TUSA), 148–9
Tigrayanism, 114, 118, 126
Tigrayan–Shoan relations, 53
Tigrinya language, 7, 9, 20, 38, 120
Tigrinya speakers, 5, 8, 8–9, 10, 12, 31, 32, 41, 68, 71, 73
Tilahun Gizaw, 148

INDEX

TNO. *See* Tigrayan People Liberation Front (TPLF)
Toshka Canal, 168
Treaty of Wichale, 61, 64
Tsazega village, 18, 41
Tunisia, 16
TUSA. *See* Tigrayan University Students' Association (TUSA)

Uganda, 170, 171, 172
Ullendorff, Edward, 8
Umm Durman, 46, 52, 55
Union of the Students of Addis Ababa University (USUAA), 148
Unionist Party (UP), 127–8, 130
United Arab Republic, 130
United Nations, 128
United States, 121
Urabi, Ahmad, 36
US Bureau of Reclamation, 167
USSR, 107
Uthman Diqna, Amir, 49
Uthman Salih Sabbe, 133

Vasco da Gama, 13
Victoria, queen, 30, 45, 48, 50, 69
Vittorio Emanuel III, 96
Voigt, Rainer, 7

Wadaju Ali, *nagadras*, 91
Wadjrat, 117
Walata-Israel, 80
Walda Selassie, Ras, 25, 26, 31, 59
Walda-Mikael, Ras, 18, 41, 42, 63, 65, 71, 149, 162–3
Wallo Muslims, 76
Wallo Oromos, 20

Wallo, 20, 22, 24, 38, 57
  Islamic revolts in, 51–2
Walqait, 156
War Office, 102
Wara-Ilu, Wallo, 40
Washington, 153
western Tigray, 112, 115, 118, 120, 150
White Nile, 169
Woki, 140–1
Wokru (town), 117
Woldeab Woldemariam, 134
World Bank, 166
World War I, 75–8
World War II, 73, 83, 99
Woyane protest, 109, 117, 148–9
  end of, 118–22
Wube Hailemariam, Dajazmach, 26, 27
Wylde, A., 68

Yeju, 24
Yekunu-Amlak Tasfai, 117
Yemen War (1962), 130–1
Yishak, Bahr Negash, 13, 14–15, 16
Yishak Yosief, 162
Yishaq, Abuna, 79
Yohaness II, emperor, 24
Yohannes IV, emperor, 9–10, 29, 31–2, 50, 52, 57, 76, 103–4
  arrangement with Menelik, 40–1
  arrangement with Menelik, 40–1
  coronation at Aksum, 31, 32–4
  defeating the Egyptian challenge, 34–7

INDEX

dominating the future Eritrea, 41–2
end of, 55–6
Ethiopia as a federation, 37–9
and Islam, 39–40
letter to Abu 'Anja, 53, 54
Mahdia threats, 45–6
unhappiness, 46–9

Zager, 140

Zagwe dynasty, 11–12
Zanaba-Warq, princess, 80, 83, 84–5
Zara Yaqob, emperor, 12, 39
Zawde Gabra-Sellasse, 139
Zawditu Menelik, 41, 53, 65, 76
Shaykh Zayd, 168
Zion, *Amba*, 60
Zoli, C., 82
Zula, 30